The Lays of Marie de France

The Lays of
Marie de France

Translated, with Introduction
and Commentary, by
Edward J. Gallagher

Hackett Publishing Company, Inc.
Indianapolis/Cambridge

For John A. Connelly
himself an accomplished storyteller and
a friend for over half a century

14 13 12 11 10   1 2 3 4 5 6 7

For further information, please address
Hackett Publishing Company, Inc.
P.O. Box 44937
Indianapolis, Indiana 46244-0937

www.hackettpublishing.com

Cover design by Abigail Coyle
Interior design and composition by Elizabeth L. Wilson
Printed at Sheridan Books, Inc.

Library of Congress Cataloging-in-Publication Data
Marie, de France, 12th cent.
    [Lais. English]
    The lays of Marie de France / translated, with introduction and com-
mentary, by Edward J. Gallagher.
        p. cm.
    ISBN 978-1-60384-188-7 (pbk.) — ISBN 978-1-60384-189-4 (cloth)
    1. Marie, de France, 12th cent—Translations into English. 2. Lays—
Translations into English.   I. Gallagher, Edward J. (Edward Joseph),
1943– II. Title.
    PQ1494.L3E5 2010
    841'.1—dc22   2009040588

The paper used in this publication meets the minimum requirements of
American National Standard for Information Sciences—Permanence
of Paper for Printed Library Materials, ANSI Z39.48–1984.

∞

CONTENTS

Acknowledgments

I was able to complete the translation of the twelve lays of Marie de France during a semester's research leave, a benefit of the Henrietta Jennings Chair at Wheaton College in Norton, Massachusetts, where I have taught for more than thirty years. I wrote the Introduction with the support of a provost's summer research grant. For the Jennings Chair, I have Provost Emerita Susanne Woods and members of the college's Faculty Chairs Selection Committee to thank; for the summer grant, I am grateful to our former provost, Molly Easo Smith, now president of Manhattanville College, Purchase, New York, and members of the Wheaton College Faculty Scholarship Committee. Professor Réda Bensmaïa, chair of the Department of French Studies at Brown University, kindly supported my appointments as visiting scholar at Brown, where I worked on this volume in the congenial atmosphere of the university's Rockefeller Library.

I am very pleased that my friend and former student Margo Vinney agreed to contribute her introduction and translation of the anonymous *Lay of Tyolet* to this volume. Her work appears here, reprinted with the permission of the editors of *Allegorica* in whose pages it first appeared in volume 3(1), 1978, pages 6–41.

I want to offer special thanks to the anonymous Hackett readers of my work who saved me from more than one egregious blunder. All remaining blunders—egregious and otherwise—are my sole responsibility. Deborah Wilkes, my editor at Hackett Publishing, has been unfailingly supportive and wonderfully encouraging. Working with her has made this experience an unexpected pleasure.

Providence, Rhode Island
21 August 2009

FOREWORD

The translations of the *Prologue* and the twelve lays attributed to the twelfth-century writer Marie de France are preceded by an Introduction to the author, her times, her works, and her literary techniques. A very selective bibliography where I have listed twelve scholarly articles, one devoted to each of Marie's lays, appears at the end of the Introduction. For each lay, I discuss in a brief commentary the characters Marie created, and I highlight what I see as important techniques, themes, symbols, and motifs used by the author. When appropriate I draw attention to parallels between and among her lays. Marie's lays are themselves quite accessible. Nonetheless, these brief postscripts may help confirm or challenge your reading, answer questions you may have, and raise others for you to consider.

Following Marie's lays, there are translations of two anonymous Breton lays: *Melion*, which, like Marie's *Bisclavret*, treats the theme of lycanthropy, and *Tyolet* (introduced and translated by Margo Vinney), which has much in common with Marie's *Lanval*.

There are two glossaries at the end of this volume: one identifying the proper names that appear in the lays, the other defining specialized terms found in these stories.

The Old French texts of the *Prologue, Guigemar, Bisclavret,* and *Yonec* appear at the end of this volume.

Introduction

The Author

Nowhere in the texts of the twelve lays translated here do we find the author's full name. Yet the lays have traditionally been ascribed in the modern era to an author who has been given the name Marie de France. The first part of that name does appear in the opening lines of *Guigemar*, the first lay of the collection: "Hear, my lords, what Marie says, who does not wish to be forgotten in her time." Interestingly enough, the most complete manuscript of the lays—British Library, MS Harley 978—contains a collection of 103 beast fables as well, and in the Epilogue to these fables their author-translator writes:

> To end these tales I've here narrated
> And into Romance tongue translated,
> I'll give my name, for memory:
> My name's Marie, I am from France.
> (Marie ai num, si sui de France)[1]

It was only in 1775 that the English scholar Thomas Tyrwhitt first claimed the author of both the *Fables* and *The Lays* to be Marie de France because of the presence of the two works in the same manuscript. For Tyrwhitt, it was obvious that the Marie of *The Lays* was surely the same person as the Marie de France of the *Fables*.[2] Once this attribution became established, scholars, always keen on finding order and connections, then decided that the same woman had translated *Saint Patrick's Purgatory*, for that religious poem, a translation into French of the Latin *Tractatus de Purgatorio Sancti Patricii* by Henry of Saltrey, contains these lines in its conclusion:

> I, Marie, have put
> The Book of Purgatory into French
> As a record, so that it might be intelligible
> And suited to lay folk.[3]

What's more, just recently June Hall McCash and Judith Clark Barban published an edition of *The Life of Saint Audrey* with introductory material suggesting that this hagiographic text too was written—in this case, once again, translated from Latin into French—by Marie de France.[4]

There is, of course, no certainty whatsoever that two, three, or all four of these works, now attributed to Marie de France, were written by the same woman. Linguistic similarities among the texts, as well as authorial concerns that the writer and her works not be forgotten, have contributed to the single-author theory. While Robert Baum as recently as 1968 went so far as to contend that, as far as his research had demonstrated, not even the canonical twelve lays of Harley 978 are incontrovertibly the work of a single author,[5] in a recent study titled *The Anonymous Marie de France*, R. Howard Bloch attempts to prove, "from within" the texts attributed to her, "not only the coherence of Marie's oeuvre," but also that "Marie is among the most self-conscious, sophisticated, complicated, obscure, tricky, and disturbing figures of her time—the Joyce of the twelfth century."[6] "Marie de France" has become and, indeed, remains, at the very least, a convenient hook on to which three and perhaps four French literary works of the second half of the twelfth century can be hung, or she is an iconic genius and a watershed figure of the High Middle Ages.

In addition to the name that scholars came to use to identify the author, some have also not been shy to theorize about the possible identity of the historical figure behind the name. Since Marie is such a common Christian name and since there was no noblewoman of the highest ranks named Marie de France known to have lived in the second half of the twelfth century, a number of other Maries have been put forth as candidates: Marie de Compiègne; Marie, abbess of Shaftsbury (half sister of Henry II); Marie de Champagne (daughter of Eleanor of Aquitaine and her first husband, Louis VII of France); Mary, abbess of Reading; Marie de Meulan; and Marie de Boulogne (daughter of Stephen of Blois, king of England from 1135 to 1154).[7] The *Encyclopedia Britannica* makes this pointed, lapidary observation about Marie de France: "Every conjecture about her has been hotly contested."[8]

What the line in the *Fables* "Marie ai num, si sui de France" ("My name's Marie, I am from France") does seem to suggest is that, because she names her place of origin as France or the Ile-de-France, the region around Paris, the writer had in all likelihood left the continent to live in Anglo-Norman England and that it was there that she wrote. As for when she wrote, some critics have argued for precise dates for at least three of Marie's putative works. Hans Runte points out that by 1925 Karl Warnke, who had edited three of Marie's texts, "had fairly well established that the *Lais* were composed before 1167, the *Fables* around 1180, and the *Espurgatoire* [*Saint Patrick's Purgatory*] after 1189. . . ."⁹ Yet in Emanuel Mickel's 1974 book-length study of Marie de France, Mickel concluded more conservatively that "Marie probably composed her *Lais* after 1155 and prior to 1200."¹⁰ Many who have studied the matter accept the idea that the "noble king" to whom *The Lays* are dedicated (see the *Prologue*) was Henry II Plantagenêt, who reigned from 1154 until his death in 1189. The second half of the twelfth century, which may strike modern readers as an exceedingly broad time frame, remains therefore the almost universally agreed upon period during which *The Lays* were composed.

The Period

Beginning a mere century after the Norman Conquest of England and a scant fifty years after the appearance of the most important French epic poem, *The Song of Roland* (c. 1095), the period from 1150 to 1200 witnessed a remarkable outpouring of cultural creativity in France. In 1924, the renowned American historian of medieval Europe, Charles Homer Haskins, wrote of the importance of this period, christening what occurred then as the "Renaissance of the Twelfth Century," because of remarkable achievements and advances in myriad fields. Among other signal developments, he noted the beginnings of Gothic architecture, the origins of the first European universities at Salerno, Bologna, Paris, Montpellier, and Oxford, as well as the emergence of the vernacular literatures.¹¹ The Adam play (*Ordo representationis Adae*), arguably the greatest vernacular drama of the French Middle Ages, dates from around 1170. Yet it was especially the verse romance, the precursor of the modern novel, that blossomed in these years. Called "romances" because they were written in the Romance tongue, rather than in Latin, these stories "recounted the exploits of knights, ladies, and noble families seeking honor, love, and adventure."¹² Outstanding examples include the five major romances of Chrétien de Troyes: *Erec and Enide* (c. 1165–1170), *Cligès* (c. 1170–1177), *Lancelot* (c. 1174–1179), *Yvain* (c. 1175–1179), and *Perceval* (c. 1179–1191).¹³ The French versions of the tale of the tragic love of Tristan and Isolde by Béroul and Thomas of England, appeared in the years around 1165 and 1175, respectively, predating by decades the German versions of the Tristan legend by Eilhart von Oberg (c. 1190) and Gottfried von Strassburg (c. 1210), and by seven centuries the perhaps better-known and widely celebrated Wagner opera about Isolde's love for her husband's nephew. From the very end of this fifty-year period comes the famously self-described "song-fable" *Aucassin and Nicolette,* the charming parodic tale of another pair of young, but less tragic, lovers.

Influences

Important elements for many of these stories entered the consciousness of twelfth-century romance writers from two sources: one popular, the other learned. The geographic proximity of the Celts and the travels of bilingual Celtic minstrels introduced the otherworldly legends and the folk tales of the continental Bretons of what is now northwest France to French-speaking audiences in northern France. Likewise, from Celtic Ireland, Cornwall, and Wales, Celtic stories came to the attention of the post-Conquest, francophone Anglo-Norman nobility and royal court. At the same time, intent on establishing the ancient pedigree of the English crown now resting, at times precariously, on the heads of the successors of William the Conqueror, Geoffrey of Monmouth, in his *Historia Regnum Britanniae* (1138), and Geoffrey's vernacular imitator Wace, author of the *Roman de Brut* (1155), offer accounts of the history of the British monarchy which highlight the legendary Celtic hero King Arthur of England. Wace, as Judith Weiss explains, expanded significantly on Geoffrey's characterization of Arthur and introduced into the legend not only the idea of the Round Table and its knights but also the image of an adulterous Guinevere involved with Arthur's nephew Mordred.[14]

The geographic settings of many of *The Lays* of Marie de France include these Celtic lands, both continental and insular. Prominent in two of her lays are Arthur and his queen (*Lanval*) and Tristan and Isolde (*Chievrefueil*). Other elements adopted from Celtic tales fill the pages of many of the lays: otherworldly creatures (fairies, werewolves, a knight who morphs into a bird and then into a woman), animals who talk, mysterious unmanned ships, enchanted rings, flowers capable of restoring both animals and human beings to life, magic potions, and more.

Love, the most prominent theme in Marie's lays, reflects yet another cultural concern of twelfth-century French and Anglo-Norman society. The origins, the precise nature, and the very existence or, at least, the

extent of the social reality behind what the nineteenth century came
to call "courtly love," and what some have even dubbed "the religion of
love," are questions that have been long debated by literary and cultural
historians. It is a generally held belief that in the late eleventh and early
twelfth centuries there developed in Provence, in southern France, a
complex ideology of love propagated by troubadours—wandering poet-
minstrels—which held that genuine love, because in that society mar-
riage was often a loveless union, was possible only outside the legal
constraints of marriage. Arranged marriages were often concluded not
for reasons of the heart but for economic, political, or other utilitar-
ian ends. Husbands often absent from home or jealous husbands who,
to avoid competition, sequestered their unhappily married wives were
conveniently displaced by amorous aspirants from among the plentiful
ranks of young, unattached knights.[15]

What makes the very idea of courtly love such a shocking concept
for that time and place is the notion that extramarital love between two
worthy lovers, who become even more worthy as a result of their love,
was championed as existing in a realm separate from and beyond the
moral strictures of Catholic orthodoxy. In some extreme examples of
this ideology, the woman assumed quasi-religious stature, as in Chrétien
de Troyes' *Lancelot,* where the eponymous hero assumes a worshipful
posture before a haughty and imperious Guinevere. "The precepts of
Provençal love," Moshé Lazar writes, "its morality, its adulterous nature,
are absolutely irreconcilable with the teachings of the Church. For the
troubadours, adulterous love, as they saw it, was not to be condemned
and did not involve any sinfulness." And he goes on to say: ". . . *fin'amors*
[the Old French term for "true love"] consists essentially of upset and
suffering; the joys resulting from this love are always provisional and at
risk, constantly thrown into question. In order to merit the love of the
lady, the lover must live for her alone, ceaselessly making every effort
to do what she wishes."[16] The ultimate objective though, as the lays
clearly show again and again, is the satisfaction of sexual desire through
the carnal union of the lovers. It must be said that Marie's treatment
of love reflects an acceptance of only some tenets of this ideology. For
her, love certainly involves suffering and usually secrecy, and she writes
approvingly of faithful lovers who engage in extramarital relationships,
or socially unsanctioned ones. Yet in several lays, couples are ultimately
united in the bonds of matrimony.

Court life, the noble classes, and knightly adventures furnish the
locus of Marie's lays. Celtic folk elements and mythological beliefs

frequently supply an exotic ambiance in which the central concerns of the lays, love and its permutations—more on this subject later in the Introduction—are examined, dissected, compared, and evaluated.

The Lay As a Literary Genre

If Chrétien de Troyes' five romances and the two Old French versions of the Tristan story constitute the medieval precursors of the modern novel, *The Lays* can be considered the medieval antecedents of the modern short story.[17] Many assume Marie de France to be the creator of this important genre. Whether this is true or not, what is undeniable is her place in literary history as the most accomplished writer of lays. A number of times, she repeats the statement that she had earlier heard the lay that she is retelling. In order that the story of what had happened—what she calls the "adventure"—not be forgotten, she has written the tale down. While originality has become a sine qua non for modern writers, the medieval aesthetic valued imitation, and so authors routinely and unselfconsciously credited their sources.

At the beginning and the end of each of her tales, Marie provides a mini-prologue and epilogue in which she both speaks of her source and describes what she has written, using terms like "lay," "adventure," "tale," and "story," but with less than absolute consistency. The opening and closing lines of *Laüstic* can serve as an example of the kinds of statements she makes here and in at least seven other lays as well (*Guigemar, Equitan, Lanval, Les Deus Amanz, Milun, Chaitivel,* and *Eliduc*). She writes at the beginning of *Laüstic*: "I shall tell you of an adventure about which the Bretons composed a lay." And then she ends with: "This tale was told; it could not be kept hidden for long. The Bretons composed a lay about it that is called *Laüstic*." She appears to be saying that a well-known tale or adventure precipitated the composition of a lay, which might well mean, as we shall see, nothing more than a piece of nonvocal music. This meaning of lay as a musical composition is explicit in only two of Marie's texts. She ends *Guigemar* with this sentence: "From this tale that you have heard, the *Lay of Guigemar* was composed, which they play on the harp and the rote; its melody is sweet to the ear." In *Chievrefueil*, she begins as in the opening of *Laüstic*: "I want to tell you the true story of the lay they call *Chievrefueil*. . . . Many have mentioned and recounted it to me. . . ." She then adds, and for the only time in the collection, besides at the beginning of

Guigemar: ". . . and I've come across it written down. . . ." So while ten of her sources seem to have been oral, for these two, *Chievrefueil* and *Guigemar*, she alludes to a written antecedent. The epilogue of *Chievrefueil* is especially noteworthy. Speaking of Tristan, one of the two main characters along with Isolde, she writes: ". . . Tristan, who knew how to play the harp quite well, created from this event a new lay, in order to recall the words of the message. . . . I have told you the truth about it in the lay I have set forth here." In the story, Tristan composed a piece of music for the harp on the subject of his message to Isolde; in her text, Marie calls what she has written a "lay" as well. One finds this same ambiguous usage of "lay" as well as "story" and "tale" in *Yonec*, where she begins by calling what she is writing "lays": "Because I have begun writing lays. . . ." But, having said that, Marie continues, reverting rather to the standard usage and calling her writings "tales" and saying, "I will certainly not be stopped by any hardship; I will recount in rhyme all the tales I know." In *Le Frêne*, she seems to say about the same thing, although somewhat less precisely: "I will tell you the *Lay of Le Frêne* according to the story that I know. . . ." Marie is more consistent in *Bisclavret*, limiting herself to the term "lay" both at the outset ("Since I've set about putting lays down in writing, I don't want to forget *Bisclavret*") and in the conclusion ("This lay about Bisclavret has been written down to be remembered forevermore").

The term "lay" then is quite a slippery one. On the one hand, among the Celts, it is believed that the term "lay" (perhaps from Old Irish *laid*, song) was first used to describe a nonvocal piece of music associated with a certain story. That story—which existed in oral, not written, form—then also became know by that same term, "lay," and was known by the same title as the title of the piece of music. Marie de France heard these narrative Celtic lays, probably in French translation, and wanted to set them down in written form in order that they not be forgotten or lost. As these Breton narrative lays migrated from oral performance and oral transmission to written versions, the term "lay" attached itself to the works of Marie and of other authors too, both named and anonymous.[18] Marie, as we have seen, refers to her sources as "lays," but she more often uses the term "tale" or "story" to refer to what she is writing. She uses the term "lay" to describe her works much less frequently. Yet the term "lay" has become, like the author's name itself, inextricably attached to the twelve narrative lays attributed to Marie de France.

It will perhaps then come as no great surprise, following this review of the vagaries of Marie's own use of literary terminology, that a totally satisfactory, succinct definition of the lay remains elusive. Marie's are narrative, as opposed to lyrical, poems written in rhyming couplets. Each line contains eight syllables, and so these rhyming couplets are called "octosyllabic." Each lay focuses on some extraordinary adventure involving in all cases a problematic love relationship in a chivalric society. The geographic setting is frequently, but not exclusively, Britain or continental Brittany. Magical or otherworldly elements play a significant role in fully half of the lays. Yet the remaining six are quite realistic and devoid of these fey elements.[19] Unlike the romance, the lay is a short narrative genre. Marie's longest lay, *Eliduc*, runs to only 1,184 lines; her shortest, *Chievrefueil*, has a mere 118 lines. In total the twelve lays contain 5,716 lines. Each one of Chrétien's five romances is longer than all twelve lays put together.[20]

The narrative lay flourished for only a brief period in the history of French literature, from the mid-twelfth century through the third quarter of the thirteenth century. Except for the twelve lays of Marie de France, scholars have not arrived at any universal agreement on the number of other extant lays, in part because they cannot agree on a definition of a lay. Donovan identifies twenty anonymous Breton lays and supplies summaries of each.[21] Translations of two of these, *Melion* and *Tyolet*, appear later in this book.

Taxonomies of *The Lays of Marie de France*

Practically every edition and translation of *The Lays of Marie de France* respects the order of the lays as they are found in British Library, MS Harley 978, the only manuscript containing all twelve lays. Whether this order was an authorial or a scribal decision is not at all clear.[22] What seems clear though is that *Guigemar*, the first lay, was intended to open the collection, because it begins with a more developed prologue than the quite brief mini-prologues of the subsequent lays. The newer *Prologue*, which precedes the entire collection, was, in all likelihood, added later. Some scholars, like Matilda Tomaryn Bruckner, hold that the final lay in the manuscript which is also the longest, *Eliduc*, was also intended by Marie to close the collection, thus positioning the two longest lays at the beginning and end of this "mini-cycle" of narrative lays.[23] *Guigemar* contains 886 lines; *Eliduc*, 1,184 lines. But, one might ask, is there any reason why the shortest lay, *Chievrefueil* (118 lines), is assigned the penultimate position? Simply from the point of view of length, with no consideration of content, there does seem to be a pattern in the alternation of longer and shorter lays, a pattern which breaks down only at the penultimate position, perhaps in order to allow the collection to close with the most substantial of all the lays, *Eliduc*, and the only one to extol the value of love in serial monogamy as a prelude to love of God. Here is the order of the lays and their length:

1.	*Guigemar*	886
2.	*Equitan*	314
3.	*Le Frêne*	518
4.	*Bisclavret*	318
5.	*Lanval*	646
6.	*Les Deus Amanz*	244
7.	*Yonec*	552
8.	*Laüstic*	160
9.	*Milun*	536
10.	*Chaitivel*	240
11.	*Chievrefueil*	118
12.	*Eliduc*	1,184

There is no pattern in the positioning within the collection of what might be called "magical" as opposed to "realistic" lays. One finds the unmistakable presence of otherworldly elements in lays 1, 4, 5, 6, 7, and 12. While out hunting, Guigemar wounds a beast, which then speaks to the hero, who has also been wounded, describing the fate that awaits the young knight. Guigemar later sails off on a self-propelling and sumptuously appointed ship devoid of any crew and lands in the country of the woman who will love him and cure his wound. In *Bisclavret*, the influence of folklore is evident in the tale of the hero transformed into a werewolf. A fairylike beauty falls in love with Lanval, one of Arthur's knights, and in the end takes her lover away with her to the mythic isle of Avalon. The medieval equivalent of performance-enhancing steroids plays a central role in *Les Deus Amanz,* where the hero's lack of moderation induces him to refuse the potion that will allow him to win the hand of his beloved by carrying her to the top of a mountain. Instead, the potion, spilled over the mountain, brings forth beauteous plants. In *Yonec,* the title character's father, Muldumarec, comes to his beloved in the form of a goshawk and transforms himself into a handsome knight and later, when required, even assumes the form of his beloved. He may be seen as the male equivalent of the fairy lover in *Lanval.* And, finally, in *Eliduc,* the hero's selfless wife resuscitates her husband's paramour using a magical red flower whose restorative powers she learned from observing the behavior of a pair of quite knowledgeable weasels.

Variations on the Theme of Love

If marvelous motifs, present in only half of the lays, do not furnish a unifying element to the entire collection, certainly the theme of love, found in all twelve lays, does fill that role. Yet even here there are significant variations to be noted. In both *Equitan* and *Bisclavret*, a wife and her lover betray a worthy husband and, for their perfidy, suffer the requisite punishment: death in *Equitan* and in *Bisclavret*, disfigurement and exile. In *Le Frêne*, *Milun*, and *Eliduc*, through the agency of a caring relative (mother, son, and wife, respectively) and after some quite vexing travails, the lovers are finally united in marriage. Yonec too, whose role in the lay of that name is restricted to the final scene, unites his parents but only symbolically, when, upon learning that his mother's jealous husband murdered Muldumarec, Yonec's father, he kills the husband and then buries his mother, dead from grief, in the same tomb with the long-dead Muldumarec. More congenial endings, where each couple goes off to live together happily, are found in the story of Guigemar, whose beloved finally escapes from her jealous husband and is then rescued by Guigemar from a knight who has become infatuated with her, and in the story of Lanval, who in the end, reunited with his fairy mistress, goes off with her to Avalon. Despite the intensity of the passion of the adulterous lovers in both *Laüstic* and *Chievrefueil*, each couple is doomed to be separated. The nightingale and the honeysuckle of each title become in the end concrete symbols of the impossibility of the survival of their love in a hostile world. *Les Deus Amanz*, in which the young man's immoderate behavior leads directly to his death and indirectly to the death of his bereft beloved, can be paired with *Chaitivel*, where the sole survivor of the quartet of knights, whose love for a coquette had been egotistically encouraged by her, rebukes her bitterly in the end for her selfishness. *Chaitivel* itself can be read as a fully developed elaboration of Guigemar's condemnation of the coquette who insists on being pursued in order to increase her reputation. The adulterous relationships of courtly lovers, then, are extolled in at least five of Marie's lays: *Guigemar*, *Yonec*, *Milun*, *Laüstic*, and *Chievrefueil*; yet in only two of these, *Guigemar* and *Milun*, does this love triumph in the end.

The unhappily married woman has been a typical figure in French love stories from medieval times to the present. One thinks, to name just a few, of Isolde in love with her husband's nephew, Racine's title character in the play *Phèdre* (1678) who lusts after her stepson Hippolytus, the adulterous heroine of Flaubert's novel *Madame Bovary* (1857), and in Mauriac's *Thérèse Desqueyroux* (1927), a sexually conflicted married woman doomed to lead a loveless existence. Marie de France studies the situation of this type of woman at length in *Guigemar* and *Yonec*, where young wives, cruelly sequestered and guarded by their much older, jealous husbands, find love with handsome young men who manage fortuitously to penetrate the confines in which these unhappy women are kept. *Milun* too engages in a twenty-year-long relationship with his beloved and the mother of his son, even after she has been married off to another man. Secrecy constitutes an essential element of these relationships, for discovery can easily lead to death, as it does in *Yonec*, or lengthy separation, as in *Guigemar*.

In the brief episode *Chievrefueil* and in *Laüstic* as well, communications between Tristan and Isolde and between the lady and her neighbor remain clandestine in order to protect the secret of their adulterous relationships. Yet their best efforts seem doomed to failure as the author reveals in the opening lines of *Chievrefueil* and as the dead nightingale clearly portends in *Laüstic*. Courtly love involves adultery and the concomitant need for absolute secrecy that is often impossible to sustain. Interestingly, even in lays involving the love between the unmarried, secrecy, so necessary in adultery, may be demanded for no particular reason, as it is by the fairy mistress in *Lanval*, who for an extended period breaks off her relationship with the eponymous hero when he reveals her existence and vaunts her beauty to the queen.

In several lays, Marie describes in some detail the overwhelming power of love. In *Guigemar*, the wound of love, symbolized by the physical wound that the hero sustains in the thigh, can be cured only by a woman willing to suffer for him. Upon hearing from the mysterious woman whom he encounters in a meadow that she loves him, Lanval is struck by love's spark, which inflames his heart. Marie depicts lovers frequently quite hesitant to express their love for fear of rejection by the object of their passion. One finds this motif in *Guigemar*, as well as elsewhere. In *Equitan*, for example, the king, struck by love's arrow and deeply wounded, is afraid to declare his love for his seneschal's wife, dreading a refusal from her. Both Eliduc and the king's daughter keep their feelings from the other, not knowing whether these feelings are shared mutually, even though his heart has become a prisoner of love and even though she has vowed to marry no one if not him.

While Marie implicitly approves of adulterous love in *Guigemar*, *Laüstic*, *Milun*, and *Chievrefueil*, one finds in *Yonec* the most audacious of any scene in all the lays demonstrating her approbation of adultery.

The unhappily married woman, in the seventh year of her imprison-
ment by her jealous husband, yearns for a love affair like those she has
heard about in old tales of love. To fulfill her wishes, the bird-knight
enters through her window, but before embarking on an affair with him,
she insists that he prove his bona fides by swearing that he believes in
God. The knight goes a step further and, so that he may receive Com-
munion, has her call the old priest who guards her. The knight assumes
her appearance, and her chaplain comes to her room to administer the
Eucharistic bread and wine to the knight as a prelude to their adulterous
liaison. Marie confirms here, and in a most striking way, her acceptance
of one of the key tenets of courtly love: its complete independence from
the moral code of the Church.

Narrative Techniques

Were it not for the *Prologue*, the brief prologue to *Guigemar*, and the
mini-prologues and epilogues of each one of Marie's lays, her readers
would have very little awareness at all of an authorial voice in these
texts. The narrative "I" intervenes quite frequently in these introducto-
ry and concluding sections of her stories. In order to explain the reason
why she writes, to advise her readers about the challenge of interpreting
her lays, and to flatter her patron, Marie added, it would seem, a formal
prologue of fifty-six lines to supplement the brief prologue (twenty-six
lines) that opens *Guigemar* and wherein she defends against the calum-
niators envious of her literary endeavors. The new *Prologue*, the subject
of much critical discussion, is, as R. Howard Bloch observes, ". . . as
close to a vernacular *art poétique* [statement of poetic doctrine] as the
High Middle Ages produced."[24] In the mini-prologue to each lay, except
in *Les Deus Amanz,* the narrator speaks in the first person, and in the
epilogues of five of the twelve lays the narrative "I" is also heard.

Very sparingly, Marie, using the figure of speech called "assevera-
tion," interjects a declaration of veracity into the body of the story she
is narrating, saying "it seems to me," or "as best I know," or "according to
the story I know." Even less frequently, she declares her desire to be thor-
ough and states her enthusiasm by writing "I do not want to forget . . ."
or "I want very much to tell you about. . . ." Marie occasionally feigns an
inability to describe any more fully an extraordinary person. In *Equitan,*
having written at length of the seneschal's wife's personality and her
beauty, the narrator concludes with: "What more can I say about her?"

In *Bisclavret*, after the beast has roundly punished his treacherous wife, Marie asks rhetorically: "Could he have done anything worse?" *Yonec* is the only lay where the narrator, like the narrator in Béroul's *Tristan and Isolde*, intervenes to express a concern for the lovers whose story she is telling. As the unhappily married woman begins her affair with Muldumarec, the narrator exclaims, "May God grant her much time in which to take her pleasure." And then, as Muldumarec is about to be wounded by the sharp spikes set by the woman's jealous husband into the window of his wife's room, the narrator exclaims: "Dear God! He was unaware of the treachery that the felons had planned." And again, at the end of *Yonec*, the narrator expresses this wish concerning the dead lovers: "May God have mercy on them!" In *Chaitivel*, the narrator expresses this wish for the three knights killed in the joust: "May God grant them His kind mercy!"

In *Lanval*, the narrator begins an explanation of the vulnerability in which foreigners find themselves with a direct address to the readers, referring to them as "My lords." It is in *Lanval* too that one finds the only striking figure of speech to come from Marie's pen, and all the more striking it is, given the paucity of rhetorical devices in general in her lays. She uses anaphora, the repetition of the name Lanval at the beginning of each of six consecutive lines, to highlight and to underscore the hero's largesse.

While hyperbole is not absent from the lays, neither is it at all so frequent as it is, for example, in the epic poems of the period. At the end of *Bisclavret*, the king embraces the eponymous hero, who has again assumed human form, more than one hundred times. Upon receiving a letter from Milun, his beloved kisses the missive one hundred times. The English princess tells her chamberlain to go to Eliduc, with whom she has fallen in love, and to greet him a thousand times for her. Later, she herself greets him six thousand times. Two thousand knights pull at their hair and their beards as a sign of grief and mourning at the death of three of the coquette's admirers in *Chaitivel*.

Other than those describing the power of love as a wound or a searing flame, similes and metaphors are rare. Lanval's beloved is more beautiful than the lily of the valley and a summer rose; her skin is whiter than hawthorn flowers. The princess, at the end of *Eliduc*, lying in a death-like state in the hermit's chapel, is said to look like a rose in bloom; her beauty is like that of a gemstone. In the *Prologue*, Marie uses blossoming flowers as a metaphor for a good story. In the old prologue at the beginning of *Guigemar*, she calls her calumniators malicious, cowardly, and felonious dogs. Marie suggests the comparative fecundity of the twin sisters in *Le Frêne* metaphorically with this sentence: "The hazelnut tree bears fruit and delights, the ash tree never bears any fruit." In *Yonec,* in the unhappily married woman's lament, she complains that "I pull and tug on a strong rope" to mean that she suffers greatly. This is the only line in any of the lays where I have changed Marie's text for ease of comprehension, replacing her proverb with another: "I have a hard row to hoe." Rare instances of litotes can be found in *Lanval* when Marie describes a conversation as "in no way common" and later writes that Lanval "was not slow in answering." In *Laüstic,* the lady's lover's reaction was "neither common nor slow" upon receiving the dead bird's body.

Characters often retell part of the plot of the lay when they explain to someone else what has already happened to them. In *Guigemar,* for example, the hero tells the lady he meets, and whom he will love, and later her husband, as well, a concise version of the tale of how he had been wounded. Near the end, the lady tells Guigemar the tale of her escape from her sequestration. In *Bisclavret,* under torture, Bisclavret's wife tells the king a concise version of the story of how she had betrayed her husband. Fairy tales and epic poetry, two other genres that developed from an oral tradition, frequently contain examples of such repetitions or brief résumés of significant highlights of earlier parts of the plot.

Not infrequently, Marie inserts maxim-like kernels of truth to state general rules reflected in particular situations. To cite just a few: "It is the wisdom of love that no one ought to try to stay rational" (*Equitan*); "Those who slander and lie about other people don't see the obvious and what can be said of them" (*Le Frêne*); "A foreigner in distress in a foreign land is very sad, when he doesn't know where to turn for help" (*Lanval*); "People cannot be so isolated nor so closely observed that they cannot find an opportunity to meet" (*Milun*); "A lord's love is not a fief" (*Eliduc*); "Whoever believes a man is quite foolish" (*Eliduc*).

Rather than engaging in narrative pyrotechnics, Marie tells her stories simply, succinctly, and straightforwardly, using only a modicum of rhetorical devices. And, as the Anglo-Norman poet Denis Piramus attests in the opening lines of his *La vie Seint Edmund le rei* (*The Life of Saint Edmund the King,* late twelfth century), Marie de France found favor among the aristocratic public of her time. He speaks of "Lady Marie who put into rhyme and assembled and composed the verses of lays, which are not at all true; and for this she is much praised, and her rhymes are admired by all, for counts and barons and knights love her and hold her dear. And they greatly love her writing, they have it read aloud, and they have them [lays] often told, and they take delight. Lays are wont to please women: who hear them willingly and in joy, for they suit their tastes."[25]

About This Translation

On the art and craft of translation, Norman Shapiro opines in the Introduction to his recent translation of *The Complete Fables of Jean de La Fontaine* that "to render formal (i.e., rhymed and metered) verse into anything but similar English is tantamount to artistic sacrilege."[26] I stand guilty as charged! Yet a prose translation, while losing the poetic structure of each line and the rhyme scheme as well, does allow for a more faithful rendition of the sense of the original, since the difficulty and the constraints of using successful English poetic conventions to approximate quite different French poetic conventions are avoided.

Other aspects of Marie's French original have also undergone modification in their migration from twelfth-century French to twenty-first-century English. As is well known, a signal feature of Old French literary texts is the shifting back and forth, for no apparent reason, between the past and present tense of verbs in telling a story set in the past. Adopting a modern convention, I have used the past tense almost exclusively in this translation of *The Lays* to narrate past events. Rather than consistently translating all of Marie's future tense verbs into the conditional, as "future in the past," I have at times retained a verb or sequence of verbs in the future, when it seemed especially appropriate to do so. The usage highlights the possible or necessary consequences of a situation or forcefully announces important upcoming events, as Marie seems to have intended.

The tendency to repeat the meaning of a verb by piling on one or two of that verb's synonyms can, in both French and English, be an effective narrative strategy. "He implored and beseeched her" underscores the character's pleading; "he declared and announced" calls one's attention to the content of the declaration being made. In a passage like "he related and explained the situation," where one of the two verbs alone could certainly suffice, the repetition does seem to add to the sense by highlighting the fact that the telling also involved giving an explanation. When Marie foretells the dénouement of *Equitan*, she uses two verbs to say that the lovers died (*mourir*, to die, and *finir*, to finish [living]). I took some liberty here to preserve the repetition and came up with "breathed their last and died." At other times, however, such repetitions may prove to be less than felicitous. Instead of a literal translation of Marie's "he spoke and said," I translated these doublets as "he spoke, saying." Likewise, "he gave and rendered" becomes "he gave back." Instead of translating Marie's "he asked and inquired" as such, I simply write, "he asked inquiringly."

When Marie's use of pronouns makes the antecedent less than obvious, I have felt free to substitute the appropriate noun, usually a proper name.

The reader will notice yet another feature of Old French narrative, and one which I have tried to preserve as much as possible: the preference for parataxis over hypotaxis. That is, rather than using coördination and subordination (hypotaxis) to show that one action followed or was caused by another, vernacular writers of the High Middle Ages often use simple juxtaposition of a series of actions, one after the other in short sentences or clauses, without any connecting words (parataxis). Here, chosen almost at random, are several passages from *The Lays*, where, for the sake of example, I have added in bold face possible words that a modern writer might have included for coördination or subordination, but that Marie has chosen not to use, and that I have therefore not added to the translation:

From *Le Frêne:* "The wedding was held in great pomp; **[and]** there was much merrymaking. Frêne was in the hall; **[yet]** she never gave any indication that this scene which she saw weighed heavily on her, or caused her any anger. **[Because]** She served very graciously in the company of the new wife. All those who saw this, both men and women, were quite amazed."

From *Yonec:* "**[Since]** Her husband was very shrewd; he realized that she looked different from the way she usually looked. **[Because]** He began to distrust his sister. He spoke with her one day and said that it was quite amazing that his wife was taking such good care of herself; **[and so]** he asked her why this was."

And also from *Yonec:* "The drawbridge was down, **[and so]** the lady entered the city still following the fresh blood through the town right to the castle. **[On her way]** She saw not a man or a woman, **[and]** not a soul spoke to her. She came to the entrance hall of the palace; she found its paving stones covered in blood. She entered a beautiful room; **[where]** she found a knight asleep. She did not recognize him, and went farther on into another, larger room. **[There]** She found a bed and nothing more, with a knight asleep on the bed; **[and so]** she continued along, and entered a third room; **[and in it]** she found her lover's bed."

And, finally, from *Eliduc:* "They took a direct route and went into the woods. They [soon] came to a chapel. [where] They called out and knocked on the door; [but since] they found no one who answered them or opened the door for them. He had one of his men make his way in, who unlocked the door and opened it. [He knew that] The saintly hermit, the perfect one, had died a week before. [when] Eliduc discovered the fresh grave. [As a result] He was quite sad, and most dismayed."

As the basis for my translation of *The Lays*, I have used this excellent edition: *Die Lais der Marie de France*, ed. Karl Warnke, Halle, Germany: Max Niemeyer, 3rd ed., 1925. As a testimony to the quality of Warnke's work, it is worth noting that Laurence Harf-Lancner prints his 1925 edition of the lays on pages facing her own modern French translation (in the bilingual Old French/modern French edition) of *Les Lais de Marie de France*, Lettres Gothiques, number 4523, Paris: Livre de Poche, 1990. Of invaluable help to me were both the Old French–German glossary in Warnke's edition of the lays and the recently published *Old French–English Dictionary*, eds. Alan Hindley, Frederick Langley, and Brian Levy, Cambridge: Cambridge University Press, 2008.

Numbers in the margins of the English versions of the *Prologue, Guigemar, Bisclavret*, and *Yonec* offer points of reference for locating corresponding passages in the Old French texts printed in the Appendix at the end of this volume.

Further Reading

There are two other widely available English translations of *The Lays:* the verse translation by Robert Hanning and Joan Ferrante (Grand Rapids: Baker Books, 1978) and the Penguin prose translation by Glyn Burgess and Keith Busby (Harmondsworth, UK, 1986). English translations of the other three works attributed to Marie de France are cited in notes 1, 3, and 4.

The best general study of the narrative lay is Mortimer Donovan's *The Breton Lay: A Guide to Varieties*, Notre Dame, IN, and London: University of Notre Dame Press, 1969.

A valuable and still quite reliable introduction to the works of Marie de France is Emanuel J. Mickel's *Marie de France*, Twayne World Author Series, number 306, New York: Twayne Publishers, 1974.

The novelist John Fowles conflated two earlier notes he had written about Marie de France into a sensitive and, at times, quite moving appreciation of her role in and her contributions to the Western literary tradition; see "*Eliduc* and the *Lais* of Marie de France," in *Wormholes: Essays and Occasional Writings*, ed. Jan Relf, New York: Holt, 1998, 152–59.

Books and articles cited in the notes to this Introduction may be of interest to readers of *The Lays*. In addition, the Web site of the Archives de Littérature du Moyen Age has a section devoted to Marie de France where a number of important English-language books and articles on the author and her works are listed at http://www.arlima.net/mp/marie_de_france.html.

Selected Bibliography

Here follows a list of twelve articles—one devoted to each of the lays. These articles are of varying lengths and offer a variety of critical approaches.

1. **Guigemar:** Ashley Lee, "The Hind Episode in Marie de France's *Guigemar* and Medieval Vernacular Poetics," *Neophilologus*, 93, 2009, 191–200.

2. **Equitan:** Sharon Kinoshita, "Adultery and Kingship in Marie de France's *Equitan*," *Essays in Medieval Studies*, 16, 1999, 41–52.

3. **Le Frêne:** Michelle Freeman, "The Power of Sisterhood: Marie de France's *Le Fresne*," in *Women and Power in the Middle Ages*, ed. Mary Erler and Maryanne Kowaleski, Athens: University of Georgia Press, 1988, 250–64.

4. **Bisclavret:** Matilda Tomaryn Bruckner, "Of Men and Beasts in *Bisclavret*," *Romanic Review*, 81(3), 1991, 251–69.

5. **Lanval:** Sharon Kinoshita, "Cherchez La Femme: Feminist Criticism and Marie de France's *Lai de Lanval*," *Romance Notes*, 34(3), 1994, 263–73.

6. **Les Deus Amanz:** Andrew Cowell, "Deadly Letters: *Deus Amanz*, Marie's *Prologue* to the *Lais* and the Dangerous Nature of the Gloss," *Romanic Review*, 88(3), 1997, 337–56.

7. **Yonec:** K. Sarah-Jane Murray, "The Ring and the Sword: Marie de France's *Yonec* in Light of the *Vie de Saint Alexis*," *Romance Quarterly*, 53(1), 2006, 25–42.

8. **Laüstic:** Robert B. Green, "Marie de France's *Laüstic*: Love's Victory through Symbolic Expression," *Romance Notes*, 16, 1974–1975, 695–99.

NOTES

[1]Marie de France, *Fables*, ed. Harriet Spiegel, Toronto: University of Toronto Press, 1994, 256–57. I have transposed the translator's clauses in the final line in order to preserve Marie's original order, but in so doing I have lost Spiegel's rhyme: memory/Marie.

[2]June Hall McCash, "Sidney Painter (1902–1960): The Issue of Patronage in Marie de France," 187. In *The Reception and Transmission of the Works of Marie de France, 1774–1974*, ed. Chantal Maréchal, Medieval Studies, number 23, Lewiston, ME: Edwin Mellen Press, 2003, 171–203. While many who write in English about *The Lays* use the French noun *Lais* to describe what Marie wrote, I have consistently used the English word.

[3]*Saint Patrick's Purgatory: A Poem by Marie de France*, trans. Michael J. Curley, SUNY Binghamton Medieval and Renaissance Texts and Studies, number 94, Binghamton, NY, 1993, vv. 2297–2300.

[4]*The Life of Saint Audrey: A Text by Marie de France*, ed. June Hall McCash and Judith Clark Barban, Jefferson, NC: McFarland, 2006. See especially pp. 3–9.

[5]Robert Baum, *Recherches sur les oeuvres attribuées à Marie de France*, Heidelberg, Germany: Carl Winter, 1968. See especially Chapter VII, pp. 147–92, where Baum's review of the disparate nature of the twelve lays of MS Harley 978 leads him to throw into question their attribution to a single author.

[6]R. Howard Bloch, *The Anonymous Marie de France*, Chicago and London: University of Chicago Press, 2003, 18.

[7]McCash, "Sidney Painter (1902–1960) . . . ," pp. 189–96, discusses who these women were and supplies arguments in favor of the identification of each one as Marie de France.

[8]*Encyclopedia Britannica Online*, s.v. "Marie de France, http://www.britannica .com/eb/article-9050909 (accessed 13 August 2009).

[9]Hans Runte, "Karl Warnke (1854–1944): A Reconstructive Approach to Marie de France's Work," 244. In *Reception and Transmission*, pp. 241–50. McCash and

Barban (p. 9) do not propose a time more specific than the late twelfth or early thirteenth century as the date for *The Life of Saint Audrey*.

[10]Emanuel Mickel, *Marie de France*, Twayne World Author Series, number 306, New York: Twayne Publishers, 1974, 19.

[11]Charles Homer Haskins, *The Renaissance of the Twelfth Century*, New York: Meridian Books, 1957, viii. [Originally published by Harvard University Press in 1924.]

[12]*The Cambridge Companion to Medieval Romance*, ed. Roberta L. Krueger, Cambridge: Cambridge University Press, 2000, 2.

[13]I have included the approximate dates of these works proposed by Douglas Kelly in his *Medieval French Romance*, Twayne World Author Series, number 838, New York: Twayne Publishers, 1993, xv–xvi.

[14]Wace, *Roman de Brut: A History of the British*, ed. and trans. Judith Weiss, Exeter, UK: University of Exeter Press, 1999, xvi–xxi. Interestingly, Wace dedicates his *Roman de Brut* to Henry II's new queen, Eleanor of Aquitaine.

[15]See Kelly, *Medieval French Romance*, p. 126, where he discusses the reasons for the distinction drawn in the *De amore* (*The Art of Courtly Love*) of Andreas Capellanus (1185) between "conjugal affection and extramarital love." Georges Duby discusses this same issue in his *Love and Marriage in the Middle Ages*, trans. Jane Dunnett, Chicago: University of Chicago Press, 1994, 60.

[16]Moshé Lazar, *Amour courtois et "fin'amors" dans la littérature du XIIe siècle*, Paris: Klincksieck, 1964, pp. 13 and 61. The English translation of these passages is mine.

[17]For a thoughtful and nuanced study of the relationship between these medieval romances and the modern novel, see the first chapter, "Rekindling Romance," in Caroline A. Jewers, *Chivalric Fiction and the History of the Novel*, Gainesville: University of Florida Press, 2000, 1–27.

[18]See Jean Frappier, "Remarques sur la structure du lai: essai de définition et de classement," pp. 23–39 and especially pp. 27–28. In *La littérature narrative d'imagination*, Colloque de Strasbourg, 22–25 avril 1959, Paris: Presses Universitaires de France, 1961.

[19]See Mortimer Donovan, *The Breton Lay: A Guide to Varieties*, Notre Dame, IN, and London: University of Notre Dame Press, 1969, 33, where, with some reservations, he proposes this dichotomy.

[20]See Frappier, "Remarques sur la structure du lai . . .", p. 23.

[21]See Donovan's second chapter, "The Late Breton Lays in French," pp. 65–120.

[22]On the question of the order of the lays, see Chapter One, "The Problem of Internal Chronology," in Glyn Burgess, *The Lais of Marie de France: Text and Context*, Athens: University of Georgia Press, 1987, 1–34.

[23]Matilda Tomaryn Bruckner, *Shaping Romance: Interpretation, Truth, and Closure in Twelfth-Century French Fiction*, Philadelphia: University of Pennsylvania Press, 1993, 157.

[24]R. Howard Bloch, *The Anonymous Marie de France*, p. 25.

[25]The translation is taken from R. Howard Block's *The Anonymous Marie de France*, pp. 13 and 24, except that I have modified his translation of the final sentence. Emanuel Mickel in his *Marie de France*, p. 15, and many others quote all or part of this well-known passage that indicates a highly favorable reception of the lays by Marie's contemporaries.

[26]Norman R. Shapiro, *The Complete Fables of Jean de La Fontaine*, Urbana-Champaign: University of Illinois Press, 2007, xviii.

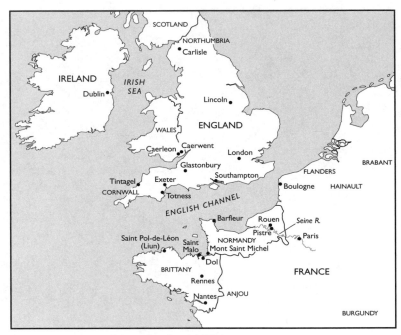

Brittany, Normandy, England, and Wales

The Lays of
Marie de France

Prologue

Anyone to whom God has given knowledge, along with fine, eloquent speech, ought neither keep that knowledge quiet nor hide it, but rather ought gladly demonstrate it. When a great good is heard widely, it immediately brings forth flowers, and when it is praised by many people, its flowers then open and bloom. According to the testimony of Priscian, the Ancients believed that as for the books that they wrote, with obscurities in them, those who were to follow them, and who were to study them, could add commentaries to what had been written down and establish their full meaning. Philosophers knew and understood intuitively that as time went by, people would have more subtle intellects and would be better able to interpret what was to be recovered in these books. Those who want to avoid vice ought to study and reflect and begin to compose weighty works; in this way they can avoid and keep themselves from great sorrow. For this reason, I began to think of some good tale to tell, transposing it from Latin into French; but this was hardly a praiseworthy endeavor, for others had undertaken the same project. I then recalled lays that I had heard. I well knew, and did not doubt, that people who first began to work on them and to promulgate them told them so that the adventures they had heard would be remembered. I have heard many of these lays which I don't want to neglect or forget. I have composed them, and have [40] spent many a sleepless night putting them into rhyme.

In your honor, noble king, who are so valiant and courtly, to whom all joy inclines, in whose heart all good things take root, I undertook to gather these lays together and to put them into rhyme and to recount them. In my heart I thought and said to myself, Sire, that I would present them to you. If it pleases you to receive them, you shall give me great joy; and because of this I shall be happy forever. Do not take me for presumptuous, if I dare to offer you this gift. Listen now to the beginning!

I. Guigemar

It weighs heavily upon the writer who works with good material if it is not handled well. Hear, my lords, what Marie says, who does not wish to be forgotten in her time. Those of whom people speak well ought to be praised. However, when there are men and women of good repute in a country, those who are envious of their good name often speak villainously of them. They want to devalue their renown; for this reason they assume the stance of a malicious, cowardly, and felonious dog who bites people out of treachery. If gossips or slanderers want to criticize me harshly, I in no way wish to abandon my work because of this; it's their right to speak ill of me.

I will recount to you rather succinctly the tales that I know to be true, from which the Bretons made lays. Following this opening, I will tell you, according to the record and what has been set down in writing, an adventure that took place long ago in Brittany.

At that time Hoël ruled this land which was often at peace, often at war. The king had a baron, who was lord over Liun. He was named Oridial. He was much loved by his sovereign, and was a worthy and valiant knight. He and his wife had two children, a son and a beautiful daughter. The girl's name was Noguent; they named the boy Guigemar. There was none more handsome in the kingdom. His mother loved him deeply and he got on marvelously with his father. When he was able to go off on his own, his father [40] sent him to serve the king. The young man was worthy and wise; and for this reason he was loved by everyone. In due course, when he came of age and intellect, the king dubbed him a knight and richly endowed him, giving him all the equipment he wished for. Guigemar left court; before going off, he gave many gifts. In order to seek fame he went into Flanders, where there was always strife and warfare. At this time one could not find such a good knight; there was not his equal in Lorraine or in Burgundy, in Anjou or in Gascony. Nature had made one mistake concerning him, for he never showed any interest in love. There was not a lady or a maiden under heaven, no matter how noble or beautiful, who would not have taken him as a lover, if he had sought her love. Many women often sought his love, but he felt no such desire; no one who knew him could imagine that he wanted to experience love. For this reason, strangers as well as his friends considered him doomed.

4

At the very zenith of his renown, this warrior-knight returned to his own country in order to see his father and his lord, his good mother and his sister, who had longed to see him. As far as I know, he stayed with his family for an entire month. He felt an urge to go hunting. That night, he called upon his knights, his huntsmen, and his hound-swains to assemble. In the morning he went into the forest to hunt, for this sport pleased him a great deal. They set [80] off after a large stag, and the dogs were let loose. The huntsmen ran ahead, the young man tarrying behind. A valet carried his bow, his hunting sword and led his hunting dog. If he had the opportunity, he wanted to use his bow before leaving the forest. In the densest part of a great thicket, he saw a doe and her fawn. This animal was completely white; it had a rack of antlers on its head. Because of the dog's barking, it bolted. Guigemar drew his bow, and let fly an arrow at the doe. He struck the doe in the forehoof. It fell instantly. The arrow rebounded: it struck Guigemar in the thigh in such a way that it went clear through and struck the horse, so that Guige-mar soon had to dismount. He fell to the ground onto the thick grass next to the doe that he had felled. The wounded doe moaned in agony. Then it spoke these words: "Ah! Alas! I am dying! And, you, vassal, who have wounded me, this is your destiny: may you never have a cure! Neither from herbs nor roots, nor by potions nor by a physician will you ever be cured of the wound you have in your thigh, until she cures you who, for love of you, will suffer great pain and great sadness such that no woman has ever suffered; and you will suffer the same for her, and all those who love, have loved, or [120] will love in the future will marvel at this. Leave here! Leave me in peace!"

Guigemar was grievously wounded and overwhelmed by what he heard. He began to think about what country he might go to in order to have his wound cured, for he didn't wish to allow himself to die. He knew quite well, and was correct in thinking, that he had never met any woman to whom he would give his love nor who would cure him of his pain. He called his valet to his side.

"Friend," he said, "go in all haste! Have my companions return; for I wish to speak to them."

The valet hurried off, and Guigemar stayed where he was. He moaned in anguish. With his shirt pulled taut he bound his wound tightly. He then mounted his horse, and left that place; he was most anxious to be far from there; he wanted none of his people to come there, to dissuade or to detain him. He went through the woods along a verdant path which led him out of the forest. On the plain he saw a mountain cliff from which water flowed steeply down to the shore below. It was an arm of the sea; there was a harbor there. In the harbor there was one solitary ship; Guigemar could see its mast. The ship was very well made, caulked inside and out, no one could find a joint. There was not a peg or a rail that wasn't made entirely of ebony; there is no gilding under heaven that is more costly. The sail was entirely of silk; when unfurled, it

[160]   was quite beautiful. The knight was very perplexed; neither in the region nor in the country had he ever heard it said that ships could anchor here. He continued along, and then dismounted; he went on board in great anguish. Where he thought he would find men charged with protecting the ship, there was none; he saw no one at all. In the middle of the ship he discovered a bed, the posts and sides of which were, in the Solomonic style, of carved gold, and inlaid with cypress and white ivory. On top of the bed was a quilt of silk with golden threads woven through it. I can't put a price on the other bedclothes; but I'll tell you this much about the pillow: were you to lay your head on it, your hair would never turn white. The sable covers were lined with crimson cloth from Alexandria. Two candlesticks of pure gold (the lesser was worth a fortune), in which two candles burned, stood on the prow of the ship. He marveled at all of this. He lay down on the bed to rest, his wound hurt. Then he got up, he wanted to leave. He could not; the ship was already on the high seas. It quickly sailed off with him. The weather was fine with a good wind, there was no going back; he was terribly sad, he didn't know what to do. It's no wonder he was distraught, for he felt excruciating pain from his wound. He had to endure this

[200]   adventure. He prayed that God would take care of him, that by His omnipotence He would lead him to a harbor and preserve him from death. He lay down on the bed, and fell asleep. That day he had come through the worst of it; before nightfall he will land in the place where he will find a cure, below an ancient city, which is the capital of this kingdom.

The lord who ruled there was very old and he had a wife, a lady of high birth, who was noble, refined, beautiful, and wise. He was exceedingly jealous since by nature old men are jealous, and every one of them abhors the idea of being cuckolded. Such is the failing of old age. He did not take lightly the necessity of having his wife watched. In the garden below the castle keep, there was a completely enclosed space. The wall was of green marble, it was very thick and high. There was but a single entry that was guarded night and day. The other side was blocked by the sea; if you had business at the castle, you could not enter or leave this place, except by boat. In order to keep his wife secure, the king had had a room carved into the wall; there was none more beautiful under heaven. At the entrance was the chapel. There was a painting that went entirely around the room. Venus, the goddess of love, was prominent in the mural; she revealed the meaning and nature of love and how people ought to embrace and serve love both well and loyally. She is tossing Ovid's book, in which he teaches how to manipulate love, [240] into a blazing fire, and she declares anathema all those who might ever read this book and follow its teachings. It was here that the wife was lodged and held. Her husband had given her a maidservant, who was loyal and well brought up; she was his niece, his sister's daughter. There was great affection between the two women; she would stay with the wife when the husband traveled. Until his return, no man or woman came there, nor did the wife go beyond these walls. An old priest with white hair and a ruddy complexion kept the key to the entry gate; he was completely impotent. Otherwise he would not have been trusted. He said Mass and served the wife at table.

That very day in the early afternoon the wife went into the garden. She had napped after lunch, and so she went outside to relax in the sole company of her maid. They looked down toward the sea; they saw the ship that sailed into the harbor at high tide; they didn't see anyone at the helm. The lady wanted to turn away and flee; her face was all red from fright; it's little wonder she was frightened. But the maid, who was wise and of stouter heart, comforted her and reassured her. They hurried in the direction of the ship. The maid removed her cloak, and boarded the ship that was quite beautiful. She found no living creature aboard, save for the lone sleeping knight. She stopped and observed him; she saw that [280] he was pale and thought he was dead. The maid turned back and quickly called her mistress. She told her the whole story, expressing great pity for the dead man she had seen. The lady replied: "Let's go see! If he is dead, we shall bury him; our chaplain will help us. If I find that he's alive, he will speak to us." They went off together, without tarrying at all, the lady in front, the maid following. When she got aboard the ship, the lady stopped before the bed. She observed the knight; she grieved for his body and his beauty. She was sad and doleful for him and said that he lost his youth in

an evil hour. She placed her hand on his chest; it felt warm and
his strong heart was beating beneath his ribs. The knight, who
had been sleeping, woke up and saw her. He was most pleased, and
greeted her; he was sure he had reached land. The lady, distraught
and in tears, answered him most courteously, and asked him how
he had come, and from what land, and if he was an exile as a result
of war.

"Lady," he said, "no, that's not why. But if you would like me
to, I will recount my story to you; I will keep nothing from you. I
am from Brittany. Today, I went hunting in the forest. I wounded
a white doe, and the arrow rebounded; it struck me in the thigh,

[320]   wounding me so severely that I feel I shall never regain my health.
The doe cried out and spoke; it cursed me terribly and then swore
that I would find no cure except at the hands of a woman. I do not
know where to find her! As soon as I heard my fate, I fled from the
forest; I saw this ship in a harbor. I did something rash and came
aboard; the ship set sail with me on board. I don't know where I've
wound up, or what the name of this city is. Fairest lady, I ask you for
God's sake, have pity on me and help me! For I don't know where to
go, I cannot steer this ship."

She answered him: "Dear gentle sir, I shall gladly enlighten you.
This city belongs to my husband as does all the surrounding terri-
tory. He is powerful and of high birth, but extremely old. If truth
be told, he is violently jealous. He has confined me to this prison.
There is but one entry; the door is guarded by an old priest: may
God grant that he burn in the fires of hell! I am sequestered here
night and day; I will never dare leave this place, unless this priest
orders it, or unless my husband asks for me. Here I have my room
and my chapel, and this maiden with me. Should you care to stay,
until you are able to travel, we will gladly take you in and it will be
our pleasure to serve you." When he heard what she had to say, he

[360]   thanked her most kindly and said he would stay with her. He got
up from the bed and stood upright; with some difficulty they helped
him. The lady led him from there to her room. They laid him on
the servant's bed, in an alcove behind a drapery that hung in the
room. They brought him water in a golden basin; they washed the
wound on his thigh. With a cloth of fine white linen they wiped
all the blood away; then they tightly bound the wound. They cher-
ished the knight very much. When their evening meal arrived, the
maid set some aside so that the knight would have enough to eat;
he ate well and drank his full. But love had struck him a mortal

blow; already there was great strife in his heart, for the lady had so wounded him that he completely forgot his homeland. He felt no pain from his wound; but he sighed mightily with pain. He asked the maid, who was supposed to serve him, to let him sleep. Leaving him, she went off. Since he had given her leave, she went to her mistress, who was feeling ardor from the same fire that ignited and inflamed Guigemar's heart. The knight remained alone. He was anxious and distraught; he didn't yet know what all this meant; nonetheless, he certainly understood that if he was not cured by this woman, his death was a sure and certain thing.

"Woe is me!" he said, "what am I to do? Shall I go to her, and shall I ask her to have pity and have mercy on this miserable wretch? If she refuses my request and if she is haughty and full of pride, I shall have to die of grief, or forever languish with this sickness." [400]

Then he sighed; a little later a different thought came to him: that it was necessary to suffer, for this was all that he could do. All night long he could not sleep, he sighed and suffered so; in his heart he kept remembering her words and her appearance, her sparkling eyes and her lovely mouth, the sweetness of which moved his heart. Inaudibly he begged her for mercy; he all but called her his beloved. Had he known how she felt and how love was torturing her, it seems to me, this would have made him quite happy; this little comfort would have somewhat eased the pain that gave him such a pallor. If he suffered because he loved her, she was in no way better off. The lady arose even before the break of dawn. She bemoaned the fact that she had been awake all night; this was the effect of love that was tormenting her. The maid, who was with her, knew from the lady's appearance that she was in love with the knight who was staying in the room waiting to recover; but she didn't know whether he loved the lady or not. The lady went into her chapel, and the maid went to where the knight was. She sat beside the bed; he spoke to her, saying this: "Friend, where has my lady gone? Why has she risen so early?" Then he fell silent, and he sighed. The maid spoke to him. [440]

"Sir," she said, "you are in love! Be careful not to hide it too much! You are able to love in such a way that your love will be well placed. He who would wish to love my mistress must have the highest regard for her. This love will be fitting, if the two of you are steadfast. You are handsome, she is beautiful!" He answered the girl: "I am stricken by such a love; I will certainly come to no good whatsoever, if I do not receive help and aid. Advise me, dear sweet friend! What am I to do about this love?"

With great tenderness, the maid comforted the knight and assured him of her help, and of all the good offices she could offer; she was most kind and gentle.

After the lady had heard Mass, she returned, not wanting to be neglectful. She wanted to know what this man whom her heart did not cease loving was doing, if he was awake or asleep. The maid called her over, and had her go to the knight. She will be quite able at her leisure to open up to him and speak her mind, whether it turns out well or badly for her. He greeted her and she him. They were both quite agitated. He dared ask nothing of her; since he was a foreigner, he was afraid that if he opened up to her,

[480] she would feel such hatred for him that she would send him away. But anyone who does not reveal weakness can scarcely expect to regain health. Love is a wound within the body, no evidence of which is seen on the outside; this is a sickness that lasts a long time, for it comes from nature. Many people consider it a jesting matter, just like those boorish courtiers who flirt everywhere, then boast of what they've done; this is not love, but folly and wickedness and lechery. Anyone who can find a loyal lover is to serve him and love him truly and do as he wishes. Guigemar was desperately in love: either he will find an immediate cure, or he will have to live as a wretch. Love gave him courage; he revealed his desires to her.

"Lady," he said, "I am dying for love of you; and so my heart is in great distress. If you do not deign to cure me, I will simply have to die. I ask you for your love; fair lady, do not in the least refuse me!"

When she heard what he had to say, she answered him appropriately. Laughing, she said: "Friend, any decision to grant your wish would be too hasty. I am hardly used to behaving in this way."

"Lady," he said, "for God's sake, have pity on me! Do not be angry if I say these things to you! A coquettish woman who makes a practice of this kind of thing insists on being pursued for a long while, to make herself more desirable, so that a man will not think that she frequently grants this kind of pleasure. But a right-

[520] thinking woman who is virtuous and sensible, if she finds a suitable man, will not be too haughty toward him, but she will love him, and will take her pleasure with him. Before anyone knows about it or hears anything about it, they will have gained a great advantage. Fairest lady, let's end this debate!"

The lady realized that he was right, and granted him her love without reservation, and so he kissed her. From then on Guigemar was at ease. They lay together and talked and they often kissed and embraced; and it is indeed fitting that they enjoyed the ultimate act to which other lovers are accustomed!

As best I know, Guigemar was with her for a year and a half. Their life was most delightful. But Fortune, always mindful of doing her duty, turns her wheel in a brief span of time, raising someone up, casting another down. Now this happened to them, for soon they were observed.

One summer morning the lady was lying beside the youth. She kissed his mouth and his face; then she said to him: "Fair sweet friend, my heart tells me I am about to lose you; we will be seen and betrayed. If you are to die, I wish to die; and if you are able to escape alive, you will know another love and I shall continue to suffer."

"Lady," he said, "do not say another word! May I never know peace or joy, if ever I turn to another! Of this, have no fear!"

"Friend, promise me this! Give me your shirt! I shall make a knot in its tail; I give you permission, wherever you may be, to love [560] the woman who is able to undo the knot and who knows how to flatten out the shirt."

He gave it to her, and gave her his word; she tied the knot in such a way that no woman would be able to undo it, unless she used scissors or a knife on it. She gave him back the shirt. He took it on condition that she likewise would keep herself secure for him, by means of a belt with which he encircled her naked flesh, tightening it somewhat round her waist. Whoever can open the buckle without smashing it and without breaking it, he urged her to love that man. Then he kissed her; and that was that.

That very day they were spied upon, seen, discovered, and found out by a malicious chamberlain whom her husband had sent. The chamberlain wanted to speak to the lady, but was unable to enter her room. It was through a window that he saw them; he went to his master and told him what he had seen. When the lord heard what he had to say, never before had he been so terribly sad. Of his right-hand men he called three. He went directly to her room; he had the door broken in. Inside he discovered the knight. Because of his uncontrollable wrath, he ordered that the knight be killed. Guigemar got to his feet; nothing dismayed him. Having grabbed hold of a massive pine branch, which they used to hang their laundry on, he confronted them. He'll bring several of them to grief. Before they close in on him, he will have inflicted great harm on them all. The lord observed him closely; questioned him and asked [600] who he was, and where he was born, and how he had gotten into this room. Guigemar told him how he had come there and how the lady had taken him in; he told him about the wounded doe's prophecy, about the ship, and about his own wound. Now he was entirely at the lord's mercy. The lord said he didn't believe him, and if things were as he said, if he could find the ship, he would then allow him to set sail. It would sadden him, if the knight survived, and he would be heartened, were he to drown. As soon as the lord had guaranteed his safe passage, they went together to the shore. They found the ship and put him aboard. The ship sailed off without delay, taking him toward his own country. The knight sighed and wept, and continually bemoaned his loss of the lady, and asked almighty God to grant him a quick death, and that he might never reach port, if he cannot again possess his beloved, whom he desired more than life itself. He was in the throes of this sadness when the ship came to the port where he had first found it. He was very near his own country. He disembarked as soon as he was able. A squire, whom he had had in his service, was riding behind a knight, holding the reins of a warhorse. Guigemar recognized him, and called to him, and the lad turned around. He saw his master, and [640] dismounted; he presented Guigemar with the horse and rode off with him. All Guigemar's friends were overjoyed to have found him again. He was held in high esteem in his country; but he was melancholy and downcast all the time. They wanted him to take a wife; but he steadfastly rebuffed them. He will never take a wife, neither for profit nor for love, unless she can unknot his shirt without tearing it. The news spread throughout Brittany; there was neither woman nor maiden who didn't come to try. None could ever undo the knot.

I want to tell you about the lady whom Guigemar loved so much. At the suggestion of one of his barons her husband imprisoned her in a tower made of dark marble. Her days were bad, her nights worse. No man alive can describe the great pain or the torment, the anguish or the sorrow that the lady suffered in this tower. I believe she was there for two years and more; she never felt any joy or pleasure there. She often lamented the loss of her beloved: "Guigemar, my lord, I was unlucky to have met you! It is preferable to die quickly than to endure this pain any longer! Friend, if I am able to escape, I will drown myself at the spot from which you set sail!" So she got up; quite bewildered, she went to the door, which she found neither locked nor barred. By sheer chance she was able to flee from the tower. No one did anything to prevent her. She came to the harbor, and found the ship that was moored to the rock where she had intended to drown herself. As soon as she saw [680] the ship, she went aboard; but she was haunted by one idea: it was here that her beloved had drowned. Because of this she could not remain standing. Had she been able to reach the gangplank, she would have allowed herself to fall into the sea. She felt a great deal of pain and distress. The ship set off, swiftly carrying her away. The ship docked in a Breton port below a magnificent and impos- ing castle. The lord of the castle was named Meriaduc. He was at war with one of his neighbors; so he had gotten up early, wanting to send forth his fighting men to wreak havoc on his enemy. He was standing at a window and saw the ship arrive. He went down a staircase and called his chamberlain. They rushed to where the ship was and, using a ladder, went on board where they found the lady who, by her beauty, resembled an enchanted creature. Meria- duc took hold of her by her mantle; he led her back to his castle. He was quite delighted with his find, for she was exceedingly beautiful. Whoever had put her on the ship was quite aware that she was of high rank. He felt love for her that was more intense than the love he had ever felt for any woman. He had an unmarried sister; in her room that was quite beautiful, he commended the lady to her care. The lady was nobly served and honored, richly dressed and outfit- ted; but she was always melancholy and dejected. Meriaduc often went to visit her, for he loved her with all his heart. He asked for [720] her love; she was not in the least interested, but she did show him her belt. She will never love any man, save he who opens it with- out destroying it. When Meriaduc heard this, he replied angrily: "There is also in this country a knight of great renown. Like you he refuses to marry because of a shirt, the right tail of which is knot- ted; it cannot be undone without using scissors or a knife. I suspect it might be you who tied this knot!" When she heard this story, she sighed, and almost fell into a faint. Meriaduc caught her in his arms. He cut the ties of her tunic; he wanted to open the belt, but he was unable to. From then on, there was no knight in the country whom he didn't have try to open the belt.

Things remained this way for quite a while until Meriaduc announced a tournament where he would face off against the enemy with whom he was at war. He had invited many knights; Guigemar was the very first among these. Meriaduc sent for him as a friend and boon companion, with the promise of a reward.

In this time of need, Guigemar must not fail to come to his aid.
Guigemar arrived richly arrayed, bringing with him more than a
hundred knights. With great honor, Meriaduc gave him lodging in
the tower of his castle. Meriaduc sent two knights with word to his
sister to ready herself and to come to him, bringing with her the
[760]   woman of whom he was so enamored. His sister obeyed his order.
The women, elegantly dressed, hand in hand, came into the great
hall of the castle; the lady was pale and pensive. She heard some-
one mention the name Guigemar; she couldn't remain on her feet.
She would have fallen to the ground had Meriaduc's sister not held
on to her. Guigemar rose at their coming; he looked at the woman
and studied her appearance and her bearing that gave him an ever
so slight start.

"Is this," he said, "my sweet beloved, my hope, my heart, my life,
the beauteous lady who loved me? Where has she come from? Who
has brought her here? What a crazy idea! I certainly know that this
isn't her at all; lots of women look alike. I'll not change my mind
needlessly. But for the sake of she whom this woman resembles, and
for whom my heart yearns and trembles, I will gladly speak with
her."

And so the knight came forward. He kissed her, and had her sit
beside him; except for asking her to sit down, he didn't say another
word to her. Meriaduc watched them; he did not much like what he
saw. Laughing, he called Guigemar.

"Sir," he said, "if you would allow it, this young woman will
attempt to unknot your shirt. She might be able to make some
headway."

Guigemar replied: "Of course, I'll allow her to try!"

He called over a chamberlain, who had the shirt in his keeping;
he told him to bring it. The shirt was handed over first to the young
[800]   maiden; but she couldn't in the least untie the knot. The lady, how-
ever, recognized the knot. Her heart was quite full of anguish, for
she'd willingly have tried her hand at it, if she could or if she dared.
Meriaduc clearly saw this; he was saddened by what he saw. He
immediately regained his composure.

"Lady," he said, "try, see if you can undo it!"

At his behest, she took hold of the shirt tail; she untied it with
exquisite dexterity. Guigemar was amazed. He did recognize her;
yet he couldn't fully believe his eyes. He spoke to her, saying this:
"Beloved, fair mortal, is it you? Tell me the truth! Let me see your
body, and the belt with which I girded you!" He put his hands on
her flanks and found the belt.

"Fairest one," he said, "what good fortune to have found you here! Who brought you to this place?"

She told him of her suffering, of the terrible pains and the sadness she had endured in the prison in which she was kept, and how it happened that she was able to escape, how she wanted to drown herself, how she found the ship, how she went aboard, and how she arrived in this port. She told him about the knight who seized her, who kept her quite honorably, but who each day asked for her love. Now her joy has returned.

"Friend, take possession of your beloved!"

Guigemar got to his feet.

"My lord," he said, "hear what I have to say! I recognize my beloved here whom I thought I had lost. By his leave, I ask and entreat Meriaduc in his mercy to return her to me! In return I will become his liegeman; I will serve him for two years or three with a hundred knights or more."   [840]

Then Meriaduc replied, "Guigemar," he said, "fair friend, I am scarcely in such distress or so distraught because of any war that I must accept your offer. I found her, I will keep her, and against you I shall fight for her."

As soon as Guigemar heard this, he ordered his men to mount quickly. He rode off, throwing down the gauntlet before Meriaduc. It weighed on him terribly that he had to leave his beloved. In town there was not a knight, who had come to joust at the tournament, whom Guigemar didn't succeed in enlisting in his cause. Each of them swore allegiance to him. They will follow him wherever he goes; anyone who fails him now will bring great shame upon himself. That night they came to the castle of the nobleman who was at war with Meriaduc. That lord gave them lodging and was joyful at Guigemar's coming and happy for his help. He was now quite certain that his war was at an end. They all rose the next morning at dawn. In their lodgings, they readied themselves. They left the town together. At their head, Guigemar led them. They came to Meriaduc's castle and they attacked it; but it was sturdy, and they failed to take it. Guigemar laid siege to the city, he would not turn back, he would take the town. So many friends and other knights fought for him that he starved out all those in the town. He took the castle and laid waste to it and killed Meriaduc, the lord of the castle. He joyously led his beloved from the castle. Her suffering had now come to an end.   [880]

From this tale that you have heard, the *Lay of Guigemar* was composed, which they play on the harp and the rote; its melody is sweet to the ear.

II. Equitan

They were very noble, those Breton barons of Brittany. In the olden days, because of the prowess, the courtliness, and the nobility of the adventures which they heard about and which happened to many men, they used to make lays in order that they be remembered, so that no one would forget them. They made one—I've heard it recounted—which ought not be forgotten, about Equitan, the most courtly ruler of the Nanz, their judge and king.

Equitan was highly respected and greatly loved in his country. He loved pleasure and love affairs; for this reason he continually engaged in chivalric acts. When it comes to love, those without understanding and wisdom are indifferent to life; it is the wisdom of love that no one ought to try to stay rational. Equitan had a seneschal, an able knight, worthy and loyal. He watched over, maintained, and dispensed justice throughout the king's domain. For no other exigency that might arise, unless it was the need to wage war, did the king ever abandon his pleasures, his hunting, his waterfowling.

The seneschal had taken a wife, because of whom great evil later befell the country. The lady was exceedingly beautiful and had had a good upbringing. She had a comely body and beautiful features; nature had a hand in forming her: her eyes were sparkling and her face lovely, her mouth beautiful, her nose most pleasing; she had radiant blond hair and a rosy complexion. She was courtly and well spoken. What more can I say about her? There was none her equal in the kingdom. The king had often heard people praise her. He often sent her greetings; he sent her riches. Without having seen her, he yearned to have her, and as soon as he could, he spoke to her. In order to enjoy himself, he went hunting secretly in the region where the seneschal lived. As he set off toward home after the pleasures of the hunt, the king took lodging for the night in the castle where the lady was. He was able to speak with her sufficiently to express both his innermost feelings and his desires. He found her to be gracious and wise, with a beautiful body and lovely face, with a friendly mien and high spirits. Love enrolled him in its service. Love let fly an arrow in his direction that left a gaping wound in his heart right where it had been aimed and had struck. He had no use for reason nor for prudence; he had been so overpowered by the lady that he was totally wretched and preoccupied. Now he had to be entirely devoted to love, unable in the least to defend himself against it. That night he neither rested nor slept, but blamed and berated himself.

"Alas," he said, "what dictate of fate led me to this place? My heart has been assailed by anguish, which makes my entire body quiver, all because of this lady whom I have seen. I feel I am compelled to love her. And if I do, I will be acting badly; she is the seneschal's wife. I owe him friendship and fidelity, just as I expect the same of him. If he somehow found out, I well know that it would weigh heavily upon him. Yet it would be much worse if I went mad because of her. Her beauty would be for naught if this woman did not know love and have a lover! What will become of her noble sentiments if she doesn't take a lover? There is no man in the world who, if she loved him, would not become much better because of this love. If the seneschal heard tell of this, it ought not bother him much at all; he cannot keep her all for himself. I truly want to share her with him!"

As soon as he had said this, he sighed, and then lay down to think. Then he spoke, saying: "Why am I tormented and distressed? I haven't known, nor do I yet know, whether she will take me as her lover; but I shall soon find out. If she feels as I do, this sorrow shall come to an end. Oh God! When will that day come? I have been trying to sleep for so long. I will never have any peace."

The king remained awake till dawn; he awaited the day in great distress. He rose and went hunting. But he soon turned back, saying he was quite indisposed. He returned to his room and took to his bed. The seneschal was saddened by this turn of events. He didn't know what the ailment was which was causing the king's fever. His wife was the true cause. Seeking pleasure and solace, the king had her come to him in order to speak with her. He opened his heart to her, he told her that he was dying because of her; she could either bring him relief or cause his death.

"Sire," the lady said to him, "I need some time to think about this. Hearing this for the first time, I am not at all sure what to say. You are a king of noble birth; I am hardly a woman of such standing that you should allow your choice of a lover to fall on me. I know for certain, and have no doubt about it, that once you've had your way with me, you will immediately cast me aside. I shall be reduced to a most sorry state. If I were to love you and grant your request, the love between us would not be apportioned equally. Since you are a powerful king and my husband holds his fief from you, it seems to me that you will think that you have the upper hand in this love affair. Love is not steadfast if it is not between equals. Of greater worth is a poor faithful man, imbued with good sense and rectitude, and greater joy comes from loving him than from loving a prince or a king who is unfaithful. If one loves higher than is fitting according to one's station, such a person is fearful of everything. The powerful man, on the other hand, believes that no one may deprive him of the mistress whom he wishes to possess by lordly authority."

Equitan then answered her: "Lady, for God's sake! Say no more! Those people are scarcely courtly lovers, but rather bourgeois hagglers, who for wealth or for a rich fief direct their efforts to disreputable dealings. Even if she owned nothing but her cloak, there is no woman under heaven whom a powerful, princely castellan would not strive to love well and faithfully, if she is wise, courtly, and noble of heart; if she values love and is not at all fickle. Those who are fickle in love and disposed to cheating are themselves betrayed and deceived. We have seen many such. It is not surprising if someone who deserves to loses out because of his actions. My dearest lady, I surrender myself to you! Don't think of me at all as a king, but as your liegeman and your lover! I declare and swear to you that I will do your bidding. Do not allow me to die because of you! You will be the sovereign lady and I the servant, you will be haughty, and I suppliant." By speaking to her in this way and begging her for mercy, the king convinced her of his love and she surrendered her body to him. By an exchange of rings they took possession of each other and mutually pledged their troth. They were faithful to their word, they loved each other deeply, then later they breathed their last and died because of it.

Their love, concealed from everyone, lasted a long time. When it was time for them to meet, when they wished to speak to each other, the king had his attendants informed that he was to be bled in private. The doors of his rooms were closed; you would not find any man so rash, unless the king had sent for him, who would ever enter. She would come under cover of darkness to see the man she loved, and she would leave again under cover of darkness. The seneschal would hold court, hearing lawsuits and appeals. The king loved her for a very long time, he had no interest in other women. He did not wish to marry anyone; he never allowed any mention of marrying. For this, his courtiers found great fault with him, such that the seneschal's wife often heard this talk of marriage. This weighed heavily on her; she feared losing him. As soon as she was able to speak with him and was supposed to enjoy herself with him, kissing, holding and embracing, laughing and enjoying the pleasures of love together, she cried constantly and grieved uncontrollably. The king asked inquiringly what this meant and what this was all about. The lady answered him: "Sire, I am crying for our love, which turns out to cause me great pain. You shall take for wife a king's daughter, and so you will abandon me. I've heard it said often and I well know it to be true. And wretch that I am, what shall become of me? Because of you, I must die; for I know of no other consolation." Because of his deep love, the king said to her: "Fairest friend, do not be afraid! Truly, I shall never take a wife, nor shall I leave you for another. Know this for certain and believe it: were your husband to die, I would make you my wife and my queen; no one shall ever cause me to fail in this." The lady thanked him for what he had said and said that she was very grateful, and if he assured her of this—that he would not abandon her for another—she would quickly seek her husband's death. It would be an easy thing to do provided that the king was willing to help her. He said that he would be willing. She will never ask anything of him, in which he will not do her bidding, whether it turns out to be foolish or wise.

"Sire," she said, "if it pleases you, go hunting in the forest in the region where I live. Stay in my husband's castle; you will be bled, and, on the third day following, you shall take a bath. My husband will have himself bled along with you and with you he shall take a bath. Tell him clearly—don't leave this out for any reason—that he will keep you company! And I shall see to it that the bathwater is heated and the two tubs brought in. I shall make his bath boiling hot; there isn't a man alive under heaven who would not be scalded and brought low as soon as he sat in it. When he is scalded to death, you will call his men and yours; and you will show them how he died suddenly in the bath." The king promised her that in all this he would do her bidding.

It wasn't three months before the king went hunting in that region. He had himself bled as a remedy for his illness, and his seneschal along with him. On the third day, he said that he would take a bath. The seneschal agreed willingly.

"You shall bathe with me!" the king said.

The seneschal said: "So be it."

The lady had the bathwater heated and the two tubs brought in. As planned, she had both tubs placed at the foot of the bed. She had the boiling water brought in, in which the seneschal was to bathe. Upon rising, this valiant fellow had gone outside seeking some diversion. The lady came to speak to the king, who had her sit beside him. They lay down on her husband's bed and joyously took their pleasure together, lying there together near the tub which was at the foot of the bed. They had the door locked and guarded; a maidservant was to be there. The seneschal returned. He knocked at the door, the maidservant kept it closed. He banged on it with such ferocity that, of necessity, she had to open it for him. He discovered the king and his wife lying on the bed, bodies entwined. The king looked up and saw the seneschal coming. In order to hide his shame, the king jumped feet first into the tub, and he was naked without a stitch on; he wasn't thinking about what he was doing. He died there scalded to death. Evil rebounded on him, while the seneschal was safe and sound. The seneschal clearly saw what had happened to the king. He took hold of his wife straightaway; he plunged her, head first, into the tub. Thus both the king and the lady died, first the king and then her. Anyone who would like to understand can derive this lesson: those who seek the misfortune of others have all the misfortune cast back upon themselves.

These events took place as I have related them to you. The Bretons composed a lay about them, about Equitan and how he died and about the woman who loved him so.

III. Le Frêne

(The Ash Tree)

I will tell you the *Lay of Le Frêne* according to the story that I know.

Long ago in Brittany, there lived two knights; they were neighbors. Powerful men and brave, valiant knights they were, and wealthy. They were close friends, from the same region. Each one had married. One of the wives became pregnant. At the appointed time when she delivered, she bore two children. Her husband was joyous and elated. Because of his joy, he shared with his good neighbor the news that his wife had given birth to two sons, with whom she too was delighted; he asked his neighbor to be a godparent to one of the children, who will take his friend's name. This nobleman sat at dinner. Now here comes the messenger! Kneeling before the high table, he delivered his entire message. The knight thanked God for the news, and gave the messenger a fine horse. The knight's wife, seated next to him at table, laughed; for she was duplicitous and proud, slanderous and full of envy. She spoke foolishly, saying to all her household within earshot: "May God help me, I greatly wonder where this honorable man got the advice to announce to my lord his shame and great dishonor, that his wife has had two sons. Both he and she are dishonored by this. We well know what must have happened: it has never been, nor will it ever be, nor might it happen that in one pregnancy a woman will have two children without two men having engendered them." Her husband glared at her and criticized her harshly.

"Lady," he said, "that's enough! You ought not speak this way at all! The truth is that his wife has always had an excellent reputation."

All the people who were in the house took note of this conversation. It was repeated often and soon known throughout Brittany. As a result of this accusation, the lady was very much despised, and was soon ruined. Every woman who heard the story, rich and poor, hated her. The messenger told all of this to his master. When he heard what had been said and repeated, he was sad and didn't know what to do; he developed an intense hatred for his honorable wife and was very suspicious of her, keeping her under scrutiny, although she merited this not at all.

Within the year the woman who had spoken so ill of the other became pregnant. She was carrying two children; and in this way her neighbor was avenged! The pregnancy went to term. Two daughters were born, to their mother's dismay. She was greatly saddened, and terribly agitated.

"Alas," she thought, "what will I do? I've lost my honor and my reputation! I will be shamed, for certain. My lord and all my family will surely never believe me, as soon as they learn what's happened; for I condemned myself when I slandered all women, when I said that there was never a woman—we never saw even one—who gave birth to twins without having slept with two men. Now I have twins; it's clear that Fortune has turned against me. Those who slander and lie about other people don't see the obvious and what can be said of them; one can speak of people as behaving in a dastardly way, who in reality behave in ways more praiseworthy than you. In order to avoid shame, I must kill one of my daughters. I prefer to make amends to God than to dishonor and shame myself publicly."

The women who were with her in the room comforted her, saying that they would not permit it; killing a child is not to be taken lightly.

The lady had an attendant, a girl from a good family, whom she had long provided for and nurtured; she very much loved the girl and cherished her. The maid heard her mistress crying, lamenting, and sorely grieving; she was most deeply touched. She went to her, and comforted her in this way.

"Lady," she said, "tears are of no avail. You will do well to stop grieving! Give me one of your daughters! I will take her away, so that you will suffer no shame, you will never see her again. I shall abandon her at a church, I'll deliver her safe and sound. Some worthy man will find her, please God, and will raise her."

The lady heard what the maid said. She was overcome with joy; and so she promised that, for this service, she would reward her handsomely. They wrapped this noble infant in a piece of very fine linen and on top of her placed a rich silken coverlet embroidered with circular designs; her husband had brought it to his wife from Constantinople, where he had traveled; they had never seen anything so beautiful. With a length of fine cord the lady tied a large ring round the infant's arm. It was made of an ounce of pure gold, into which a ruby had been set; the band of the ring was decorated all around with filigree. Those who find the child will truly know from these signs that she is highborn. The maid picked the child up, then left the room. That night when all was quite still, she stole away out of town. She took the high road that led into the forest. She continued through the woods. With the child she continued on, never straying from the road. Quite far along, on her right she heard dogs barking and cocks crowing; she knew she had found a town. She quickly headed in that direction, toward the sound of the barking dogs. The maid came to a fair and prosperous town. In this town there was an abbey, rich and well endowed. To the best of my knowledge, it was nuns who lived there, governed by an abbess. The maid saw the church, the tower, the walls, and the belfry. She was soon at the church door, where she stopped. She lay the child she was carrying down and knelt down quite humbly. She began to pray.

"God," she said, "for the sake of your holy name, Lord, if it pleases you, keep this child from harm!"

When she had finished her prayer, she looked behind her. She saw an ash tree, broad with dense foliage and finely branched, supported by four trunks; it had been planted there to give shade. She took the child into her arms, and rushed toward the ash tree. She placed the child in its branches; then she left; she entrusted the child to the one true God. The maid returned home; she recounted to her mistress what she had done.

At the abbey there was a porter who would open the church doors, by which people in the neighborhood entered who wanted to attend services. He rose early while it was still dark. He lit the candles and the lamps, he rang the bell and opened the doors. He noticed pieces of clothing on the ash tree, and thought that someone had stolen them and left them there; he noticed only the clothing, nothing else. As soon as he could he went to the tree, he touched the clothes and discovered the child. He gave thanks to God, and then took the child, not wanting to leave it there. He immediately took the child to his lodge. He had a daughter who was a widow; her husband was dead, she had an infant still in the cradle whom she was nursing. The porter called out to her.

"Daughter," he cried out, "wake up, wake up! Light some candles and lay a fire! I've brought an infant, which I found out there in the ash tree. You must suckle it with your milk, warm the child, and bathe it!"

She followed his orders. She lit a fire and took the child, she warmed it well and bathed it, and then with her milk she nursed it. She noticed the ring on the infant's arm; she and her father examined the beautiful, rich silk. They knew for certain that the child was wellborn. The next day after Mass, as the abbess was leaving the church, the porter came to speak with her. He wanted to tell her the story of his discovery of the foundling. The abbess ordered the child brought before her exactly as she had been found. The porter returned to his lodge. He brought the child willingly, and showed her to the lady abbess, and having scrutinized the child closely the abbess said that she would raise her as her niece. She strictly forbade the porter to reveal what he knew about the child. So the abbess raised the child. Because she had been found in an ash tree, they gave her the name Frêne which is what people called her.

The lady abbess passed the baby off as her niece. In this way the child remained hidden for a long time; the young girl was raised within the abbey close. When she had reached her seventh year, she was tall and beautiful. As soon as she was of an age to understand, the abbess had her instructed; for she loved this child very dearly and cherished her, and dressed her quite sumptuously. When she came to the age when nature endows young girls with beauty, there was not another maiden in Brittany so beautiful or so refined. She was gracious and well schooled both in demeanor and in speech. There was no one who saw her who did not love her and hold her in marvelous esteem. Powerful men came to see her. They asked the abbess to introduce them to her beautiful niece and to allow her to speak with them.

In Dol there lived a noble lord; neither before nor since has there been a better man. I'll tell you his name: in his country they called him Gurun. He had heard of this girl, and he began to love her. He went to a tournament, returning by way of the abbey. He asked to see the girl; the abbess allowed it. He found her to be beautiful and learned, wise, graceful, and well mannered. If he cannot have her love, he will consider himself a wretch. He was troubled, and didn't know how to proceed; for if he returned again and again, the abbess would notice; and he would never be able to gaze on the girl with his eyes. He thought of a solution; he will enrich the abbey, he'll donate much of his land, continually increasing his donation, for he wanted to return to the abbey, to visit often, and to spend time there. To become part of the community he gave the abbess much of his wealth; but there was another reason than to receive God's pardon. He often went to the abbey. He spoke to the girl; he implored her so much, and made promises so often, that she gave him what he asked for. When he was sure of her love, he spoke quite seriously to her one day.

"Dear," he said, "now that you have made me your lover, do come away with me! I think and believe that you must know that if your aunt discovered the truth, she would be very distressed; if you got pregnant while here with her, she would be exceedingly angry. If you take my advice, you will come away with me. Certainly I will never fail you, I will provide for you regally."

She who loved him dearly acquiesced to his wishes. She went away with him; he led her to his castle. She took with her her silk coverlet and her ring; she might find them useful one day. The abbess had given them to her and had told her the circumstances of her arrival at the abbey. She was found sleeping in the ash tree; the one who left her there had given her the coverlet and the ring. The abbess received nothing else with the girl; she raised her as her niece. The girl had kept these objects and had locked them in a chest. She took the chest along with her, not wanting to leave it or forget it. The knight who led her from the abbey cherished her greatly and loved her deeply, as did his liegemen and all his servants; there wasn't one, great or small, who did not love her and cherish her and honor her because of her noble nature.

She had been with the knight for a long time when his vassals, committing a great error, turned against him. They often urged him to marry a noblewoman and to abandon the one he was with. They would be happy if he had an heir who after his death could take possession of his lands and all his goods; they would consider it a grave ill if, on account of a concubine, he abandoned the possibility of having a child with a legitimate wife. They will never consider him their lord, nor ever serve him willingly, if he does not accede to their wishes. He assured his knights that he'd follow their advice and take a wife. Now they pondered where to find him a wife.

"Sir," they said, "quite near us there is a nobleman, one of your peers. He has a daughter who is his heir; you will be able to have much land from her. The girl's name is Coldre; there is no more beautiful a maiden in this country. For Frêne whom you will abandon you will have in exchange Coldre. The hazelnut tree bears fruit and delights, the ash tree never bears any fruit. We will seek out this maiden and, please God, we will present her to you."

They were intent on this marriage and secured the permission of all parties. Alas, what a misfortune that these two noblemen did not know of the true relationship of these girls who were twin sisters! Frêne's identity had been concealed; her lover married the other. When she learned that he had chosen a wife, she never showed any displeasure. She served her lord cordially and did honor to all his household; yet the knights of the household and the squires and the grooms grieved greatly for Frêne because they were to lose her.

On the day chosen for the marriage ceremony, the lord invited his friends and the archbishop of Dol was there, who held that archiepiscopal see from this lord. They brought his betrothed to him, her mother was there with her. Her mother was fearful of the girl for whom this lord felt such love, fearful that she would, if she could, come between him and his new wife. The mother will try to get her out of the house, by advising her new son-in-law to marry the girl off to some nobleman; in this way she felt she would be rid of her.

The wedding was held in great pomp; there was much merrymaking. Frêne was in the hall; she never gave any indication that this scene which she saw weighed heavily on her, or caused her any anger. She served very graciously in the company of the new wife. All those who saw this, both men and women, were quite amazed. Her mother observed her most closely, admiring her and, in her heart, loving her. Her mother thought: if she had known Frêne's character and who she was, Frêne would not have been undone because of her other daughter, nor would her lord have been taken from Frêne.

At night Frêne went to where the bride was to sleep in order to prepare the bed. She removed her cloak. She called the chamberlains, and instructed them how her lord wished the bed to be prepared, for she had seen it done many times. When they had readied the bed, they spread a blanket over it. The blanket was made of worn-out silk. Frêne looked at it. It seemed to her that it was scarcely good enough; this weighed heavily on her heart. She opened a chest and took out her coverlet. She spread it out on her lord's bed. She did this in order to do honor to him, for the archbishop was there, as was his duty, to give his blessing to the newlyweds with the sign of the cross. The mother led her daughter into the room when it was ready. She wanted to prepare her for bed, and so she told her to undress. She saw the coverlet on the bed, never had she seen one so lovely, save only the one she had given to the daughter whom she had abandoned. Thereupon she remembered her daughter; her entire being trembled. She called the chamberlain to her side.

"Tell me," she said, "on your word, where was this lovely coverlet found?"

"Lady," he replied, "I'll certainly tell you. Our lord's mistress brought it, and spread it out over top of the blanket which did not seem good enough to her. I believe the coverlet belongs to her."

The lady called for Frêne, who came to her. Frêne removed her cloak and her mother began to speak to her: "Fair friend, keep nothing from me! Where did you find this lovely coverlet? How did it come into your possession? Who gave it to you? Tell me, who?"

The girl answered her: "Lady, my aunt, the abbess who raised me, gave it to me; she told me to keep it. Those who sent me to her to be raised gave me both this and a ring as well."

"Dear, may I see the ring?"

"Certainly, lady, most willingly."

So she brought the ring to her, and the woman looked at it closely. She very well recognized it and the coverlet which she had seen. There was no doubt about it, she knew and believed that Frêne was her daughter. Before everyone present she declared this and hid nothing: "You, fair friend, are my daughter!"

From the emotion that she felt, she fell into a faint. When she came out of her swoon, she immediately sent for her husband; and he arrived in great consternation. When he entered the room, his wife threw herself at his feet and then embraced them tightly; she asked his pardon for her crime. He understood nothing of her plea.

"Lady," he said, "what are you talking about? Between us, there is no such thing as a crime. Whatever you're talking about, I forgive you! Tell me what's troubling you!"

"My lord, since you have pardoned me, I will tell you everything: listen carefully! Long ago out of vileness I said terrible things about a neighbor woman. I spoke ill of her twin children, and in so doing dishonored myself. The truth is, I got pregnant, and delivered two daughters, one of whom I hid. I had her abandoned at a church, and with her your silk coverlet and the ring you gave me when first we ever spoke together. I can no longer keep all this from you; I have found the cloth and the ring. In this house I have recognized our daughter, she whom I had lost through my folly. And now she is a young woman, worthy, wise, and beautiful, whom the knight loved, who has married her sister."

Her husband said: "I am overjoyed at this news; I have never been so pleased. Since we have found our daughter, God has given us great joy, before allowing this sin to be made worse."

"Daughter," he said, "come here!"

The girl was delighted at what she had heard. Her father would wait no more; he sought out his son-in-law, and he sent for the archbishop to whom he told the story. When the knight learned the truth, his joy was without bounds. The archbishop advised that they do nothing more that night; in the morning he will annul the marriage, and will marry Frêne and the knight. This is what they consented to and what they did. In the morning the couple was unjoined. Afterward he married his beloved, and her father gave her away to Gurun, for whom he had the warmest feelings. He divided his fortune in two. He and his wife were at the ceremony with their daughter as was proper and fitting. Another lavish marriage ceremony took place; it would be a strain for a wealthy man to pay for what they served at the grand celebration they arranged. Because of the joy of the girl whom they had found in this way, and who looked as beautiful as a queen, they too felt great joy. When they returned to their own country, they took along with them Coldre, their daughter, who was given in marriage sumptuously.

When the story of what had happened was known, the *Lay of Le Frêne* was composed and named for her.

IV. Bisclavret

(The Werewolf)

Since I've set about putting lays down in writing, I don't want to forget *Bisclavret*. Bisclavret is the Breton name; the Normans call him Werewolf.

In bygone days, people used to hear, and it often used to happen, that many men became werewolves and took shelter in the woods. Werewolves are wild beasts; so long as they are in this state, they wander about in vast forests, devouring men and doing great harm. I'll now let that matter drop; I want to tell you about Bisclavret.

In Brittany there lived a baron, whom I've heard praised as exceptional. He was a goodly knight and handsome and he acted nobly. He was valued by his lord and loved by his neighbors. He had a noble wife who had a kind face. He loved her, and she him. But she was greatly troubled by one thing: each week he would disappear for three entire days and she didn't know where he went or what became of him. Nor did any of her household know anything either. Once, when he came back home joyously happy, she asked him this inquiringly: "My lord," she said, "dear sweet friend, I would gladly ask you something if I dared, but I fear your wrath more than anything else."

When he heard this, he took hold of her neck and pulling her close to him, he kissed her. "Lady," he said, "ask your question! There's nothing that you can ask about, that I won't tell you if I know the answer." [40]

"In truth," she said, "I'm relieved. I am so distraught, my lord, on the days you are away from me. I feel such pain in my heart because of it and have such fear of losing you that, if I don't find solace soon, I will surely die. Do tell me where you go, what you do, and where you stay. I suspect you are in love and if that's true, what you are doing is wrong."

"Lady," he said, "for God's sake, please. If I tell you, evil will befall me. For you will stop loving me and I will be lost if that happens."

When the lady heard this, she took it very seriously. She asked him often, wheedling and cajoling him, so that he did explain his activities to her. He kept nothing from her. "Lady, I turn into a werewolf. I go into the thickest woodlands of that vast forest and I live off prey and plunder."

When he had told her everything, she asked quizzically whether he stripped his clothes off or whether he went about fully clothed.

"Lady," he said, "I go about stark naked."

"Tell me, for God's sake, where do you leave your clothes?"

"Lady, that I will not tell you, for if I were to lose them and if someone saw me like that, I would always remain a werewolf. There is no denying, I would be helpless until my clothes were returned to me. For that reason, I don't want it known where I leave my clothes."

[80]   "My lord," the lady answered him, "I love you more than anyone. You ought not hide anything from me, nor be at all afraid of me; that would not be a sign of love. What have I done, what sin have I committed that you should fear anything from me? Tell me the truth! You'll be doing the right thing!"

She tormented him so much and so put upon him that he couldn't do anything else, and so he told her.

"Lady," he said, "at the edge of the woods, near the path I take, there is an old chapel, which has often served me well. Under a bush, there is a large, hollowed-out stone. I leave my clothes under that bush until I come back home."

The lady heard this strange story; her face was quite flushed from fear. She was frightened by this tale. She thought a lot about how she might leave; she no longer wanted to lie next to her husband.

Nearby there lived a knight who had loved her for a long time and who had often asked and implored her for her love and who had often done favors for her. (She had never loved him, nor given him any encouragement.) She sent for him and revealed her feelings to him. "Friend," she said, "be glad! What has been eating away at you, I will grant without delay; truly you will meet no resistance. I give you my heart and my body; take me as your lover!"

[120]   He thanked her warmly and promised to be faithful to her and she bound him to her by oath. Then she told him where her husband went and what he became. She told him all about the route her husband took into the forest; she sent him in search of his clothes. In this way, Bisclavret was betrayed and greatly harmed by his wife. Since people knew that he often disappeared, they all now assumed that he had gone away for good. People asked about him and inquired after him, but they weren't ever able to learn anything

at all about him, and so they had to drop the matter. The lady then married the knight who had long loved her.

And so a whole year went by, until the king went hunting in the forest and came to the very spot where Bisclavret was. When the dogs were let loose, they located Bisclavret. The huntsmen and the dogs pursued him all day until they almost caught him and would have torn him to pieces. As soon as he saw the king, he ran toward him to beg for mercy. He took hold of the king's stirrup, kissed his leg and his foot. At this sight, the king was sore afraid; he called out to all his men. "My lords," he said, "come here and look at this wondrous sight: see how this beast humbles himself! It has human intelligence, he is begging for mercy. Keep all the dogs away and make sure that no man strikes the beast! This beast has reason and understanding. Make haste! Let's be off! I'll give safe conduct to the beast; and I'll hunt no more today." [160]

The king turned toward home at that moment. Bisclavret went along behind him, staying very close to him, not wanting to be separated from him; he had no desire to leave the king. The king led him to his castle. He was very happy and most pleased with what had happened, for he had never before seen anything like this; he found the beast to be quite astonishing and held him in great affection. He ordered all his retainers to take care of the beast for love of the king and not to harm him in any way, nor was he to be hit by any one of them, but was to be given food and drink. They all willingly took care of him; each night the beast slept among the king's men, near the king. There was no one who didn't hold him dear, for he was so gentle and so tame. He never did anything untoward. Wherever the king went, the beast was anxious to serve him. He followed the king every day; it was obvious that he loved him.

Now listen to what happened next. To an assembly that the king held, he summoned all his barons, those who held their fiefs from him, in order to serve the king fittingly and to make the gathering noteworthy. The knight who had married Bisclavret's wife went to court richly dressed and nicely turned out. He didn't know nor did he ever think that he'd find Bisclavret so close. But as he approached the palace, Bisclavret saw him and ran toward him at top speed. With his teeth, he grabbed the knight and pulled him toward him. He would have done great harm if the king had not [200] called the beast and threatened him with a switch. Twice more that day Bisclavret again tried to bite the knight. Many of those at court were astonished because Bisclavret had never done anything like this before to any man he had encountered. Everyone in the household said that the beast had hardly done what he had done without cause. The knight must have mistreated Bisclavret in some way for him to seek such vengeance. That's how things remained until the assembly concluded and the barons took their leave and returned to their castles. To the best of my knowledge the knight whom Bisclavret had attacked was among the first to leave. It's no surprise that Bisclavret hated him.

It was hardly long—this is what I've heard—before the king who was wise and kind went into the forest where he had found Bisclavret, and Bisclavret went along with him. As night fell and the king set off toward home, he sought shelter in the region. Bisclavret's wife learned about this. The next morning, elegantly dressed, she went to speak to the king, and she brought him rich presents. When Bisclavret saw her coming, no man was able to restrain him. He ran toward her as if he was enraged. Listen to how he took his revenge! He ripped the nose off her face. Could he have done anything worse? From all sides people threatened him; they were about to cut him to shreds, when a wise man spoke to [240] the king: "Sire," he said, "listen to me! This beast has lived with you; now there isn't one of us who hasn't observed him all this time and who hasn't often been quite close to him. Never before has he attacked anyone nor shown any hostility toward anyone except toward the woman I see here; by the loyalty I owe you, his anger is directed only against her, and against her husband as well. This is the wife of the knight whom you held so dear, who has been missing for so long now; we don't know what became of him. So put her to the question, inflict pain, until she tells you why this beast hates her. Make her say what she knows! We have seen many strange things happen in Brittany."

The king took his advice. He seized the knight; and he took the woman and made her suffer great pain. As much from torture as from fear, she confessed the entire story about her husband: how she had betrayed him, how she had taken his clothes, and the tale he had told her about where he went and what he became. Because she had taken his clothes, he had not been seen in the kingdom; she believed, and had every reason to believe, that the beast was Bisclavret. The king asked for the clothes. Whether she wished to or not, she had them brought and given to Bisclavret. When they [280] had been put before Bisclavret, he paid no attention to them at all. The king called the wise man who had advised him earlier. "Sire, you are not doing this right. There is no way the beast will put on his clothes in front of you nor change his beastly appearance. Don't you know what that would mean? He feels very great shame about all this. Have him taken into your bed chamber along with his clothes; and let's leave him there alone for a while. If he turns into a man, we'll certainly notice."

The king himself led Bisclavret into the room and, upon withdrawing, had all the doors closed. When some time had passed, the king re-entered the room accompanied by two barons. All three entered the room. On the king's own bed, they found the knight asleep. The king rushed to embrace him, hugging and kissing him more than a hundred times. As soon as the knight had recovered, the king restored all his lands to him; he gave him even more than I can say. His wife was driven from the country and sent into exile. The man, for whom she had betrayed her husband, went along with her. She had a number of children who were quite recognizable by their faces and their resemblance to her: many women descended from her—this is the truth—were born without a nose and so they lived their lives noselessly.

The tale that you have heard is true; have no doubt about it. This lay about Bisclavret has been written down to be remembered forevermore.

V. Lanval

I shall recount to you the story of another lay just as it happened. It was about a very valiant vassal; in Breton they call him Lanval.

Arthur, the noble and courtly king, was staying at Carlisle, because of the Scots and the Picts who were devastating the country; quite often they would come into the land of Logres and ravage it. The king was staying there at Pentecost in the summer season. He gave a great many rich gifts. He gave women's hands in marriage and distributed lands to both counts and barons and to the knights of the Round Table (of these there are no equal in the entire world!). He gave to all with the exception of one single knight who had served him. This was Lanval. The king did not remember him, nor did any of his court express concern for him. Just about everyone envied him for his valor, for his largesse, for his beauty, and for his prowess; some who showed him the appearance of affection, if ill luck befell this knight, would never show any concern for him. He was a king's son, of high birth, but far from his ancestral land. He was a member of the king's household. He spent all his wealth; for the king gave him nothing, nor did Lanval ask him for anything. And so Lanval was in a real predicament, he was very sad and most downcast. My lords, don't be surprised: a foreigner in distress in a foreign land is very sad, when he doesn't know where to turn for help.

The knight I am telling you about, who had served the king so well, mounted his horse one day, and went off to enjoy himself. He went out from the town all alone, and came into a meadow. He dismounted near a stream, but his horse trembled uncontrollably. He unsaddled it and the horse went off; he allowed it to frolic in the field. Folding his cloak under his head, he lay down to rest. He was most downcast because of his situation, nothing in his life pleased him. From where he was lying, he looked downstream toward the river, and he saw two damsels approaching; he had never seen more beautiful women. They were richly dressed and tightly laced in lovely tunics of deep crimson; they had the most beautiful faces. The elder carried a basin of pure gold, perfectly wrought—I am, without question, telling you the truth—the other carried a towel. They went directly to where the knight was lying. Lanval, who was very well brought up, got to his feet at their arrival. First they greeted him, and then told him the message they brought.

"Sir Lanval, my lady, who is very noble and beautiful, has sent us to you; you are to come with us! We shall lead you safely. See, her pavilion is nearby!"

The knight went with them; he took no account of his horse that was foraging in the meadow. They led him as far as the tent, which was very beautiful and well appointed. Queen Semiramis never had more wealth or more power or more knowledge, and the Emperor Octavian could not afford even the right flap of this tent. A golden eagle sat atop the tent; of this I cannot guess the price, nor the price of the cords nor of the stakes that held the flaps. There was no king under heaven who could afford all this, no matter how much money he might spend. The lady, inside this tent, surpassed in beauty the lily of the valley and the blossoming rose that blooms in the summertime. She lay on a most beautiful bed (the bedcovers were worth a castle), dressed only in her shift. Her body was most lovely and comely. To keep warm, she had put over herself a costly mantle of white ermine, covered in crimson cloth from Alexandria; her entire side was bare, as were her face, her neck, and her breasts; her skin was whiter than hawthorn flowers. The knight advanced, and the lady spoke to him. He sat at the foot of the bed.

"Lanval," she said, "fair friend, it was for you that I left my own country; I have come seeking you from afar. If you are valiant and courtly, neither emperors, nor counts, nor kings will have had as much joy or good fortune as you; for I love you above all others."

He looked at her, and saw how beautiful she was. Love struck him with its spark, which lit up and inflamed his heart. He answered her fittingly.

"Fairest one," he said, "if it pleased you and if I felt the joy of your wanting to love me, there is nothing you could order that I would not do to the best of my ability, be it utterly foolish or wise. I will do your bidding; for you I will forsake everyone else. I never wish to leave you; this is what I most desire."

When the lady heard what this knight who could love her so much had said, she gave him her love and her heart. Lanval was now on the true path! Then she gave him a gift: simply by wishing for it, he will not want for anything that he desires. He may give and spend liberally, she will grant him what's needed. Lanval is well provided for now: the more mightily he spends, the more gold and silver will he have.

"Friend," she said, "now I caution you, and command you and beseech you: do not speak of this to any man! I shall tell you the crux of the matter: if this love were known, you could no longer see me nor take possession of my body."

He answered her that he would certainly do whatever she commanded. He lay in the bed beside her; now Lanval was well ensconced with her! They tarried in bed until nightfall, and he would have stayed longer, if he could have and if his beloved had agreed.

"Friend," she said, "get up! You cannot stay here any longer. Go; I will stay. But I will say one thing to you: whenever you wish to speak with me, you will never think of any place, where one could meet his beloved without reproach and without villainy, where I will not come to you in order to satisfy all your desires. No man, save you, shall see me nor will anyone else hear me speak."

When he heard this, he was overjoyed; he kissed her, then he got up. Those who had brought him to the tent provided him with rich garments. When he was dressed in these, there was not a more handsome youth under heaven; he did not look in the least foolish or common. They gave him water to wash his hands and a towel to dry them; then they served him dinner. He supped with his beloved; he refused nothing. He was served most courteously, and he dined with great joy. There was one entire course that especially pleased the knight, for he often kissed his beloved and embraced her tightly. When they had gotten up from table, the damsels brought him his horse. He was well served; they had cinched the saddle well. He took his leave, mounted, and headed toward the town. He often looked back. Lanval was quite agitated; he rode along preoccupied with his adventure and full of doubt. Astonished, he didn't know what to think; he didn't believe that what had just happened was true. He came to his lodgings; he found his men handsomely dressed. That night he entertained well; yet no one knew the source of the wherewithal. No needy knight was living in town whom he didn't have come to his lodgings. He saw to it that they were treated richly and well. Lanval gave fine presents, Lanval freed prisoners, Lanval dressed minstrels, Lanval bestowed great honors, Lanval spent lavishly, Lanval distributed gold and silver: there was no stranger nor close friend on whom he did not bestow gifts. Lanval was joyous and pleased. As often as he wanted, he could see his beloved, who was totally at his beck and call whether during the day or at night.

From what I know, that same year after the feast of Saint John as many as thirty knights had gone to enjoy themselves in an orchard beneath a tower in which the queen was staying. With them was Gawain and his cousin, the handsome Yvain. The noble and valiant Gawain, who was so well loved by all, said this: "By God, my lords, we did an injustice to our companion Lanval, who is so generous and courtly and whose father is such a powerful king, for we have not invited him along." They then turned round, and went to Lanval's lodgings, and prayed him to join them.

Together with three of her ladies-in-waiting, the queen was leaning at a recessed window. She saw the king's retinue, recognized Lanval, and watched him. She called one of her ladies; she told her to tell the most elegant and the most beautiful young women of her household to go with her into the garden to amuse themselves with the men of the king's company. She led thirty or more young ladies down the stairs. The knights showed great joy at their arrival, and walked toward them. They took the young women by the hand; their conversations were in no way common. Lanval went off on his own, at some remove from the others. He was very anxious to hold his beloved, to kiss her, to embrace her, to feel her close to him; little did he value other people's joy, if he could not in turn enjoy his own pleasure. When the queen saw that he was alone, she went to him straightaway. She sat down beside him, spoke to him, and opened her heart to him.

"Lanval, I have honored you very much and cherished you and loved you. You may have all my love; now tell me what you desire! I offer my love to you; you ought to be very happy because of what I'm doing!"

"Lady," he said, "let me be! I have no interest in loving you. I have served the king for a long time, I do not wish to break faith with him. Neither for you nor for your love will I betray my lord!"

The queen got angry, she was furious, and she spoke without thinking.

"Lanval," she said, "I am quite convinced you are scarcely interested in such pleasures. People have often told me as much, that you have no liking for women. You like handsome young men, and it's with them that you take your pleasure. Villainous coward, wicked deceiver, you have ill served my lord, who has suffered you to be near him. I do think he will lose God's love because of this!"

When he heard this he became quite distressed. He was not slow in answering her; he said something in anger, which he later often regretted.

"Lady," he said, "I do not show any competence whatsoever for such a calling. But I do love a woman who is to be prized above all the women I know, and I am loved by her. And I'll say this to you: let me tell you quite openly that any one of the maidens who serves her, even the very poorest one, is more worthy than you, my queen, in body, visage, beauty, in knowledge and in goodness!"

The queen left at once, and returned to her room in tears. She was exceedingly sad and angry because he had reviled her so. Ill, she took to her bed, and said she would never get up again if the king did not do right by her in the matter of the complaint she would make.

The king, after a most enjoyable day, came back from hunting in the forest. He entered the queen's room. As soon as she saw him, she bemoaned her lot, fell at his feet, begged for mercy, and said that Lanval had shamed her by soliciting her love. Because she had rebuffed his advances, he had belittled and reviled her terribly, boasting that his beloved was so graceful, noble, and charming that the poorest of that woman's chambermaids was more worthy than the queen. The king became terribly angry and swore this oath: if Lanval cannot defend himself in court, the king will have him burned at the stake or hanged. The king left the room; he called for three of his barons, and sent them to get Lanval, who was sad and sick at heart. He had returned to his lodging; he had already realized that he had lost his beloved, for he had disclosed their liaison. He was all alone in his room, deep in thought and full of anguish. He called for his beloved endlessly, but for naught. He lamented and sighed, from time to time he fell into a swoon; then a hundred times he begged for mercy, and asked his beloved to speak to him. He cursed his heart and his tongue; it's a wonder he didn't take his own life. He could not cry out or howl, thrash about or tear at his hair enough for her to take pity on him and allow him simply to see her. Alas, how will he manage to go on?

Those whom the king had sent to him arrived, and they told him to come to court without delay because the king had summoned him. The queen had accused him. Lanval went to court in the saddest state; had he had his way, they would have killed him. He came before the king. He was very downcast, quiet, and mute; he looked to be in great distress. The king said to him angrily: "Vassal, you have grievously wronged me! You embarked on a most vile affair to bring shame on me and to revile me and to slander the queen. You are a foolish braggart! Your beloved is so very noble that her maidservant is more lovely and more distinguished than the queen."

Lanval, maintaining that he had not sought the queen's favors, defended himself against every word of the king's accusation that he had dishonored and shamed his lord; but he admitted the truth of what he had said about the beloved of whom he boasted. He was bereft because of all this, for he had lost her. He told them he would do whatever the court decided. The king was very angry with him. So that people might not interpret what he did in any unfavorable way, the king sent for all his barons to advise him on what he ought to do. The barons followed his orders: whether they liked the situation or found it distasteful, they all convened and they judged and resolved that Lanval was to have his day in court. He was to offer guarantors to his lord, that he will await his trial and appear in person; and the court will be augmented, for at present there were none there except from the royal household. The barons returned to the king, and explained the matter to him. The king asked for guarantors. Lanval was alone and distraught, he had no family or friends. Gawain came to him and, along with all his friends, declared himself his guarantor. The king said to them: "I accept your role as guarantors based upon whatever each one of you holds from me, lands and fiefs." Once Lanval was secured by guarantors, there was nothing more to do. He went back to his lodging. Knights escorted him; they reproached him and castigated him harshly for grieving so, and they cursed such a mad kind of love. Every day they returned to see him because they wanted to know whether he was eating and drinking; they very much feared that he might go mad.

On the appointed day, the barons were gathered. The king and the queen were present, and the guarantors had brought Lanval. All of them were very sad for him; I think that there were a hundred such who would have done all in their power to have him acquitted without trial; he had been charged most unjustly. The king asked for a summation of the accusation and of the defense; now everything was in the hands of the barons. They had come to judge; they were most downcast and troubled by this worthy foreigner who was in such a predicament among them. Many wanted him condemned since their lord wished it. The Duke of Cornwall said this: "As for us, we will surely not falter; for whether one cries or sings, justice must proceed. The king spoke against his vassal, the one I have heard you call Lanval; he accused him of an act of perfidy and indicted him on a charge of calumny, concerning the love he boasted about, which so angered the queen. No one accused him except the king. By the faith I owe you, which certainly requires the truth, he ought never have to respond, if not for this fact: that a man owes his lord honor in all matters. Lanval will swear an oath about it, and the king will turn him over to us. And if he can offer his proof, and if his beloved comes forward, and if what he said about her is true, which is why the queen became angry, he will certainly be pardoned since he will have said nothing about the queen out of contempt for her. And if he cannot offer proof, this is what we will have to say to him: he will be excluded from all service to the king, he must go into exile." They sent for the knight, and they declared and announced to him that he must have his beloved come forward in order to defend and protect him. He told them he could not; he would never have any help from her. These men, who expected no help for Lanval, returned to the judges, whom the king was pressing hard to render their verdict, for the queen was waiting.

As they were about to conclude, they saw two damsels approaching at an amble on two handsome palfreys. They were very lovely, and clothed in nothing but crimson silk draped over their naked flesh. The judges contemplated them with pleasure. Gawain, along with three knights, went to Lanval, and spoke to him; he pointed the two maidens out to him. Gawain was very pleased, he beseeched Lanval to tell him whether one of these was his beloved. Lanval said to him: "I don't know who they are, nor where they are from, nor where they are going." The women continued to approach on horseback, such that they dismounted right before the high table where Arthur the king was seated. They possessed great beauty, and they spoke courteously.

"May the God who made the light and the darkness protect and keep King Arthur! King, have rooms readied and hung with curtains, where our lady may stay; she wishes to take lodging with you."

He willingly granted them this favor, and called two knights who led the women up to their rooms. They said no more at this time.

The king asked his barons for their verdict and their judgment and said that they had angered him greatly by having taken so much time.

"Sire," they said, "we made a decision. Because of the women whom we saw we have not been able to reach a final verdict. We shall now begin to hear the case again."

They therefore reconvened quite perplexed, amid much commotion and quarreling.

In the midst of all this uproar, they saw coming down the path two maidens elegantly outfitted (dressed in lovely silk with gold embroidery and riding on two Spanish mules). The vassals felt great joy at this sight, and said among themselves that the valiant and brave Lanval was now exonerated. Gawain, leading his companions, went to him.

"Sir," he said, "be of good cheer! For God's sake, speak to us! Coming toward us are two very elegant and very beautiful women. One is surely your beloved!"

Lanval answered quickly and said that he didn't recognize them, nor did he know them, nor had he loved them. The two women arrived just then; they dismounted before the king. Many of those present praised them highly for their bodies, their faces, and their complexions; each was a more worthy beauty than ever the queen was. The elder of the two was courtly and wise, she announced her message most properly.

"King, do have rooms prepared for us where our lady may be fittingly lodged; she is coming here to speak with you."

He ordered that they be taken to the women who had come earlier. They had no need to be concerned about their mules; there were enough servants who took care of them and stabled them. When he had acquitted his obligation toward the women, the king then ordered all his barons to render their judgment; this business had dragged on too long. The queen was angry because of this delay, and for much too long she had not been able to eat. Thereupon they truly set to judging the case, when a lady seated on a horse came riding into town; in the entire world there was none so beautiful. She was riding a white palfrey, which carried her along nice and gently; its neck and head were well formed; there was no more noble beast under heaven. The palfrey was richly equipped; no count or king under heaven could have bought it without selling or mortgaging his land. The lady was dressed in a white linen shift and a tunic, laced on both sides in such a way that the entire side of her body was exposed. Her body was comely, with low-slung hips, her neck was whiter than snow on the branch; her eyes were sparkling, her face fair, a beautiful mouth, a most pleasing nose, dark eyebrows, and a lovely forehead and curly hair, rather blond; a golden thread does not shine so lustrously as her hair does in the daylight. She had wrapped the ends of her dark crimson mantle around her. She held a sparrow hawk on her wrist, and a greyhound followed along after her. A noble squire stood beside her, carrying an ivory horn. They came along the street most pleasingly. Such great beauty had not been seen in Venus, who was a queen, nor in Dido, nor in Lavinia. There was in town neither highborn nor low, neither old nor young, who, as they saw her coming along, did not go out to look at her. About her beauty, there was no exaggeration. She came slowly. The judges who saw her were astonished; there was not a single one of them who looked at her who was not set aglow with true joy. There was not an old man at court who did not turn his eye toward her with pleasure and who would not have served her willingly, had she wanted him to. Those who loved Lanval came to him, and told him about the lady who had come, and who, God willing, would deliver him.

"Dear companion, a woman is coming here, but she does not have auburn or brown hair; she is the most beautiful woman in this world, more beautiful than all others in it."

Lanval heard this, raised his head; indeed he recognized her and he sighed. Color returned to his face; he was anxious to speak.

"By my faith," he said, "this is my beloved! Now I don't mind if they kill me, if she does not have pity on me. I am cured, by the very sight of her."

The lady entered the palace; never had such a beautiful woman come there before. She dismounted before the king, so that she was clearly seen by everyone. She let fall her mantle, so that they might see her better. The king, who was very well mannered, immediately went toward her, and all the others honored her and strove to serve her. After they had examined her closely and sufficiently praised her beauty, she spoke in such a way that it was clear she did not wish to stay.

"Arthur," she said, "and these barons whom I see here, hear me! I have loved one of your vassals. There he is! It is Lanval! He was accused in your court; I do not in the least want things to go badly for him because of what he said. Know well that the queen was wrong; never did he solicit her love. If he can be acquitted because of me for the boasting he did, may he be exonerated by your barons!"

What they decided lawfully, the king agreed to accept. There was not a single one who did not declare that Lanval had substantiated all that he had said. He was exonerated by their decision, and the lady left. The king was unable to convince her to stay, despite the number of those ready to serve her. Outside the chamber there stood a large step made of dark marble from which knights in heavy armor mounted their horses as they left the king's court. Lanval climbed onto the stone. When the maiden came out of the door, in a single bound Lanval jumped onto the palfrey behind her. He went with her to Avalon, according to what the Bretons say, to a most beautiful island; it was to there that the young man was carried off. No one heard any more about this, and about this I don't know anything more to say.

VI. Les Deus Amanz

(The Two Lovers)

In olden days in Normandy, a much talked about adventure took place involving two young people who loved each other, and who died because of that love. The Bretons composed a lay about it; it was given the title *Les Deus Amanz* [*The Two Lovers*].

The truth is that in Neustria, what we call Normandy, there is a towering mountain, of remarkable height; the two young people lie buried beneath it. On one side of the mountain, a king who was lord of the Pistrians had a city built with great care; he had it named for his Pistrians and so he had it called Pistre. The name has endured ever since; the city and its houses are still there. That region which is called the Vale of Pistre is well known to us. The king had a daughter, who was a beautiful and a very refined young woman. Except for her, he had no sons or daughters; he loved and cherished her exceedingly. She was sought after by powerful men, who would willingly have wed her; but the king did not want to give her in marriage, for he could not do without her. The king had no other recourse: he was with the girl night and day; and since he had lost the queen, he was consoled by her. Many took exception to this situation; his own court criticized him for it. As soon as he heard that people were talking about this, this weighed on him very much; he was greatly saddened. He began to think how he could prevent anyone from asking for his daughter's hand. He announced and decreed it far and near: let him who wished to wed his daughter know one thing for certain: it was foreordained and foretold that he would carry her in his arms to the top of the mountain outside the city, without ever stopping to rest. When this decree was known and the news had spread throughout the region, quite a few tried, without achieving anything. There were those who made an effort and were able to carry her to the midpoint of the mountain, but could go no farther; they had to leave her there. For a long time she remained unsought after, for no one cared to ask for her hand.

In this land there was a young man who was noble and handsome, the son of a count. In order to succeed and to establish a better reputation than all others, he took up the challenge. He frequented the king's court and quite often stayed there; he fell in love with the king's daughter, and spoke with her on many occasions, asking that she grant him her love and that she become his beloved. Because he was valiant and courtly and because the king held him in such high esteem, she did grant him her love, and for this he humbly thanked her. They spoke together often and loved each other faithfully, and they concealed their love as best they could so that no one would become aware of it. This need for prudence distressed them greatly; but the young man conclud-ed that it was preferable to tolerate these frustrations than to be rash and thereby ruin everything. He was tormented by his love. Then it happened on one occasion when the young man, who was both valiant and handsome, came to see his beloved that he revealed to her and complained of his frustration. With anxiety, he asked her to run away with him, for he could no longer tolerate the torment. He well knew that if he asked her father for her hand, the king would not want to give her away, unless the young man succeeded in carrying her in his arms to the top of the mountain. The girl said to him: "Beloved," she said, "I certainly know there is no way you can carry me to the top of the mountain; you are not strong enough. If I run away with you, my father will be both sad and angry, he could not live on without great suffering. Truly, I love him so much and hold him so dear that I would not want to anger him. You need to consider some other course of action, for I do not wish to entertain this one. I have a relative in Salerno, she is a for-midable woman, with a vast income. She has lived there for more than thirty years, and has practiced the physician's art for so long that she is most knowledgeable about medicinal drugs. She knows herbs and roots so well that if you agree to go see her and take along with you a letter from me and explain to her your venture, she will aid and advise you. She will supply you with such elixirs and furnish you with such potions that they will fully fortify you and give you great strength. When you return to this country, you will ask my father for my hand. He will treat you like a child, and will tell you about the terms of the agreement that he will give me to no man, regardless of the efforts he exerts, if he can-not carry me up the mountain in his arms without stopping; and you will accept these terms gladly, for it cannot be otherwise." The young man heard the girl's statement and her counsel; he was delighted, and thanked her. He bid his beloved farewell.

He went into his own country. He quickly gathered together fine clothes and money, horses and beasts of burden. The young man took along with him some of his closest friends. He would spend time in Salerno in order to speak with his beloved's aunt. He gave her the let-ter from his beloved. As soon as she had read it all the way through, she had him stay with her until she got to know him thoroughly. She fortified him with medicines. She gave him a potion. He will never be so exhausted nor so weary nor so weighed down, that it will not refresh his body as soon as he drinks it, even his veins and his bones, so that he will have exceptional strength. He then brought back to his own country the potion that he had poured into a phial.

The young man was joyous and happy when he returned home, and did not stay long in his own country. He went to the king to ask for his daughter; he will take her and carry her to the top of the mountain. The king did not refuse him in the least; but he thought him quite mad, because of his tender age. Many valiant, wise, and worthy men had attempted this feat, who were unable to achieve a successful outcome. He announced and fixed a date for him. The king sent for his men and his friends and all those he could gather; he left no one out. They came from all parts because of the king's daughter and the young man, who was to undertake the feat of carrying her to the top of the mountain. The girl prepared herself; she limited her eating and often fasted in order to lose weight, which would help her beloved. The day on which everyone gathered, the young man was first to arrive; he did not in the least forget his potion. The king led his daughter onto a prairie near the Seine, where a great crowd was assembled. She had put on nothing but a shift. The young man took her in his arms. Well aware that she had no intention of thwarting his efforts, he gave her the little phial to carry which contained all of his potion; but I fear it will avail him little, for in him there was no sense of moderation. He set off with her at a rapid pace; he got up to the midpoint of the mountain. Because of the joy he felt from holding her, he did not remember his potion; she had the impression he was tiring.

"Friend," she said, "do take a drink! I know for sure that you are tiring. In this way, you will recover your strength!"

The youth replied: "Fair one, I can tell that my heart is quite strong. As long as I am able to take three steps, I will on no account stop, not even just long enough to take a drink. These people would shout at us, their uproar would distract me; soon they would impede me. I do not wish to stop here!"

When he was two-thirds of the way up, he almost fell over. The girl often implored him, saying: "Beloved, drink your medicine!" He wanted neither to listen to her nor to believe her. Suffering great pain, he continued his climb with her in his arms. He arrived at the summit, having so exerted himself that he fell down and did not get up. His heart had burst from his chest. The girl looked at her beloved, and thought that he had fainted. She knelt down beside him, wanting to give him his potion; but he was unable to speak to her. In this way he died, as I've told you. She lamented his loss with loud lamentations. Then she threw the phial which contained the potion, spilling its contents. Soon the mountain was quite damp from it; the entire region and the country were made better by this; people discovered many fine herbs there that sprang from this potion.

Now I'll tell you about the girl. Because she had lost her beloved, she had never before been so bereft. She stretched out beside him on the ground, she took hold of him and held him in her arms, and often kissed his eyes and his mouth. Her grief at his loss pierced her heart. The girl who was so noble, wise, and beautiful died on this spot. The king and those around him, when they realized that the young couple was not coming down the mountain, went in search of them, and found them. The king fell down in a faint; when he was able to speak, he expressed his great grief, and so did the foreigners there. They kept watch over the bodies for three days. They sent for a marble sarcophagus, and laid the two young people in it. On the advice of those present, they buried them on the mountain, and then they all withdrew.

Because of what had happened to these young people, this mountain is called the Mountain of the Two Lovers. All this happened just as I have recounted it to you; the Bretons composed a lay about it.

VII. Yonec

Because I have begun writing lays, I will certainly not be stopped by any hardship; I will recount in rhyme all the tales I know. I have in mind and I want to tell you about Yonec: of his birth, and about his father and how his father first visited his mother. He who engendered Yonec was named Muldumarec.

In the Britain of yore there lived a powerful man, who was old and decrepit. He was lord of Caerwent and of all the surrounding lands. That city is located on the Duelas, where in the past ships sailed. The lord was advanced in years. Since he possessed a substantial estate, he took a wife in order to have a child, who after his death would be his heir. The girl who was given in marriage to this powerful man was well born, wise, refined, and most beautiful; he loved her very much for her beauty. Why would I say another word about it? She had no equal as far as Lincoln, nor from there to as far away as Ireland. He who gave her away in marriage to this old man committed a grievous sin. Because she was beautiful and noble, the old man put a great deal of effort into keeping watch over her. He sequestered her in his tower, in a large room with a stone floor. He had a sister, she was old and widowed, and without a husband; he lodged her with his wife in order to keep his wife under strict control. There were other women there too, I believe, in another room of their own; but the wife never spoke with any of them, without the old woman's consent. [40]

He kept her in this condition for seven years (never did they have a child), she never left the tower to visit either relative or friend. When the husband went to bed, there was neither chamberlain nor porter who dared enter his room, nor carry a candle before him. His wife was in great distress. From crying, sighing, and weeping, she lost much of her beauty like any woman who has no concern for her appearance. She wanted no more for herself than a quick death.

It was early April when the birds are singing. The husband rose one morning, and left to go into the woods to hunt. He woke the old woman too and she closed the doors after him. She followed his orders. Carrying her psalter in her hand, she went into another room where she wanted to read the office. The wife awakened and in tears looked at the bright sunlight. She noticed that the old woman had left the room. She grieved and sighed and in tears lamented.

47

"Wretch," she said, "cursed be the day I was born! My fate is most dire. I am imprisoned in this tower, I shall not leave it except at my death. What does this jealous old man fear who keeps me in such strict confinement? He is irrational and frightened, fearing each day to be betrayed. I am unable to go to church or assist at

[80]   Mass. If I could speak to people and go off with someone to enjoy myself, I would show him a friendly mien, even if I had no inclination to. May my family and all others be cursed who gave me to this jealous husband and married me to his flesh! I have a hard row to hoe! He will never die! When he was to be baptized, he must have been plunged into the river of hell; strong are his nerves, strong his veins, all full of pulsing blood. I have oft heard it said that in the old days those who were downcast used to find adventures in this country, which heartened them. Knights found maidens to their liking, noble and beautiful ones, and ladies found handsome and courtly lovers who were courageous and valiant, so that no blame fell on these ladies, for no one besides them saw their lovers. If this could happen or if it was ever so, if ever it happened to anyone, may God, who has power over everything, answer my prayer!"

After she had lamented in this way, she saw the shadow of a great bird through a narrow window. She didn't know what this could be. It flew into the room. It alighted at her feet and seemed to be a goshawk that had molted five or six times. It stood before the woman. After it had been there awhile and she had observed it closely, it turned into a handsome and distinguished knight. The

[120]   lady was astonished. Seized by violent emotions, she trembled, became sore afraid, and covered her head. The knight was very courtly and was the first to speak.

"Lady," he said, "do not be afraid, the goshawk is a noble bird. Even though the secret things are hidden from you, please be reassured, and take me as your lover!"

"I came here," he continued, "for this reason. I have loved you for a long time and in my heart I have greatly desired you; I have never loved any woman but you and never shall I love any other. But I would have been unable to come to you or to leave my country, if you hadn't asked for me. Now I am able to be your lover!"

The lady felt reassured; she uncovered her head, and spoke. She answered the knight and said that she would take him as her beloved if he believed in God, and, if he did, their love would be possible. He indeed possessed extraordinary beauty; in her entire life she had never seen such a handsome knight and will never see another one so handsome.

"Lady," he said, "you have spoken well. I would not want there to be on my account any accusations, bad faith, or suspicion for any reason at all. I believe firmly in the Creator who redeemed us from the affliction into which Adam, our father, cast us, when he bit into the bitter apple; He is and will be and always was the way and the light for sinners. If you doubt me on this, send for your chaplain! [160] Tell him that you have suddenly taken ill, and you wish to have celebrated the service which God established in the world, by which sinners are saved. I will assume your appearance; I will receive the Body of the Lord our God, and I will recite my entire creed. In this way, you will not doubt me!"

And she replied that he had spoken well. He lay beside her in the bed; but he did not want to touch her, or embrace her, or kiss her. At that moment, the old woman returned. She found the lady awake, and told her it was time to rise, she wanted to bring her her clothes. The lady told her she was ill; she asked her to alert the chaplain and have him come to her immediately, for she was in great fear of her own death.

she listened to the knight

The old woman said: "Now, be patient! My master has gone into the woods; no one may enter here except me."

The lady was in the greatest distress; she pretended to faint. The old woman observed this with alarm. She unlocked the door to the room, and sent for the priest, who came as soon as he was able, carrying the Body of Christ. The knight received the host, and drank the wine from the chalice. The chaplain withdrew, and the old woman secured the doors.

The lady lay beside her lover; I never saw such a lovely couple. When they had sufficiently laughed and satisfied the desires of the flesh and spoken of their love, the knight took his leave; he wished to return to his country. She asked him sweetly to return to her [200] often.

"Lady," he said, "whenever you wish it, I shall always be here within the hour. But do be moderate so that we are not caught unawares. This old woman will spy on us night and day and will betray us. She will become aware of our love and will inform her lord about it. If this happens as I predict, and if we are betrayed in this way, I will not be able to escape at all, but will have to die."

Thereupon the knight went off, and left his beloved full of joy. In the morning she rose quite recovered, and spent the week

cheerfully. She took great care for her appearance; she completely
regained her beauty. Now she was more content to stay in her room
than to engage in any other diversion. She often wanted to see
her lover and to take her pleasure with him; as soon as her hus-
band left, either day or night, early or late, she had her lover all
to herself. May God grant her much time in which to take her
pleasure! Because of the intense joy that she felt, and because she
was able to see her beloved often, her appearance changed entirely.
Her husband was very shrewd; he realized that she looked different
from the way she usually looked. He began to distrust his sister. He
spoke with her one day and said that it was quite amazing that his
wife was taking such good care of herself; he asked her why this
[240]   was. The old woman said that she knew nothing (for no one could
speak to his wife and she had neither lover nor friend), except that
his wife stayed alone more willingly than she used to. This she had
noticed. The husband then answered her.

"By my faith," he said, "this is what I think. Now you must do
one thing! In the morning after I have gotten up and after you've
closed the doors, pretend to leave, allowing her to lie alone. You
will be in a secret place and you will watch and observe what it can
be that gives her such great joy and whence it comes."

After this conversation they separated. Alas! What ills will
befall those on whom they wish to spy in order to betray and entrap
them!

Three days later, this is what I've heard, the husband pretended
to leave on a journey. He told his wife the tale that the king had
summoned him by letter, but that he would return quickly. He left
the room and locked the door. Then the old woman awoke, she
placed herself behind some drapes; she will be quite able to see and
hear what she sought so much to know. The wife lay down, but did
not fall asleep, for she desired her lover so very intensely. He came,
without delay, within the agreed-upon limit of one hour. Together
they partook of very great joy by both what they said and what they
did, until it was time to get up, and time for him to leave her. The
[280]   old woman saw him, and observed how he came and how he left.
She was sore afraid at what she saw: first a man and then a gos-
hawk. When the husband, who had scarcely gone far, returned, the
old woman spoke to him and revealed the truth about the knight,
and the husband became greatly concerned. He hurried to have
traps made to kill the knight. He had large iron spikes forged and
had the points which jutted out sharpened; there was no sharper

razor under heaven. When the spikes were ready with the points
all sticking out, he had them installed, positioned closely together,
in the window casement, through which the knight entered when
he came to meet his beloved. Dear God! He was unaware of the
treachery that the felons had planned!

   The next day at dawn, the husband got up and said that he
intended to go hunting. The old woman saw him out; then she
went back to bed, for it was not yet light. The wife was awake,
waiting for him whom she loved so faithfully, and said that now
he would surely be able to come and spend plenty of time with
her. As soon as she called for him, he wasted no time in coming.
He flew in through the widow; but there were the spikes! His body
was pierced through by one of them, red blood gushed out. He felt
he'd been wounded unto death, pulled himself from the spike, and
came into the room. Before his beloved's eyes, he lay on the bed;
all the sheets became covered in blood. She saw the blood and   [320]
his wound, she was frightened and full of anguish. He said to her:
"My dearest love, I am losing my life for love of you! I clearly told
you that this would happen and that your behavior would kill us."
When she heard this, she fell into a faint; for a time she appeared
to be dead. He comforted her gently and said that grieving served
no purpose. She was pregnant by him with a child, she will have a
son who will be courageous and valiant, and who will be a comfort
for her. She will give him the name Yonec. He will avenge both   Yonec
his father and his mother, he will kill his enemy. The knight could
remain no longer, for blood flowed continuously from his wound.
He left in great sorrow. She followed him lamenting loudly. She
went out through a window; it's a wonder that she wasn't killed,
for she jumped from a height of twenty feet. She was naked under
her nightgown. She followed the trail of blood, which the knight
left behind on the road where she was. She traveled along this road
and held to it, until she came to a hillock. There was an entrance
into this hillock, and it was awash in blood; she could see nothing
beyond this point. She felt certain that her lover had gone into
this opening. She quickly followed. She found herself in total dark-
ness. She continued straight ahead until she came out the other
side of the hillock and into a most beautiful prairie. She saw that   [360]
the grass was covered with blood, and so she was very frightened.
She followed the trail of blood across the prairie. Quite nearby she
saw a city. It was completely surrounded by a wall. There was not a
house, nor a hall, nor a tower that didn't appear to be made entirely

of silver; the buildings were very sumptuous. On the approach to the town there were marshlands and forests and enclosed lands. In the other direction a river flowed all round the castle; ships docked there, and there were more than three hundred in port. The drawbridge was down, the lady entered the city still following the fresh blood through the town right to the castle. She saw not a man or a woman, not a soul spoke to her. She came to the entrance hall of the palace; she found its paving stones covered in blood. She entered a beautiful room; she found a knight asleep. She did not recognize him, and went farther on into another, larger room. She found a bed and nothing more, with a knight asleep on the bed; she continued along, and entered a third room; she found her lover's bed. The bedposts were of pure gold; I couldn't guess the cost of the bedclothes; the tapers and the candelabra, which burned night and day, were worth all of any city's gold. As soon as she saw him, she recognized the knight. She went toward him full of fright; she fell

[400]   into a faint on top of his body. He greeted the lady whom he deeply loved; wretched, he continually bemoaned his fate. When she woke from her faint, he comforted her sweetly.

"Dearest one, in God's name I beg of you, go! leave here! I shall die forthwith, at midday; there will be such mourning here when that happens that, if you were to be discovered, you would be terribly mistreated. It will be clearly known among my people that they have lost me because of my love for you. For you, I am sad and worried!"

The lady said to him: "Beloved, I prefer to die together with you than to suffer woes with my husband! If I go back to him, he will kill me."

The knight calmed her. He gave her a ring, and told and instructed her that as long as she kept the ring, her husband would recall nothing she had done, nor would he treat her harshly. He handed over and entrusted his sword to her; then he declared and insisted that no man be allowed to touch it, but that she keep it for his son. When he has come of age and has become a noble and valiant knight, she will go to a celebration and will take him and her husband along. They will come to an abbey; near a tomb that they will see, they will hear the tale of the knight's death and how he was killed in perfidy. Then she will give her son the sword. The young man will be told the story of his birth and who his father

[440]   was; and everyone will observe what he does. When the knight had told her all this in detail, he gave her a beautiful tunic, and

Yonec's destiny

told her to put it on. Then he had her leave him. She set off, car-
rying the ring and the sword which gave her comfort. She had not
gone a half a league, when, at the edge of the city, she heard the
church bells toll and heard wailing from the castle for their lord
who was dying. She knew for certain that he had died; because of
the sorrow she felt, she fainted four times. And when she came out
of her faint, she headed toward the hillock. She entered it, passed
through, and returned to her own country. She remained for years
and years together with her husband, who found no fault with her
for what she had done, nor did he abuse her, nor did he scorn her.

Her son was born and was well nurtured and well cared for and
much loved. They named him Yonec. In the kingdom one could not
find a young man so handsome, so courageous or so valiant, so gen-
erous or so liberal. When he had reached adulthood, they dubbed
him a knight. Now hear what happened in that same year!

On the feast of Saint Aaron, which was being celebrated at
Caerleon and in several other towns, the husband had been sum-
moned there along with his friends according to the customs of
the country; he dressed richly and took along his wife and his son. [480]
Thus it happened, they went forth. But they didn't know where
they were going; they had a young servant with them, who led
them along the right road, until they came to a castle; there was
none more beautiful in all the world. There was an abbey attached
to the castle with many religious. The young man who led them
to the feast gave them lodging there. In the room, which was the
abbot's, they were treated with honor and well served. The next day
they went to hear Mass; then they wished to leave. The abbot came
to speak with them; he strongly enjoined them to stay, he would
show them the dormitory, the chapter house, and the refectory.
Since they were comfortably lodged, the husband acquiesced.

When they had dined that day, they went to see the rooms of
the abbey. They came to the entrance to the chapter house. They
saw a large tomb covered with a silk cloth, with ring designs and a
diagonal stripe of rich gold embroidery. Twenty candles burned at
the head, the foot, and alongside the tomb. The candelabra were
of pure gold, the censers were of amethyst, by which the tomb was
incensed all day long out of great respect. They asked inquiringly of
those who were from this country what tomb this was and who was
buried in it. The local people all began to cry and through their
tears said that he was the best knight, the strongest and the brav-
est, the handsomest and the best loved, who had ever been born [520]
into the world.

"He was the king of this land; there was never a kinder ruler. In Caerwent he was attacked and killed for love of a woman. Ever since we have had no lord, but we have long awaited a son whom he fathered with the woman, such was his word and his charge."

When the wife heard this news, she called to her son in a loud voice.

"Dearest son," she said, "you have heard how God led us to this place! It is your father who lies here, whom this old man unjustly killed. Now I give and entrust to you his sword; I have kept it long enough."

Within everyone's hearing she told him that the knight had fathered him and that he was his son, how he used to come to her, and how her husband betrayed him; she told him the entire story. She fell into a faint on the tomb; and in this swoon she died. She never spoke another word. When her son saw that she was dead, he cut off his stepfather's head. Thus he avenged his father and his mother with the sword that had been his father's. As soon as this happened and was known throughout the city, they treated the woman with great honor and took her and laid her in the tomb next to the body of her lover. May God have mercy on them! Before they left the tomb, they made Yonec their lord.

[560]   Those who heard this adventure a long time afterward made a lay about it, and about the pain and sadness that this couple suffered for love.

VIII. Laüstic

(The Nightingale)

I shall tell you of an adventure about which the Bretons composed a lay. It is called *Laüstic*, as best I know, that's what they call it in their country; it's *Rossignol* in French and *Nightingale* in proper English.

In the countryside near Saint Malo there was a famous town. Two knights lived there and each had a fortified manor house. Because of the goodness of the two barons, the town had a good name. One of the barons had married a wise, refined, and elegant woman. She took pride in herself and adhered to custom and had good manners. The other baron was a young man, well known among his peers for his prowess and his great valor. He was eager to act honorably. He frequently fought in tournaments and spent much money, giving to others what he possessed. He was in love with his neighbor's wife. He entreated her, begged her, and was of such fine character that she loved him above all others, as much because of all the good things she had heard about him, as for the fact that he lived so near to her. They loved each other wisely and well, hiding their love and taking such precautions as not to be discovered, or impeded, or suspected. And they succeeded because their residences were close to each other. They had adjoining houses, great halls, and towers; there were no barriers or partitions save one high wall made of dark stone. When the lady stood at the window of the room where she slept, she was able to speak to her lover who was in his house, and he to her. They could exchange objects by throwing or flinging them. They were hardly displeased about anything (they were both content) except for the fact that they could not meet when they wished to, because the lady was under strict surveillance, when her lover was in residence. But they did have some recourse; at any time of night or during the day, each was able to speak to the other; no one could prevent their going to the window and their seeing each other in this way. They loved each other for a long while, until one summer when woodlands and fields were again verdant and meadows were again in flower, and the birds sang of their joy most sweetly among the flowers. It is no wonder that those who are in love devote themselves to love to their hearts' content. I will now tell you the truth about the knight-lover: he devoted himself to love with all his might, and the lady too, as they conversed and looked at each other. At night when the moon was out and her husband was asleep, the lady would get up from beside him and put on her tunic.

She would go to the window to see her lover who she knew would be at his, for he spent his time as she did. She would stay at the window for most of the night. Each would feel such delight at the sight of the other, even though they could have no other pleasure than this. She stood at the window so frequently, got up from bed so often that her husband got angry and asked her on many occasions why she got out of bed and where she went.

"Sir," the lady answered him, "those who have not heard the nightingale sing have known no earthly joy; that's why you see me standing here. At night I hear it singing so sweetly that it is a great delight to me; it pleases me so much and I yearn so much to hear it that I cannot sleep a wink."

When her husband heard this, he let out an angry, sardonic laugh. He could think of just one thing: how to trap the nightingale. There was no valet in his household who wasn't concocting a trap, a net, or a snare. Then they set them throughout the garden. There was not a hazelnut or a chestnut tree in which they didn't hang snares or put down birdlime, until they trapped and caught the nightingale. As soon as they had caught the nightingale, it was turned over still quite alive to their lord. He was quite pleased when he took possession of it. He went to his wife's room.

"Lady," he said, "Where are you? Come here! Speak to us! I have caught the nightingale which has kept you awake so much. From now on you'll be able to sleep peacefully; it will not awaken you again!"

When the lady heard this, she was sad and troubled. She asked her husband for the bird. He killed it out of wickedness. With his two hands he wrung its neck; he did this most villainously. He threw the carcass at her, bloodying the front of her tunic just a bit above her breasts. Then he left the room. The lady held the tiny corpse. She cried bitterly and cursed all those who had betrayed the nightingale by making traps and snares, for they had deprived her of great joy.

"Alas," she said, "woe is me! I will no longer be able to get up at night nor go to stand at the window, where I used to see my lover. I know one thing for certain, he will think that I am faint of heart. I must decide on a plan of action. I shall in fact send him the nightingale, and explain to him what has happened." With gold thread she embroidered a bit of silk fabric with writing; she wrapped the little bird in it. She called one of her valets. She entrusted him with her message, and sent him off to her lover. The valet came to the knight and greeted him in the name of his mistress, and recounted to him the entire message and presented him with the nightingale. When the valet had told him and showed him everything, and after the knight had listened attentively, he was saddened by the story; but he was neither common nor slow in his reaction. He had a small casket made. They used neither iron nor steel for it; it was all of pure gold set with fine stones, both precious and costly; it had a well-fitting lid. He placed the nightingale inside it; then he had the reliquary sealed, and henceforth kept it with him always.

This tale was told; it could not be kept hidden for long. The Bretons composed a lay about it that is called *Laüstic*.

IX. Milun

Anyone who wants to tell diverse tales must begin in different ways and speak so reasonably that what is said is pleasing to people. Here I shall begin *Milun* and I shall state succinctly why and how the lay so named was created.

Milun was born in South Wales. Since the day he was knighted, not a single knight had been able to unhorse him. He was a fine knight, noble and brave, well mannered and proud. He was famous in Ireland, and in Norway, and in Jutland; many were envious of him in Logres and in Scotland. He was much beloved for his courage and honored by many princes. In his country there was a baron, whose name I do not know. He had a daughter, a beautiful and refined girl. Having heard of Milun, she fell deeply in love with him. She told him by way of a messenger that, if he wished, she would love him. Milun was delighted with this news and he thanked her for it; he gave her his love willingly and his word never to stop loving her. He sent her a quite lovely reply. He gave fine gifts to the messenger and promised him his friendship.

"Friend," he said, "now, find a way for me to speak to my beloved and a way to hide our secret. You'll take my golden ring and give it to her from me. Whenever she wishes, come for me and I will return with you to her."

The messenger took his leave and then departed. He returned to his mistress. He gave her the ring, and told her that he had done what she had commanded. The girl was overjoyed for the love thus offered her. Outside her room in a garden where she used to spend her time she and Milun often arranged to talk together. Milun came there so often and loved her so much that the girl became pregnant. When she became aware of her condition she sent for Milun and began to lament. She told him what had happened and how, for having done such a thing, she had lost her honor and her good name. She will suffer dire consequences; she will be tortured with a sword or sold off into some other country. Such was the custom of the Ancients and it was still in force at this time. Milun said he would do whatever she advised.

"When the child is born," she said, "you will take it to my sister who is married and who lives in Northumbria, she is a wealthy woman, noble and wise, and you will inform her both by letter and by the words of a messenger, that this is the child of her sister, who, because of this child, has suffered much pain. She is to make certain that the child is well cared for, whether it is a boy or a girl. I shall hang your ring round the child's neck and I'll send along a letter. Therein will be written the name of the child's father and the story of its mother. When the child has grown and has reached the age of reason, she is to give it the letter and the ring and is to tell the child to keep them till the child is able to find its father."

They held to this plan, and the time came for the girl to give birth. An old woman who served her, and who shared everything with her, hid her and protected her, so that there was never any indication—either said or seen—of this birth. The girl gave birth to a beautiful son. Around his neck they attached the ring and the letter in a silk pouch to keep it well hidden from all. Then, wrapped in a white blanket, the infant was laid in a cradle. Underneath the infant's head they put a fine pillow and over him a coverlet trimmed all round with marten fur. The old woman gave the child to Milun who was waiting for her in the garden. He ordered his men to carry the child away faithfully. They stopped seven times each day in villages they came upon to have the child nursed, to bathe it, and to change its linen. They followed the road exactly until they entrusted the child to his aunt. She welcomed the child joyfully. She took the sealed letter. When she discovered who the child was, she cherished him deeply. Those who had brought the child returned to their own country.

Milun left his own lands to increase his renown and augment his fortune. His beloved remained at home. Her father betrothed her to a baron, a very rich man in their country, very powerful and quite famous. When she learned this news, she was sad beyond description and often lamented Milun's absence, for she feared she would be mistreated for having had a child; her intended would know it immediately.

"Woe is me," she said. "What shall I do? Will I take a husband? How will I manage? I am no longer a virgin; I shall forevermore be a maidservant! I didn't think it would be like this; I thought rather that I would have my beloved, and we would always keep our relationship a secret and never would I hear it mentioned elsewhere. It would be better for me to die than to live; but I am hardly completely free, rather I have around me a number of retainers, old and young, my attendants, who always detest noble love and who take pleasure in sadness. So I am obliged to suffer, wretch that I am, since I am unable to die."

At the appointed time, her new husband led her off.

Milun returned to his country. He was quite sad, and most pensive, he suffered greatly, and could not hide it; but he took comfort in this: that nearby his country was she whom he loved so much. Milun began to ponder how he might send word to her, in such a way that it would not be noticed, letting her know that he had returned to his country. He wrote his letter and sealed it. He owned a swan that he loved very much; he attached the letter to its neck, concealing the letter in the bird's feathers. He called one of his squires, and entrusted him with his message.

"Go quickly," he said. "Change your clothes! You will go to the castle of my beloved. You will take my swan with you. See to it and make certain that the swan is passed along to her by either a servant or a serving maid."

The squire followed his orders and left immediately, taking the swan. He was able to get to the castle by the most direct route he knew. He passed through the town, and came to the main door of the castle. He called the porter over to him.

"Friend," he said, "listen carefully! I am a fowler, whose trade it is to catch birds. In a field below Caerleon I caught a swan in my snares. To gain the goodwill and protection of the lady of this house, I wish to make a present of it, so that I will not be bothered or harassed in this country."

The porter answered him: "Friend, no one may speak with her; nonetheless, I will go see whether there is a place where I may lead you, where you might be able to speak with her."

The porter entered the great hall and found but two knights there; they were seated at a large table, engaged in a game of chess. He quickly returned to the fowler whom he guided in such a way that no one heard him, saw him, or knew he was there. The porter came to her room and called out; a serving maid opened the door for them. They came into the lady's presence and offered her the swan. She called one of her valets. Then she said to him: "Now see to it that my swan is well cared for and that it has enough to eat!"

"Lady," said he who had brought the swan, "no one save you may receive this magnificent gift; notice how lovely and pleasing it is!"

He gave it to her, placing it into her hands. She accepted it most joyously. She caressed its neck and its head, she felt the letter under its plumage, she blanched as the blood drained from her face and she trembled; she knew well that the letter was from her beloved. She had the fowler given a gift and ordered him to go.

When the room was empty, she called a serving maid. Together they unfastened the letter; the lady broke the seal. In the opening line she saw "Milun." She recognized her beloved's name; crying, she kissed the letter a hundred times, before she was able to continue reading. At the beginning of the letter she saw the words that Milun had ordered to be written down about the terrible pains and the sadness that he suffered day and night. Now it was entirely in her hands whether he died because of her or was cured. If she could come up with a ruse that would allow him to speak with her, she should reply to him in a letter, and send the swan back to him. First she was to have the swan well cared for, then have it fast such that it ate nothing for three days; she was to attach the letter to its neck; and allow him to fly off; he would return to where he first lived. When she had reread the entire letter and understood what Milun had written there, she allowed the swan to rest and gave it plentiful food and drink. She kept it in her room for a month. But now, hear what happened! By art and guile she managed to get ink and parchment. She wrote a letter that pleased her, and sealed it with a signet ring. She made the swan observe its fast; she hung the letter around its neck, and let it loose. The bird was famished and wanted to eat; it quickly returned to the place where it had first been nurtured, to the city and into the house. It swooped down at Milun's feet. When he saw the swan, he was very happy; happily he took it by its wings. He called his steward, and had the swan given food. He removed the letter from around its neck. He examined it from beginning to end, he rejoiced at what he found written and at her greeting: "She can have no joy without him; and he is to tell her what his intentions are in the same way, that is, by means of the swan!" He did so immediately. Milun and his beloved continued this exchange for twenty years. They used the swan as a messenger, they had no other communication, and they had the swan fast before they allowed it to fly. Be assured: the one to whom the swan flew fed it. They did manage to meet several times. People cannot be so isolated nor so closely observed that they cannot find an opportunity to meet.

The woman who raised their son (he had been with her for so long that he was now of age) had him dubbed a knight. He was a very noble lad. She gave him the letter and the ring. Then she told him who his mother was and her relationship with his father, and how he was a goodly knight, so courageous, brave, and strong. No one in the country was his better in prestige or in valor. When she instructed him he listened intently, he rejoiced upon learning of his father's reputation; he was pleased with what he heard. He reflected and said to himself: "Little does a man value himself, being the son of such an esteemed father, if he does not set for himself a higher goal beyond his own land and his own country." He had all that was needed. He remained there only that evening; the next day he took his leave. The lady gave him much advice and admonished him to do good; she gave him a large sum of money.

He went to Southampton with all speed and set sail. He came to Barfleur and went from there directly into Brittany. There he spent money and engaged in tourneys; he made the acquaintance of powerful men. He never engaged in any battle where he was not considered the best. He befriended poor knights; he gave them what he won from the rich and he took them into his service, and spent his money very freely. Never did he willingly tarry. From every land in that part of the world he carried away fame and repute; he was noble and knew much about honor. The news of his virtue and of his fame reached his own country: a young man had crossed the seas in order to seek fame, and then accomplished so much by his prowess, by his goodness, and by his largesse that those who did not know his name everywhere called him Peerless. Milun heard his praises and the good things said about him. He was very saddened, and complained bitterly about the knight who was so worthy, for as long as Milun was able to travel and bear arms and joust, no one born in Milun's country ought to be so esteemed or extolled. He thought of one thing: he will quickly cross the sea and will fight this knight in order to discredit and degrade him. It was out of anger that he wanted to fight; if he can unhorse him, he will have finally shamed him. Then he will go in search of his son who has left his country, but what has become of him, he does not know.

He let his beloved know his plan, he wanted to have her leave to go. He told her of his feelings, sending her a sealed letter, as far as I understand, by way of the swan; he asked for her opinion. When she heard of his plan, she thanked him and expressed her gratitude, since in order to seek and find their son and to demonstrate his own ability he wished to leave the country, she didn't in any way wish to impede him. Milun heard the reply and equipped himself richly. He crossed into Normandy, and from there into Brittany. He fought against many men and frequently sought out tournaments; he often enjoyed sumptuous lodgings and gave generously to others.

As best I know, Milun remained in this country for an entire winter. He kept a number of good knights in his service until Eastertide when they again began to enter tournaments, to engage in battles and disputes. At Mont Saint Michel, there assembled Normans and Bretons, knights from Flanders and from France, but scarcely any Englishmen. Milun, who was brave and strong, was the first to arrive. He sought out the good knight. There were many there who told him where he had come from and who showed him his arms and his shields. They all showed these to Milun who examined them closely. They all gathered for the tournament. He who sought a fight soon found one; he who sought out conflict could soon lose or win in fighting an opponent. I want to tell you this much about Milun: he did very well in these combats and he was held in high esteem that day. But the young knight I'm telling you about won more praise than all the others, none could be compared with him in fighting or in jousting. Milun saw him performing so well, urging his steed forward and attacking head-on. Despite Milun's envy of him, he greatly admired this young knight. Milun entered the lists against him, the two jousted one against the other. Milun struck the knight so violently, that his lance veritably shattered into pieces, but without at all vanquishing his adversary, who now rode back and, striking Milun, knocked him off his horse and onto the ground. Through Milun's visor the knight saw his hair and beard, all white; he was sorely distressed at having unhorsed him. He took Milun's horse by the reins, and standing before him returned his horse to him. Then the young man said to him: "Sir, remount! I am most painfully saddened for having done such a wrong to a man of your years." Milun jumped onto his horse with great joy.

When the young knight handed him back his horse, Milun recognized the ring on the knight's finger. He spoke to him, saying: "Friend, listen to me! Tell me, for the love of God almighty, what is your father's name? And what is yours? Who is your mother? I must know the truth. I have seen much in my many travels, and visited other lands to joust and to do battle; never from the blow of another knight have I fallen from my horse! You have defeated me in a joust; I admire you beyond measure!" The youth replied: "I will tell you all that I know of my father. I believe he was born in Wales and that his name is Milun. He fell in love with the daughter of a powerful lord; I was conceived in secret. I was sent to Northumbria; there I was raised and educated. An aunt of mine raised me, and then kept me with her, giving me arms and a horse, and sending me to this land. I have lived here for quite some time. I have thought about it and it's my intention to cross the sea quickly and to return to my own country. I wish to know my father's situation and his intentions concerning my mother. I will show him a certain gold ring and I will give him such proofs that he will not be able to send me away, but will love me and hold me dear." When Milun heard him say these things, he could listen no longer; he suddenly leapt forward and grabbed the young knight by the hem of his coat of mail.

"Oh God!" he said. "I am restored to life! Truly, friend, you are my son. Some time ago, I left my country in order to seek you and to find you."

When the knight heard this, he dismounted, and kissed his father tenderly. They showed their affection for each other and said such things to each other that those who observed them shed tears of joy and compassion. When the tournament ended, Milun departed; he was anxious to speak at length with his son, and to explain his feelings to him. They lodged together that night. In great joy they made merry with many other knights in attendance. Milun told his son how he fell in love with the young man's mother, and how her father married her off to a baron from her own country, and how he continued to love her and she him deeply, and how he sent messages by means of the swan, who carried his letters that he would not have entrusted to any person. The son replied: "Truly, dearest father, I will reunite you and my mother. I will kill the man to whom she is married and I will see to it that she marries you."

That was the final word that night and the next day they readied themselves. They bade farewell to their friends, and set off for their own country. With fair sailing weather and a strong wind, they had a speedy sea crossing. As they continued their journey, they encountered a serving lad. He came on behalf of Milun's beloved, and wanted to cross to Brittany; she had sent him. His task was now shortened. He gave Milun a sealed letter. The lady had written him to return and not to delay. Her husband had died; Milun was to return in all haste! When he heard the news, it seemed to Milun to be too good to be true. He showed his son the letter and read it to him. There was neither hindrance nor delay; they continued until they came to the castle where the lady lived. She was delighted with her son who was so valiant and noble. They did not send for any relatives; without consulting anyone, their son united the two of them, giving his mother to his father. They lived henceforth, in great joy and in great tenderness.

About their love and their joy, the Ancients created a lay; and I, who have put it down in writing, am delighted to have recounted it.

X. Chaitivel

(The Unfortunate One)

I was prompted by the desire to remember a lay that I heard. I shall tell you the adventure and give you the name of the city where it originated, and what it was called. They call it *The Unfortunate One*, yet there are many who call it *The Four Lamentations*.

In Brittany in the city of Nantes, there lived a lady who was much esteemed for her beauty and her learning and for all the social graces she possessed. There was no knight in the region worth his mettle who, having seen her once, did not fall in love with her and woo her. She could scarcely love them all, yet she hardly wanted them to die of love. It would be preferable to seek the love of all the women in a country than to take bread from a fool, for the fool wants to strike out in haste. If a lady obliges everyone, of everyone she retains the goodwill; however, if she doesn't want to listen to them, she ought not revile them, but keep them dear and honored, show them devotion, and praise them to their satisfaction. The lady, whose story I wish to tell, whose love was so often sought because of her beauty, and because of her worth, was kept busy in this way night and day.

In Brittany there were four barons, but I am unable to furnish their names. Although not very old, they were very handsome, worthy and valiant knights, generous, courtly, and liberal with their money; they were highborn and exceptionally admired in that country. These four loved this lady and took pains to succeed; each one did his utmost to possess her and her love. Each one sought her for himself, putting all his effort into this; there wasn't one of them who didn't think himself more successful than others in this endeavor. The lady was quite sensible. She gave herself over to thought and reflection in order to ascertain and to know which one it would be best to love. Because they were all of great consequence, she was unable to determine the best one. In choosing one, she didn't want to lose the other three; she retained a friendly demeanor for each one, showing signs of affection to each, sending each of them messages. None knew about the others; in any case, none was able to abandon her. Through appropriate service and entreaties each believed he could best succeed. In knightly combat, each one wanted to be first in fighting well, if he could, in order to please the lady. Each one considered her his beloved, wore the love tokens she had given him—a ring, or a sleeve, or a pennon—and each invoked her name. She loved all four and held on to them, until one Eastertide, a tournament was announced that would take place before the city of Nantes. In order to joust with the four lovers, there arrived from other countries Frenchmen, Normans, knights from Flanders and from Brabant, from Boulogne and from Anjou, and others who were neighbors from close by; all gladly came to Nantes. They had stayed for a long time. On the eve of the tourney they exchanged blows ferociously. The four lovers were armed and left the city; their companions followed after them, but the weight of the undertaking fell to the four. Those from elsewhere recognized them by their banners and their shields. They sent against them two knights from Flanders and two from Hainault, ready to charge; there wasn't one who didn't want to have the battle joined. The four lovers saw them coming toward them, they had no urge to flee. With their lances lowered, straightaway each one chose his opponent. They struck with such ferocity that the four foreigners were unhorsed. The four lovers had no need for mounts, so they left them riderless; they took their stand against the unhorsed knights whose companions came to their aid. In the melee that this rescue engendered, many sword blows were struck. The lady was in a tower, she watched her knights and their companions closely. She saw her lovers demonstrating remarkable competence; she didn't know which one to prize the most.

The tournament began, the line of battle grew, and became quite thick. Many times that day, battle was joined before the city gates. The four lovers fought well, so that they prevailed over all there, until nightfall when they were to part company. Too impetuously they threw themselves into the fray, far from their companions; for this they paid dearly: for three of them were killed and the fourth was injured, wounded by a lance that went through his thigh and into his body and came out the other side. They had been struck from the flank and all four had been felled. Those who had mortally wounded them threw their shields onto the field; they were sorely saddened by what they had inadvertently done to them. A din arose and lamentations, never had such mourning been heard before. The inhabitants of the city came to the site, they didn't fear the adversaries. Grieving likewise for the dead were two thousand knights who unlaced their neck protectors, and pulled at their hair and their beards. The mourning among them was universal. Each knight was placed on his shield, they were carried into the city to the lady who had loved them. As soon as she learned what had happened she collapsed to the ground in a faint. When she regained consciousness, she lamented the loss of each by name.

"Alas," she said, "what shall I do? Never shall I know joy! I loved these four knights and I desired each one for himself; there was great goodness in each of them. They loved me more than anything. Because of their beauty, their prowess, their worth, and their generosity, I made them focus their love on me; I didn't want to lose all of them by choosing one of them. I do not know which of them I ought to pity the most; I do not wish to hide my thoughts or to pretend. I see one wounded, three are dead; I have nothing left in the world that consoles me! I shall have the dead buried, and if the wounded one is capable of recovering, I shall willingly take pains to secure able doctors for him."

She had him carried to her rooms. She then had the others readied for burial; with great tenderness, she had the bodies richly and sumptuously prepared. She made generous offerings and presents to a very prosperous abbey where they were buried. May God grant them His kind mercy! She summoned wise physicians, and she had the knight, who lay wounded in her room, put under their care until he recovers his health. She would go to see him often and would comfort him most tenderly; but she missed the three others and felt great grief because of them.

One summer's day, after dinner, the lady was speaking to the knight. Thoughts of her deep bereavement came back to her; and because of this she lowered her head and her eyes. She gave herself over to intense reflection. The knight observed her closely; he realized that she was deep in thought. He gently asked her: "Lady, you are upset! What are you thinking of? Do tell me! Forsake your sorrow, you should take heart!"

"Friend," she said, "I was thinking about and recalling your companions. A woman of my station, no matter how beautiful, noble, or wise, will never love four such men at the same time, nor lose them in a single day—excepting you who, alone among them, were wounded and in great danger of death because of this. Because I loved you all so much, I want my bereavement enshrined in memory. I shall make a lay about the four of you and I shall entitle it *The Four Lamentations*.

As soon as the knight heard this, he quickly corrected her: "Lady, make your new lay and call it *The Unfortunate One*! And I wish to demonstrate to you that it ought to have this title. The others have been dead for some time now and spent their entire lives in the great torment they suffered because of the love they bore for you. But I, who escaped with my life, am quite wretched and confused, I often see, coming and going and speaking with me morning and evening, she whom I love most in the world, yet I can experience no joy either from kissing or from embracing or from other favors, save speaking with her. A hundred such pains cause me to suffer, it would be better for me to die. For this reason, the lay will be named for me: it will be called *The Unfortunate One*. Whoever calls it *The Four Lamentations* will be altering its real title."

"In truth," she said, "I'm willing. Henceforth, we shall call it *The Unfortunate One*."

And so the lay was begun and then completed and recounted. Some of those who disseminate it call it *The Four Lamentations*. Each of the names suits it well, for the material allows this; *The Unfortunate One* is the customary name. It ends here, there is no more: I heard no more about it, I know no more about it, no more of it shall I recount to you.

XI. Chievrefueil

(The Honeysuckle)

It pleases me very much and indeed I want to tell you the true story of the lay they call *Chievrefueil*, how it was composed, why, and what its origin is. Many have mentioned and recounted it to me, and I've come across it written down; it's about Tristan and the queen, about their love which was so true, and because of which they suffered so much pain, only to die of it on the same day.

King Mark was angry, nay, furious, with his nephew Tristan; he exiled him from his land because of the queen whom he loved. Tristan went into his own country. He went to South Wales where he was born, he could not return for an entire year; but then he exposed himself to death and destruction. Don't be at all surprised, for he who loves faithfully is very sad and pensive, when his sexual desires are unsatisfied. Tristan was sad and pensive, and so he left his own country. He went straight to Cornwall where the queen was. He stayed in the forest all alone, not wanting to be seen by anyone. At dusk when it was time to find shelter for the night, he came forth. He took shelter for the night with peasants and poor folk. He inquired of them how the king was behaving. They told him they had heard that by proclamation the king's barons had been ordered to come to Tintagel. The king intended to hold court, they should all be there at Pentecost; there will much joy and merrymaking, and the queen will be with the king.

Tristan heard this news, he was very pleased. She would not be able to go to Tintagel without him seeing her pass by. The day on which the king was to travel, Tristan returned to the woods, to the road he knew the royal cortege would take. He cut off the branch of a hazelnut tree, and whittled it to give it four sides. When he had shaped the staff he carved his name with his knife. If the queen sees it—she was very observant—*when* she sees it, she'll surely recognize the staff of her friend. When he had come to her another time, she had become aware of him in this way. This was the meaning of the message that he had sent and announced to her: for a long while he had been there and waited and stayed to watch and decide how he might see her, for without her he could not live. They were just like the honeysuckle clinging to the hazelnut: when it entwines itself, attaches itself, and winds itself all about the trunk, they are able to adhere together; but if anyone later wants to detach them, the hazelnut quickly dies and the honeysuckle likewise. "Beauteous friend, so is it with us: neither you without me, nor I without you!"

The queen came along on horseback. Looking carefully ahead of her, she spotted the staff, and read all that was written. She ordered the knights accompanying her who rode along with her to stop immediately: she wanted to dismount and rest awhile. They followed her command. She went some ways off, leaving her entourage; she called her servant, the most faithful Brangien, to accompany her. The queen strayed a little from the road. In the woodland she found him whom she loved more than any living being. They took great pleasure together. He spoke with her with complete abandon, and she told him what she desired; then she showed him how they might make peace with the king, for Tristan's exile, precipitated by an accusation, weighed so heavily on the king. Then she went away, leaving her friend; but at that moment of separation, they both began to weep. Tristan returned to Wales to wait for his uncle to call him back.

Because of the joy which he felt upon seeing his beloved and because of what he had written which the queen had read out, Tristan, who knew how to play the harp quite well, created from this event a new lay, in order to recall the words of the message. I'll name it succinctly: the English call it *Gotelef*, the French name it *Chievrefueil*. I have told you the truth about it in the lay I have set forth here.

XII. Eliduc

I shall tell you in its entirety the tale of a very old Breton lay, to the best of my knowledge and exactly as I understand the true facts.

In Brittany there was a brave and noble knight, bold and mighty. His name, as far as I know, was Eliduc; there was no more worthy man in the country. He had a wife, who was noble and wise, of high birth, and of aristocratic lineage. They had been married for a long time, and loved each other loyally; but then, because of a war, it happened that he went off seeking gain as a mercenary; there he fell in love with a girl, who was the daughter of a king and queen. The maiden's name was Guilliadun, the kingdom boasted of none more beautiful than she. The wife, in turn, was called Guildeluec in her country. In honor of these two, the lay is also entitled *Guildeluec and Guilliadun*. It was initially entitled *Eliduc* but, in fact, the title was changed, for the story on which the lay was based happened to the women. I will tell you the true story just as it happened.

Eliduc had as his master the king of Brittany who loved him greatly and cherished him, and Eliduc served the king faithfully. Whenever the king had to be away, Eliduc protected his land; the king depended upon him for his prowess. For this reason much good fortune came to Eliduc. He was able to hunt in the forests; there was no royal forester presumptuous enough to dare to prevent him nor to complain about it even once. Out of envy for his good fortune, as it often happens to people, he was slandered and denounced and lost favor with his lord who sent him away from court without giving him any explanation. Eliduc didn't know why this had happened. He often begged the king to listen to his defense and not to believe the slanderers, saying he had served him most willingly; but the king did not answer him. He wanted to hear nothing about it, and so, it behooved Eliduc to leave. He went to his home and sent for all his friends. He disclosed to them the ire which the king, his lord, felt for him. He had served the king well and to the best of his ability, and the king ought not now be ungrateful. The peasant, when in a quarrel with his ploughman, says, by way of a maxim, that a lord's love is not a fief. He is wise and shrewd who shows loyalty to his lord; to his good neighbors, love. He didn't want to stay in this country, but said this: he would rather go across the sea; he will go into the kingdom of Logres and spend some time there. He will leave his wife on his domain; and he will order his men, as well as all his friends, to watch over her loyally. He settled on this decision, and so he

71

equipped himself splendidly. His friends were terribly sad at his leaving them. He took with him ten knights, and his wife accompanied him a ways. At the moment of her husband's departure, she displayed a great deal of sorrow; but he assured her that truly he would be faithful to her. He then left her. He followed the road before him, came to the sea, and crossed it; he arrived at Totness.

In this land there were numerous kings who were in conflict and at war with one another. In this land, near Exeter, there lived a very powerful man. He was an old man, advanced in years. He did not have a male heir born of his flesh; he had a daughter of marriageable age. Because he refused to marry her off to a peer of his, this man was at war with him, and was laying waste to his entire realm. He had besieged him in his castle. There was not a man in the castle so bold as to dare to ride out against the king's enemy in order to engage in combat or in a skirmish. Eliduc heard of this situation. He didn't wish to continue any further on his way, since he had found a war in this place; he wished to stay in this country. He wanted to help, as best he could, the king who was so distressed, overwhelmed, at the mercy of his enemy; and to remain in his employ. Eliduc sent envoys to the castle and in his letters informed the king that he had left his own country and had come to aid him. But he asked him what the king desired and if he did not wish to engage him, to grant him safe passage through his lands, so that he could seek gain as a mercenary elsewhere. As soon as the king saw the messengers, he felt great affection for them and held them in the highest regard. He summoned his constable and promptly ordered him to ready an escort and to bring the baron to court; and to prepare lodgings where he and his men could stay; and to have made available and turned over to them as much as they might spend in a month. The escort was readied and sent to get Eliduc, who was received with great honor; he was very welcomed by the king. His lodgings were in the house of a burgher, who was very wise and obliging; he turned over to his guests his beautiful room hung with tapestries. Eliduc had himself well served. To his meals he invited the less well-off knights who were lodged in the town. He ordered all his men that there be none so bold as to accept any gift or money during the first forty days.

On the third day of his stay a report went through the town that their enemies had come and had spread out into the countryside; they were now ready to attack the town and to come right up to the gates. Eliduc heard the tumult among the people who were bewildered. Straightaway he armed himself, and his companions did the same. There were fourteen mounted knights lodged in the town (a number of others had been

wounded and many others had been taken prisoner). These knights saw
Eliduc mount up. They went to their lodgings to arm themselves; they
went out through the city gates with him, not waiting for any call to
arms.

"Sir," they said, "we shall go with you and shall do what you do!"

He answered them: "Thank you! Would there be any one of you here
who knows of a difficult, narrow passage where we could attack them? If
we lie in wait for them here, we will perhaps engage in battle, but this
will be to no avail. Who has other advice?" They said to him: "Truly,
Sir, in a thicket near these woods, there is a narrow road, by which they
withdraw. When they have gotten their booty, they return this way;
they often go back unarmed, riding on their palfreys, in this way put-
ting themselves in danger of dying outright. One could soon hurt them,
humiliate them, and reduce them to a sorry state." Eliduc said to them:
"Friends, I pledge you on my faith: he who does not often go to such a
place, where he assumes that he will lose, will never gain any spoils or
increase his reputation. You are all men of the king and you are to bear
him true faith. Come with me where I go, and do what I do! I assure you
in good faith that you will encounter no misfortune, as far as I can help
it. If we can make some gains, this act of bringing ruin to our enemies
will redound to our credit." The king's men had faith in this promise,
and they led Eliduc to the woods. They lay in ambush near the road,
waiting for the enemy to withdraw along it. Eliduc showed and taught
and explained everything to them, how they were to charge the enemy
while shouting war cries. As soon as the enemy had entered the nar-
rows, Eliduc challenged them. He called upon all his companions and
summoned them to fight well. They rained down blows fiercely, not in
the least sparing the enemy, who were completely startled, soon routed,
and in flight. They were vanquished in a short time. Their constable
was captured and many other knights (whom the king's knights handed
over to their squires); there were twenty-five knights on the winning
side who captured thirty of the enemy. They captured a great deal of
equipment; they carried off marvelous spoils. They returned overjoyed;
they had accomplished a great deal. The king was in a tower, sorely
afraid for his men; he complained bitterly about Eliduc, for he thought
and feared that Eliduc had traitorously abandoned his knights. They
all approached together, completely weighed down, laden with booty.
There were many more returning than had gone off; for this reason
the king didn't recognize them and so he was full of doubt and uncer-
tainty. He ordered that the gates be closed and that men take to the
battlements to let fly arrows and spears; but they'll have no need to do

that. The knights had sent a squire ahead riding hard, who told the
king of the adventure and informed him about the mercenary: how he
had defeated the enemy and how he had comported himself. Never was
there such a knight. He had captured their constable and had taken
twenty-nine others prisoner, while wounding and killing a great many
others. As soon as the king heard the news, he was overcome with joy.
He came down from the tower and went to greet Eliduc. He thanked
him for his feats of arms, and Eliduc delivered the prisoners over to him.
To the others he dispensed the spoils; he kept for himself but three
horses that were allocated to him; he gave away all of his share on this
occasion, distributing it all both to prisoners and to the other knights.

After this feat that I've told you about, the king loved Eliduc dearly
and cherished him. For an entire year, the king kept with him Eliduc
and those who had accompanied him. He received pledges of loyalty
from Eliduc and made him protector of his domain.

Eliduc was courtly and wise, a handsome knight both valiant and
generous. The king's daughter had heard mention of his name and had
heard tell of his good deeds. With one of her personal chamberlains as
intermediary she asked, requested, and entreated him to come relax
with her, to chat, and to get acquainted; she was quite surprised that
he had not visited her. He replied that he would come, and gladly get
to know her. He mounted his horse, taking one knight with him; and
went to speak with the young woman. As he was to enter the room,
Eliduc sent the chamberlain ahead, while he tarried a bit, until the
chamberlain returned. With a gentle manner, a friendly expression, and
a quite noble demeanor, Eliduc spoke most affably, and thanked Guil-
liadun, the young woman, who was most beautiful, for having wanted
to send for him to come speak with her. She took him by the hand, they
sat down on a bed and spoke of many things. She looked intently at his
face, his body, and his demeanor and thought that everything about
him was pleasing. She held him in the highest regard in her heart. Love
delivered its message inviting her to love him, making her blanch and
sigh. But she didn't want to speak to him about this, fearing that he
would consider this a flaw. He stayed there for some time; he then took
his leave and left. She allowed this reluctantly; he left nonetheless. He
returned to his lodgings. He was completely dejected and preoccupied;
he was terribly agitated because of this beautiful maiden, the daughter
of his lord the king, who had spoken to him so sweetly and because she
had sighed. He was terribly disturbed that he had been in the country
for so long without having seen her often. As soon as he said this, he
repented: he remembered his wife, and how he had assured her that he
would be faithful to her and conduct himself honorably.

The maiden who had now seen him wanted to have him as her lover. Never had she held another in such esteem; if she can, she will take him as her lover. And so, she spent a sleepless night, unable to rest or to sleep. She rose at dawn the next day and went to the window. She summoned her chamberlain, and revealed to him all her thoughts.

"Truly," she said, "things are not good with me! I have fallen into a lamentable situation: I am in love with the new mercenary, the goodly knight, Eliduc. Unable to close my eyes for sleep, I have had no rest this night. If he wishes to love me sincerely and to affirm that with his body, I shall completely satisfy his desires, and he will be able to obtain great benefits from this, he shall be king in this country. He is so wise and so courtly, that, if he does not love me sincerely, I shall have to die from profound sorrow." When she had told him what she wished to say, the chamberlain whom she had summoned gave her his loyal counsel for which one ought not criticize him.

"Lady," he said, "since you love him, send him a message. Send him a belt or a ribbon or a ring, if that pleases you. If he receives it cordially and is happy about the message, you will be certain of his love! There is no emperor under heaven, who, if you wanted to love him, would not be utterly delighted about it." Having heard his advice the young woman replied: "How shall I know from my gift if he is inclined to love me? I never met a knight, whether he loved or he hated, who had to be begged to be willing to keep a gift that someone had sent him. I would very much hate it were he to mock me. However, by their mien one can understand others. Make ready and go!"

"I am," he said, "quite ready."

"You shall take him a gold ring and you shall give him my belt! You shall greet him for me a thousand times!"

The chamberlain went off. She was in such a state that she almost called him back, yet she let him go, and she began to worry: "Alas! How my heart has been overpowered by a foreigner! I do not know whether he is highborn. If he leaves soon, I shall remain here dejected. I foolishly set my mind on him. I never spoke with him until yesterday and now I am asking for his love. I think that he will reproach me. If he is courtly, he will be grateful to me, (now everything is entirely up in the air!) and if he cares not a bit about my love, I shall consider myself disgraced; I shall never know joy in my life."

As she worried, the chamberlain went in great haste. He came to Eliduc. Privately, he conveyed to him the greetings that the maiden had sent, and presented him with the ring and gave him the belt. The knight expressed his thanks to her. He put the gold ring on his finger, and girded himself with the belt; the servant said no more to him, and

Eliduc asked nothing of him but offered him something of his own. The servant took nothing, and left. He returned to the young woman, and found her in her room. He greeted her in the name of Eliduc who sent her thanks for her gifts.

"All right," she said, "keep nothing from me! Does he wish to love me sincerely?"

He answered her: "I think so: the knight does not act without thinking; I judge him to be courtly and wise, and someone who is quite able to hide his feelings. I greeted him on your behalf and presented him with your gifts. He girded himself with your belt, tightening it appropriately around his waist, and put the ring on his finger. I said no more to him, nor he to me."

"Did he accept them as love tokens? Otherwise, is it possible I have given myself away?"

The servant said to her: "To tell you the truth, I don't know. Now hear what I do have to say: if he did not wish you the very best, he would not have accepted anything from you."

"You are speaking in jest," she said. "I am quite aware that he doesn't hate me. I never did anything to offend him, except love him ardently; and if for this he wishes to hate me, he is deserving of death. Neither through you nor through another, do I ever wish to ask anything of him until I speak with him; I want to show him myself how my love for him torments me. But I don't know whether he will remain here." The chamberlain responded: "Lady, the king has engaged him by oath to serve him loyally for one year. You will have ample time to make your feelings known to him." When she heard that he was to stay, she was overjoyed, and very pleased that he was staying. She knew nothing of the pain he felt since meeting her. He never felt any joy or delight, except when thinking of her. He felt great distress, for he had promised his wife, before leaving his country, that he would love no one but her. Now his heart was utterly captivated. He wanted to remain loyal, but he could in no way free himself from loving the young woman, Guilliadun, who was so lovely, and from wanting to look at her and to speak to her and to kiss her and embrace her. But he would never seek a love which would bring him dishonor, as much because he wished to keep faith with his wife as because he was the king's man. Eliduc was greatly tormented. He mounted his horse without delay and called his companions to him. He headed to the castle to speak with the king. He will see the maiden if he can: she is the reason why he set off. The king had gotten up from eating, and gone into his daughter's room. He began to play chess with a knight from abroad seated at the other side of the chessboard, who was to teach the game to his daughter. Eliduc entered. The king greeted him in a friendly way, and had him sit down next to him. He called his daughter and said to her: "Young lady, you ought to get to know this knight and show him the very warmest welcome; among five hundred, there is no better knight." When the girl heard what her father commanded, she was exceedingly happy. She rose and called Eliduc, they sat down at some distance from the others. Both were stricken by love. She dared not speak to him, and he feared speaking to her, except to thank her for the presents she had sent him, never had he had such cherished gifts. She answered the knight that she was very pleased at this; she had sent him the ring, and the belt as well, because she had granted him her body. She loved him with such a love that she wanted to make him her husband and if she cannot have him, he should know one thing for certain: she will never have any living man. Now he was to reveal his feelings to her.

"Lady," he said, "I am very grateful to you for your love, it gives me great joy. Since you have prized me so, I ought to be extremely happy; and as far as I am concerned these sentiments will not remain unreciprocated. I am to remain in the king's service for a year. He has my word on that. I shall not leave for any reason, until his war has been concluded. Then I shall return to my country, for I do not wish to remain if I am able to go with your leave."

The girl replied: "Friend, thank you so much! You are so wise and courtly, you will have decided before then what you wish to do with me. I love you and trust you more than anyone."

Each had great faith in the other. For the time being, they said nothing more. Eliduc returned to his lodgings; he was quite happy, having done quite well. He was often able to speak with his beloved, there was great affection between them. Eliduc so committed himself to the war that he captured and detained the adversary at war with the king, and freed the entire country. He was highly prized for his prowess, for his good sense, and for his liberality. Things had gone exceedingly well for him!

During this time, three messengers had been sent abroad in search of him, sent by his master who was distressed and aggrieved, troubled and in danger and in the process of losing all his castles and of seeing all his land laid waste to. He had quite often repented of having sent Eliduc into exile. He had received bad advice concerning Eliduc and had judged Eliduc badly. He had chased from his country and into permanent exile the traitors who had accused and slandered Eliduc and sown seeds of discord. Because the king was in great need, he sent word urging and entreating Eliduc by the faith that he had sworn the king, when the king had accepted his homage, that he come to his aid; for the king was in dire need.

Eliduc received the news. He was most upset on account of the girl, for he loved her desperately, and she him passionately and wholeheartedly. But there was between them no licentiousness, no wantonness, nor villainy; their entire amorous relationship consisted of wooing and conversing together and of exchanging fine gifts. This was her intention and her hope: she fancied having him all to herself and keeping him if she could; she did not know that he had a wife.

"Alas," he said, "I have behaved badly! I have stayed too long in this country! Woe unto me that I ever saw this land! Here I have loved a girl most dearly, the king's daughter Guilliadun, and she me. If I have to leave her, one of us will have to die, or it may be both of us. And yet I must leave; by letter my lord has sent for me and by my oath enjoined me, as has my wife as well by my promise to her. Now it behooves me to keep faith! I cannot in the least stay, but shall go as required. Were I to wed my beloved, Christianity would not tolerate it. Everything is going badly in every way. Oh God, leaving is so difficult! Regardless of those who may see it as a fault, I shall do right by her; I shall bend to her will and follow her advice. Her father, the king, has a lasting peace, I don't think anyone will again wage war against him. Because of my master's need I will ask leave of the king before the day agreed upon as the end of my time in this country. I will go to speak with the maiden and explain my entire situation; she will tell me her wishes and I shall follow them as best I can."

The knight wasted no time; he went to ask leave of the king. He related and explained the situation to him, he showed the king the letter and read him the message from his lord who, in distress, had sent for him. The king heard the summons and the news that there was no question of Eliduc's remaining; he was sorely distressed and concerned. He offered Eliduc much of what he possessed, a third of his realm and his treasure in abundance were Eliduc to stay; he will do so much for him so that Eliduc will praise him forever.

"By God," Eliduc said, "at this time because my lord is so distressed and has called me from so distant a place, I shall leave to help him, and will under no circumstances stay. If ever you have need of my services, I shall willingly come back to you with a large contingent of knights."

The king thanked him for this and kindly granted him leave. The king put all the wealth of his household at Eliduc's disposal, gold and silver, dogs and horses, and fine and beautiful silken garments. Eliduc took of this in moderation. Then quite fittingly he said to the king that he would quite gladly go to speak to his daughter, if it pleased the king. The king replied: "That would please me quite a bit." He sent a squire ahead who opened the door to the room. Eliduc went off to speak to her. As soon as she saw him, she called out to him and greeted him six thousand times. He sought advice about his situation, which he explained to her concisely. Before he had told her everything or asked for or taken his leave, she fainted from grief and lost all her color. When Eliduc saw her unconscious, he began to grieve. Crying most tenderly, he kissed her mouth repeatedly; he took her into his arms and held her, until she came out of her faint.

"By God," he said, "my sweet love, let me speak to you a little: you are my life and my death, and you are my absolute solace; for this reason I am asking you that there be a pledge between us. I am going to my country out of necessity, I have taken leave of your father; but I shall do your bidding, regardless of what may happen to me."

"Take me with you," she said, "since you don't wish to stay here! If not, I shall kill myself; I shall never know joy or happiness."

Eliduc, who loved her most deeply, responded gently: "Fairest one, until the end of the agreed upon period, I am truly bound by oath to your father (if I were to take you with me, I would be disloyal to him). I swear to you in good faith and I guarantee that if you give me leave and grant me a delay by naming a day, if you wish me to return, nothing in the world will hold me back, so long as I am alive and healthy. My life is entirely in your hands."

She felt great love for him; she gave him a date and fixed the day to come back and to take her away. They felt great sorrow at the moment of separation; they exchanged their gold rings and softly kissed each other.

He went down to the sea. The wind was up, he soon made the crossing. When Eliduc returned home, his king was joyously happy, as were his friends, his relatives, and others, and above all his good wife, who was most beautiful, wise, and noble. But at all times Eliduc was despondent because of the love which had overtaken him. Never on account of anything that he saw did he feel joy or give the appearance of being pleased. He will never know joy until he sees his beloved again. He acted strangely. Because of this, his wife had a heavy heart, not knowing at all what this portended; she grieved in silence. She would often ask him, if he had heard from someone that she had acted wrongly or behaved badly while he had been out of the country; she would gladly make amends before his men, whenever he wished.

"Lady," he said, "I do not accuse you of any unseemly behavior or of any wrongdoing. But in the country where I have just been I made a pledge and swore to the king that I would return to him, for he has great need of me. Once my king is at peace, I shall not remain here more than a week. I shall have to suffer great hardships, before I can return. Truly, I will feel no joy on account of anything I may see, until I go back there, for I do not wish to break my word." Then the lady let him be. Eliduc was with his lord, helping him greatly and being of inestimable value; the king followed the advice given by Eliduc who watched over the entire country. But when the deadline approached which the maiden had set, he took pains to make peace, and to reach a settlement with all his enemies. Then he readied himself for travel and chose those he wished to take along. He took only two much-beloved nephews of his and one of his chamberlains (who had been in on their secret and had carried messages for them) and his squires; he had no need of anyone else. He had these men give their word and swear to keep this entire matter secret.

Waiting no longer, he put to sea. They made the crossing quickly. He arrived in that country where he was most desired. Eliduc was quite shrewd, lodging far from the harbor, not at all wanting to be seen, or discovered, or recognized. He prepared his chamberlain and sent him to his beloved, and informed her that, true to his word, he had come back; that night when all was in darkness, she was to leave the town; the chamberlain would be with her, and Eliduc would meet her. The chamberlain had completely changed his clothes. He went very quickly on foot; he went directly to the city, where the king's daughter was. He made every effort and did all he could so that he gained entry to her room. He greeted the girl and told her that her beloved had come. As soon as she heard the news, having been all sad and dismayed, she lovingly shed tears of joy and kissed the chamberlain a number of times. He told her that at dusk she was to go with him. They spent all day in this way carefully planning their journey. That night when all was still, they left the town, the young man and the girl with him; there were none but these two. She was sore afraid that someone might see her. She was dressed in a silk garment finely embroidered with gold, and a short cloak fastened over it.

At the distance of an arrow's flight from the city's gate, there was a woods, in the midst of a lovely parkland. Her beloved, who had come for her, waited for them below the palisade. The chamberlain led her to him, Eliduc dismounted and kissed her. They were overcome with joy at this reunion. He had her mount a horse, and he mounted, taking the reins, he rode off with her swiftly. They came to the harbor at Totness. They went aboard the ship immediately; there were only his men and his beloved, Guilliadun. They had a fair wind and fine sailing weather, calm and settled. But as they were to make land, there was a storm at sea, and the wind rose up before them which tossed them far from the harbor; their mast was split and shattered and their sail was completely rent asunder. They devoutly implored God, Saint Nicolas and Saint Clement, and Mary, the Blessed Mother, that she ask her Son for help to spare them from death and enable them to come to safe harbor. Now forward, now backward, thus they sailed along the coastline. Shipwreck was imminent. One of the sailors shouted out loudly: "What are we doing? Sir, you have with you here on board she who is the cause of our death. We shall never reach land! You have a legally wedded wife and in addition to her you are bringing another one, in spite of God and in spite of His law, in spite of what is right and in spite of the promises you have made. Let us toss her into the sea, so that we may land at once." Eliduc heard what he had said, he was almost overcome with rage.

"Son of a whore," he said, "wretch, villainous traitor, don't say another word!'

Had Eliduc been able to leave his beloved, the sailor would have paid most dearly. But Eliduc took her in his arms and comforted her as best he could, given the sickness she had because of the sea and because she had heard that her beloved had a wife, other than her, in his country. She fell on her face in a faint, completely pale and without color. She remained in this faint, neither coming out of it nor breathing. He who was fleeing with her thought she was surely dead. He grieved terribly. He got up, and went straight to the sailor. He struck him with the oar, knocking him flat out. Taking him by the feet he threw him overboard; the waves carried the body away. Since he had thrown him into the sea, Eliduc took the rudder. He steered and held the ship on course, such that he made port, and reached land. As soon as they had arrived safely, he weighed anchor and lowered the gangplank. She still lay in a faint, looking as if she was dead. Eliduc was overcome with grief; his wish then was to join her in death. He asked his companions what advice each wanted to give him about where to take the girl, for he cannot leave her, until she is buried with great honor and a beautiful service, and in consecrated ground; such is her right as the daughter of a king. His companions were completely perplexed and gave him no advice. Eliduc began to ponder where he might take her. His castle was close to the sea, he could be there by dinnertime. It was surrounded by a forest, thirty leagues wide. A holy hermit lived there and had his chapel in this forest; he had been in the forest for forty years. Eliduc had spoken with him often. It is to him, he said, that he will take her to be buried in his chapel; he will give him enough of his land to found an abbey and install a community of monks, of nuns, or of canons, who will pray continuously for her. May God have mercy on her! He had his horses brought, and ordered all his men to mount. But he had them pledge that this would not be revealed by them. He carried his beloved with him, seated in front of him on his palfrey.

They took a direct route and went into the woods. They came to the chapel. They called out and knocked on the door; they found no one who answered them or who opened the door for them. He had one of his men make his way in, who unlocked the door and opened it. The saintly hermit, the perfect one, had died a week before. Eliduc discovered the fresh grave. He was quite sad, and most dismayed. His men wanted to dig the grave into which he was to lay his beloved, but he had them back off. He said to them: "This is not to be. First I shall take counsel about this with the wise men of this country, on how I can exalt this place either with an abbey or a church. We shall lay her out before the altar and commend her unto God." He had her clothes brought, they immediately constructed a bed; they lay the maiden on it and left her for dead. But when it came time to leave, he thought that he would die of grief; he kissed her eyes and her face.

"Fairest one," he said, "please God that I never bear arms nor stay alive in the world! Beautiful friend, cursed be the day that you saw me! Dear sweet one, cursed be the day you followed me! Fairest one, you would of course be a queen, were it not for the true and fine love with which you loyally loved me. Because of you, I have a very grieving heart. The day on which I bury you, I shall become a monk; each day at your tomb I shall ease my sorrow. With that, he left the maiden, closing the door of the chapel.

He sent a message to his home, announcing to his wife that he was coming, but saying that he was weary and worn out. As soon as she heard this, she was most delighted. She readied herself to go meet him. She received her husband warmly but little joy came to her from this, for he never had a friendly look or a good word to say. No one dared speak to him. He had been at home for two days. He would devoutly hear Mass early in the morning, then ride off alone. He would go into the woods to the chapel where the young woman lay. He would find her motionless, neither having regained consciousness nor breathing. Given this, he found it quite remarkable that her flesh appeared fair and rosy; she had not lost her color, except for being a bit wan. He would cry most bitterly and pray for her soul. When he had finished his prayer, he would return home.

One day as he left church, his wife had him spied on by one of her servants; she promised him much—she would give him many horses and weapons—if he followed her husband and observed from afar where he went. The servant followed her orders. He entered the woods, going along behind Eliduc without being seen by him. He paid attention and saw clearly that Eliduc went into the chapel; he heard him lamenting. Before Eliduc came out of the chapel, the servant had returned to his mistress. He told her everything he had heard: her husband's grieving, his wailing, his lamentations in the hermitage. Her entire disposition changed upon hearing this. The lady said: "We shall go there immediately! We shall examine the entire hermitage! I believe my husband is supposed to travel; he is going to court to speak with the king. The hermit died recently; I am well aware that my husband loved him, but he would never act this way because of him nor manifest such sorrow." For the moment, she let the matter rest.

That same day after the noon hour, Eliduc went to speak with the king. His wife took the servant with her, who led her to the hermitage. When she entered the chapel and saw the bed and, on it, the maiden, who looked like a rose in bloom, she uncovered her and saw her trim body, her long arms and white hands, and her slender fingers, long and smooth. She now realized the truth about why her husband was grieving. She called the servant forward and showed him this wondrous sight.

"Do you see this woman," she said, "whose beauty is like that of a gemstone? This is my husband's beloved, for whom he grieves so. By my faith, I am scarcely surprised, when it is such a beautiful woman who has died. Partly because of pity, partly because of love, I shall never feel joy again. She began to cry and to lament the death of this girl. She sat crying before the bed. A weasel came running out from under the altar; and, because the weasel had walked across the girl's body, the servant struck it with a staff he was carrying and killed it. He threw the weasel into the middle of the floor. In an instant, as the weasel's companion came rushing in, it saw the place where the creature lay. It circled around its companion, poking it a number of times with its paw. When it couldn't succeed in making its companion get up, it seemed to show signs of grief. It ran from the chapel and went to gather some herbs in the woods. With its teeth it took hold of a flower, all red in color. It returned quickly. It placed the flower into the mouth of its companion, whom the servant had killed, so that the weasel was instantly brought back to life. The lady observed all this. She shouted to the servant: "Catch it! Throw your staff, my good man! Don't let it get away." And he threw it, hitting the weasel and causing it to drop the flower. The woman rose and picked it up. She turned back quickly. She placed this stunningly beautiful flower into the girl's mouth. It was there for a very short time, when the girl regained consciousness and began to breathe; then she opened her eyes and spoke: "Oh God!" she said, "I have slept so much!"

As soon as the wife heard her speak, she began to thank God. She asked the girl who she was and the girl replied: "Lady, I was born in Logres, I am a daughter of a king of that country. I loved a knight mightily, the good mercenary, Eliduc. He brought me here with him. He committed a sin in deceiving me! He had a wife, but did not tell me and never gave me any inkling of it. When I heard about his wife, the pain which I felt caused me to fall into a faint. Shamefully he abandoned me, helpless, in a strange land. He betrayed me, I don't know why. Whoever believes a man is quite foolish!"

"Fairest one," the lady answered, "no living creature in all the world can give him any joy; anyone will tell you that this is true. He believes that you are dead, his grief is profound; each day he has come to see you, I do think he found you unconscious. I am in fact his wife; my heart is sorely pained for him. Because of the sadness he was manifesting, I wanted to know where he was going. I followed after him, and discovered you; I am delighted that you are alive. I'll take you along with me and will deliver you over to your friend. I want to give up my rights to him completely and so I shall take the veil." The lady comforted her in this way and took her away with her.

She readied her servant and sent him to find her husband. The servant traveled until he found him. He greeted him in a fitting way and told him in detail his wife's adventure. Eliduc mounted his horse, even without waiting for any companion, and returned home that night. When he saw his beloved alive, he thanked his wife tenderly. Eliduc was most delighted, he had never before been so happy. He kissed the girl often and she him, most sweetly; together they rejoiced very much. When his wife saw their expressions, she spoke to her husband imploring and beseeching him to grant her leave to separate from him; she wished to become a nun in order to serve God. Would that he give her a portion of his land where she might build an abbey, and would that he take as his wife she whom he loves so much, for it is neither seemly nor does the law of God allow one to have two wives. Eliduc consented and willingly gave her leave; he will do all that she wishes and will give

her part of his domain. In the woodlands near the castle attached to
the chapel and the hermitage, she had her church constructed and her
monastic compound built. He endowed the place with much land and
great wealth, she will certainly have all that is needed. When the lady
had everything quite ready, she took the veil, along with thirty other
nuns. She established their mode of life and composed the rule of her
order.

Eliduc took his beloved as his wife; the celebration on the day that
he wed her was marked by great pomp and a beautiful ceremony. They
lived together for many years and there was between them a most per-
fect love. They bestowed rich gifts and made splendid charitable offer-
ings, until they turned toward God. Near the castle on the other side,
Eliduc wisely and with great care had a church built, donating the bulk
of his land and all his gold and all his silver; there he installed his
own men and others of very deep piety to live in the monastery and
observe its rule. When all had been made ready, he scarcely delayed:
together with them he entered, surrendering himself to the service of
God almighty. He installed his wife whom he loved so dearly with his
first wife, who received her like her sister and showed her very great
respect. She encouraged her to serve God and instructed her in the rule
of her order. They prayed to God for their beloved that God might grant
him His good pardon, and he in turn prayed for them. He sent them
messages inquiring how they were faring and asking whether each one
had found solace. Each of the three strove to love God with deep fidelity
and they all had a happy death, thanks be to God, the true divinity.

The ancient, courtly Bretons composed this lay about the adventure
of these three in order to remember what one ought not forget.

Commentaries on *The Lays*

On the *Prologue*

Marie discusses her writerly role in this celebrated preface to *The Lays*. With no hint at all of standard authorial modesty, she unabashedly contends that anyone possessing knowledge and endowed with eloquence ought to demonstrate that knowledge. Her allusion to Priscian, the sixth-century Latin grammarian, has been interpreted in various ways, but Donovan has made a critical distinction between what Priscian wrote and the way in which Marie interprets what he said as it applies to her. There seems to be no doubt about the meaning of her reference to Priscian's statement that he will correct in his *Institutiones grammaticae* the obscurities found in the works of ancient grammarians: "the Ancients believed that as for the books that they wrote, with obscurities in them, those who were to follow them, and who were to study them, could add commentaries to what had been written down and establish their full meaning." It is the precise meaning of Marie's next sentence that has eluded critics or, at least, been open to various interpretations. Marie wrote: "Philosophers knew and understood intuitively that as time went by, people would have more subtle intellects and would be better able to interpret what was to be recovered in these books." Donovan admits frankly that the meaning of Marie's sentence remains ambiguous: ". . . either she will rework clearly and meaningfully certain obscure Breton lays, or . . . she considered the twelve lays in their present form as so obscure that future readers will want to add to them and clarify any meaning implicit in them."[1]

This idea that there was something in texts that needed to be recovered or uncovered or interpreted recalls especially the biblical exegesis of the early Church Fathers. In Chrétien de Troyes' preface to his *Lancelot*, he makes a similar distinction between the story he will tell (the "matter" of his romance) and the meaning or significance (the "sense"). He admits that he was supplied with both the matter and the sense by his patroness Marie de Champagne. K. Sarah-Jane Murray points out that in the opening lines of *Erec and Enide* too, Chrétien speaks of the need to unlock the lessons hidden within his book.[2]

In her *Prologue*, Marie de France tells her readers that she first considered translating texts from Latin into French—a literary activity in which she will engage later when writing *Saint Patrick's Purgatory* and *The Life of Saint Audrey*. In saying that through creative writing people "can avoid and keep themselves from great sorrow," is she speaking in general terms, or has she herself turned to writing as a remedy for some sorrowful situation in her life? Since we know nothing about the author's life, it is impossible to say. What Marie does clearly assert is that she chose some lays that she had heard and which, so that they would be remembered and not lost, were worth writing down. She adds that composing them required intense and extensive work on her part. She ends her *Prologue* with a standard trope, as she offers her literary effort to the unnamed "noble king," possibly Henry II Plantagenêt, king of England.

Curiously *Guigemar*, her first lay, begins as well with a prologue, wherein she again invokes the importance of memory, but this time, it is she, as an author—who here gives her name, which she does not give in the *Prologue*—who does not want to be forgotten in her time. In fact, she insists that she will not abandon her work on the lays even if she is criticized by envious calumniators, whom she calls malicious, cowardly, and felonious dogs anxious to bite others out of treachery. She concludes by underscoring the concision of her lays, stating that she will retell succinctly the tales or adventures she knows and from which the Bretons had made lays.

NOTES

[1]Mortimer Donovan, *The Breton Lays: A Guide to Varieties*, Notre Dame, IN, and London: University of Notre Dame Press, 1969, 17. See his pp. 13–25 for a full discussion of Marie's references to Priscian.

[2]K. Sarah-Jane Murray, *From Plato to Lancelot: A Preface to Chrétien de Troyes*, Syracuse, NY: Syracuse University Press, 2008, 182.

On *Guigemar*

Marie portrays the young hero Guigemar as a paragon of chivalric virtues: noble, valiant, handsome, and well liked by all. He has, however, one flaw, because of which his friends judge him to be doomed. He lacks any interest whatsoever in love, and this mistake of nature confirms his resemblance to the paradigmatic classical example of this type, Theseus' son Hippolytus, the Greek youth after whom his stepmother Phaedra lusted, who, like Guigemar, eschewed love, throwing himself instead enthusiastically into activities like riding and hunting. *Guigemar*, more than any other of Marie's lays, chronicles the sentimental education of this youth on what will be a painful journey to adulthood. His mortal wounding of a hermaphroditic doe may well symbolize his hostility to sexuality, but his is an untenable position, for to be fully human is to love, and as Marie teaches here and in a number of her other lays, to love is to suffer. The arrow that fells the doe rebounds and pierces Guigemar's thigh, tellingly creating a wound in the region of the hero's sexual organs. The doe in its death throes announces to Guigemar that this wound will be healed only by a woman who will suffer great pain and sadness for him and he for her.

Unsure of where to find such a woman, Guigemar comes to the coast, where he discovers a solitary unmanned ship and on its deck a luxurious bed, richly adorned and worthy of King Solomon. As he stretches out on the bed to rest and to ease his pain, the ship sets off, and the hero's journey—both physical and emotional—begins.

He is destined to arrive in a land whose king, old and jealous, and fearful of being cuckolded, has married and then imprisoned a beautiful, young unnamed wife, creating a triangular relationship repeated later in *Yonec*. The wife is guarded by an impotent old priest, whose physical condition presents no sexual threat to the husband, and she is served by the king's niece. All the walls of her room itself are painted with the secular equivalent of the didactic statues, paintings, and stained glass windows of a church. Here, Venus, the goddess of love, is depicted throwing into the fire one of Ovid's books, in all likelihood, the *Remedia amoris*, wherein the author gives advice on how to manipulate love. The goddess declares anathema all those who might ever read this book and follow its teachings. With this visual aid, the husband constantly admonishes his wife against frivolous love affairs. It will take Guigemar himself to convince the wife, whose hesitancy might well be an effect of Venus' lesson, of the value of a relationship with someone like him.

As the wife and her servant care for Guigemar's wound, share their food with him, and hide him safely in the woman's room, the wound in his thigh is soon eclipsed by a more significant, yet invisible, wound. His thigh wound now causes him no pain at all, but he sighs mightily in pain nonetheless, for it is the lady who has now wounded him grievously. She too burns with the same ardor from the fire of love that has inflamed Guigemar's heart. In these descriptions of the beginnings of love, Marie adopts the traditional vocabulary of love as a wound and as a burning fire. The wound of love will be cured only by the person who has caused the wound. Each of the two lovers suffers silently at first, not knowing whether there exists a reciprocity of feelings. The wife's female companion plays the traditional role of the go-between who facilitates the union of the two neophytes at love. This first lay contains the most detailed description of love's beginnings of any lay. Marie describes love as a wound hidden in the body and thus unseen. It is therefore a sickness that lasts a long time. To be cured, Guigemar, the intrepid hero, must take an emotional risk and declare his love or live as a wretch. It is the very love he feels that gives him the courage to reveal his desires to the woman, yet she hesitates. He cautions her against being coquettish, insisting that a virtuous and right-thinking woman ought to love a man she judges likely to be a loyal lover. (In *Chaitivel*, Marie will provide a much fuller condemnation of coquettishness.) The wife, her resistance overcome, accepts Guigemar as her lover, and they enjoy, in Marie's somewhat prudish periphrastic expression, "the ultimate act to which other lovers are accustomed!"

Their love idyll lasts a year and a half and is ended by the workings not of Venus but of another goddess, Fortune, who inexorably turns her wheel, casting some down while raising others up. The agents of Fortune's change in their fate are the husband's spies, who will have the same role in *Yonec* and who observe and denounce the lovers. These are Marie's equivalents of the evil-sayers of Provençal love poetry who are the traditional enemies of true love. Sensing the imminent exposure of their clandestine liaison, the lovers exchange love tokens, pledging and signifying their undying loyalty to each other. She ties a knot in his shirt; he girds her waist with a belt. The wearer will be able to love whoever can untie the knot or undo the belt. Such love tokens proliferate in the lays and serve as concrete symbols of lovers' loyalty and fidelity which for Marie are among the essential traits of true love.

A series of highly unlikely events follows, echoing in another register the mythic elements described earlier in this lay, like the talking doe and the unmanned ship. The jealous husband, upon hearing Guigemar's tale of his arrival on board that mysterious ship, allows him to escape and to sail home on the selfsame ship that, by coincidence, awaits him at the shore. The lovers will now suffer a two-year separation, until the wife one day tries the door of her room which she conveniently finds unlocked. Intending to drown herself in the sea at the spot where Guigemar's ship had docked, she finds that ship moored there once more and waiting to take her to Brittany, Guigemar's homeland. Yet more sorrow awaits her. She is seized by a knight who covets her, yet who respects her and treats her virtuously. Guigemar has been melancholy and downcast (and, one could add, quite passive and listless) since his return, and the lady too, held captive now by Meriaduc, is constantly pensive and dejected. In this second part of the lay, Marie replicates the wretched conditions of Guigemar and the unhappily married woman before their meeting and their eighteen-month clandestine liaison. Upon seeing his beloved, Guigemar doubts that it is even she, opining somewhat surprisingly that many women look alike. In response to Meriaduc's taunt, the lady tries and easily undoes the knotted shirt, and Guigemar effortlessly unfastens her belt. Yet an impediment to their union still remains: Meriaduc refuses to release her. A resolution is possible only after Guigemar—now acting decisively—kills Meriaduc. At last, after three and a half years, the lovers' suffering comes to an end, and as the dying doe had predicted: "all those who love, have loved, or will love in the future" will now marvel at their story.

Marie's first lay constitutes a mini-*Bildungsroman*, the story of the sentimental education of the hero who learns to love and whose one glaring and unnatural flaw, his indifference to love, is remedied only after he accepts to suffer for the sake of another who also, in her turn, accepts to suffer for him.

On *Equitan*

Marie's second lay, like *Guigemar*, presents the story of a love triangle, once again involving a married couple and the wife's male lover. The author, however, signals to the reader that this tale will be unlike *Guigemar* in significant ways, for at the outset she states that great evil will befall the country because of the woman in this lay. Marie supplies thumbnail sketches of all three principals. Equitan, the king, loves pleasure and amorous affairs, leaving governance to his seneschal. The seneschal is described as able, worthy, and loyal. His wife is exceedingly beautiful, courtly, and well spoken. There is no woman her equal in the country. Even before seeing the seneschal's wife, Equitan yearns to possess her because he has heard her praised so. This same motif of falling in love before ever seeing the object of that love will be found in at least four other lays: *Le Frêne, Lanval, Yonec,* and *Milun.*

At their first meeting, the effect of the woman's beauty on Equitan is immediate. The wound of love is caused by Love's arrow that strikes the king in the heart. Overpowered by this love, Equitan realizes, nonetheless, that to love this woman would be wrong, because in so doing he will betray his loyal seneschal. Yet, despite this conflict of loyalties, life without her will drive Equitan mad, and so he rationalizes that she needs to have a lover in order to actualize her noble sentiments, that loving her will make Equitan a better person, ennobled by her love, and that his seneschal ought not be troubled about sharing his wife with the king.

While not an unhappily wedded wife like the lord's wife in *Guigemar,* the seneschal's wife too hesitates to accept Equitan's offer of love, for she also is unused to such requests. It soon becomes clear, however, that her hesitancy is not prompted by virtue or propriety, but rather by the marked disparity in their social status, an issue unknown to Guigemar and his beloved. Because Equitan is a king, this woman fears that once he has his way with her, and thus satisfied, he will discard her. Without having to say it, she has to know that such is often the fate of royal mistresses. And so her rule for love is simple: love is not steadfast if it is not between equals. Equitan goes her one better, pledging to assume the inferior position of the male lover found in the most extreme examples of the courtly love ethic. Equitan will be Lancelot to the wife's Guinevere. He describes himself as her liegeman, her servant, and a suppliant; she will be haughty and his sovereign lady. At the end of this scene, as in the opening of the lay, Marie foretells the consequence of this love: ". . . they loved each other deeply, then later they breathed their last and died because of it."

They will, in fact, die not because of this love itself but rather because of the concern that continues to haunt the lady that the king will abandon her. Her fear in this regard will soon be realized not because he loves anyone else but because, like Gurun's barons in *Le Frêne,* Equitan's barons soon insist that he marry in order to provide an heir. Assuring her that he has no intention of marrying, Equitan adds sincerely, but imprudently, that were the seneschal to die, he would make her his wife and his queen. That is all she needs to hear; she will seek her husband's death if Equitan will help. Like Adam taking the fruit from Eve and biting into it at her urging, Equitan, as he had promised her earlier, will obey her in all things and willingly do her bidding. In absolute thrall to this woman, he has lost all rationality and moral sense.

The wife's plan to scald her husband to death as he enters a tub filled with boiling water proceeds as planned. Unable though to moderate their passion even at this critical time, Equitan and the wife are surprised by the seneschal who enters the room as they lie naked and entwined on the king's bed before which stand the twin bathtubs. Wishing to hide his shame, Equitan jumps feet first into the tub of boiling water. The seneschal then plunges his faithless wife head first into the same caldron. Along with Bisclavret's wife and her new husband, Equitan and the woman he loves and with whom he dies constitute the two anomalous couples of Marie's lays, for they are punished not for loving but in retribution for their dastardly, murderous plan against a worthy spouse.

At the end of *Equitan*, as she does at the end of most of her *Fables*, but for the only time in *The Lays*, Marie states the lesson taught by this story; namely, that "those who seek the misfortune of others have all the misfortune cast back upon themselves." So the primary lesson is not that their adulterous love in itself is fatal—even Equitan realized that it was wrong to betray his seneschal by loving the seneschal's wife—but rather that their decision to kill the loyal husband is a vile plan. The wife had called for equality between the lovers; the immoderate king went too far, ceding total control to the lady, with a promise to obey her in all things whether wise or foolish. Her plot to kill her husband and Equitan's willingness to help her sealed their fate. Had she not feared losing him and had the seneschal's wife trusted in Equitan's promise of fidelity, as Guigemar and his beloved each trusted in the good faith of the other, the outcome might have been quite different, but Marie had already told that tale in *Guigemar*. In *Equitan*, she tells a rather disturbing variant.

On *Le Frêne*

Le Frêne begins with a reprise of the theme of the "trickster tricked," so powerfully developed and seen to have such fatal consequences at the end of *Equitan*. The heroine's mother, having accused her neighbor of having slept with two men because the woman has just given birth to twins, subsequently gives birth herself to twin daughters. The distraught new mother of these unwanted twins, the consequence, by her own statement, of debauchery, explains that Fortune has turned against her, whereas Marie states more damningly that those who slander others don't see the obvious and what can be said of them.

Fearing social disgrace more than eternal damnation, the woman decides that her only salvation lies in killing one of her daughters. Her women, more temperate, set a higher threshold for justifying infanticide, contending that killing a child is not to be taken lightly. They convince the new mother to abandon one of her unwanted daughters at the door of a church. And so, early on, the stage is set for a later recognition scene when the women attach to the infant's arm a fine gold ring into which a ruby is set and place a rich coverlet on top of her. They do this to signal to those who discover the foundling that she is of high birth. Clearly more concerned for the child's welfare than the infant's own mother, the maid who abandons her prays that God will keep the child safe. The sexton who discovers the child in the ash tree near the church door, his daughter who nurses the child, and the abbess who adopts her as her "niece" all treat the child with more humanity and compassion than the girl's own mother.

This entire episode constitutes the prelude to the love story at the center of *Le Frêne* in which Gurun falls in love with Frêne sight unseen, asks for her love, and begs her to go off with him after she accepts him as her lover. She remains his mistress for a long time until Gurun's men insist that he marry in order to produce a legitimate heir. In what seems like a rather matter-of-fact decision, Gurun, unlike the resistant Equitan, agrees to take a wife.

The long prelude to this love affair—the story of one twin as foundling—now seems justified as Coldre, Frêne's sister, is chosen as Gurun's bride. Avoiding a facile dénouement, Marie does not allow the recognition scene to take place before the wedding of Coldre and Gurun. It is only on their wedding night that the mother sees on the newlyweds' bed the coverlet, a gift to her from her husband's visit to Constantinople, and used, in fact, to protect her abandoned daughter.

Frêne had lovingly used it to replace a threadbare bed covering unworthy of the spouses' first night together. When asked, Frêne shows her mother the golden ring as well.

The mother asks her husband's pardon for her crime of child abandonment. To remedy a new dilemma created by Gurun's marriage to his mistress's sister, the archbishop, who had performed the ceremony, announces that he will annul the marriage in the morning. He does this—on what grounds, it is not clear—and then marries Gurun and Frêne.

Gurun's compliant decision to marry another, Frêne's quiet acceptance of her fate as the abandoned mistress, and her willingness to serve her lover and his new wife remain disquieting elements of this lay, despite the apparent happy ending. Frêne's self-sacrifice and her self-effacing personality recall the similar behavior of Guilliadun, the remarkably accommodating wife of Eliduc in the final lay of the collection. The focus on Frêne's parents in the closing section of the lay and their joy at finding their daughter seems to mollify the uneasiness the reader feels about Gurun's behavior. Even Equitan had steadfastly refused to marry when pressed to do so by his barons in order to remain faithful to the seneschal's wife. Not so Gurun.

On *Bisclavret*

In *Bisclavret*, both the husband and the wife seem ideally matched at first: he is an exceptional knight, noble and handsome; she too is noble, as well as beautiful. And they share a mutual love. There is, however, one cloud in this otherwise clear sky, just as there was one single and singular flaw in Guigemar's otherwise flawless personality. Bisclavret's wife, who suspects his hebdomadal absences to be the result of an amorous dalliance, fears losing him to another woman. While the secret of his absence has nothing to do with marital infidelity, he knows for certain that breaking his silence will have a devastating effect, for she will stop loving him. But he also realizes that an even more damaging revelation would be to tell her or anyone where he leaves his clothes when he metamorphoses into a werewolf. It is at this moment in their conversation that the theme of love becomes central. Bisclavret's wife elicits answers from him by invoking the need for total honesty as a sign of his love for her and by reminding him that he has nothing at all to fear from her.

Just as fear of losing Equitan had prompted the seneschal's wife's murderous plan, so too fear of Bisclavret's lycanthropy—despite his wife's assurances to him of love and security—causes her to take as her lover and co-conspirator a knight who had often unsuccessfully sought her love, but for whom she has no feelings. Having used protestations of love to pry her husband's secrets from him, she uses love—or more precisely the promise of her heart and body to her new lover—to dispose of Bisclavret who, deprived of his clothes, is condemned permanently to lupine mutism.

To correct any reader who might harbor some sympathy for this woman's desperate solution when confronted with her husband's dark secret of a double life, Marie now recounts the charming episode describing the werewolf's encounter with the king. All of the creature's interactions with the king and his court suggest that this is a creature both tame and gentle, and endowed with human emotions. Marie provides picturesque descriptions of courtiers willingly caring for the beast who at night sleeps near the king and who always appears anxious to follow and to serve the sovereign.

It comes as no great surprise to the reader, but as a shock to the king and his intimates, when Bisclavret tries three times in one day to bite the knight who has married Bisclavret's timorous wife. The sole explanation they can offer is that this knight must have mistreated the beast. They are right, yet without knowing the full story. Bisclavret's subsequent encounter with his wife surely constitutes, even for the reader, one of the most terribly brutal scenes in any of the twelve lays. Just as Bisclavret has had to lead an inhuman existence since the theft of his clothes, now his wife whose nose he has ripped off her face with his fangs will live henceforth horribly deformed.

The court sage alone manages to see a pattern in the beast's puzzling behavior, without understanding the reason for the beast's anger. That this otherwise gentle creature has attacked both the wife of the good knight who had mysteriously disappeared and her new husband must have an explanation. Under torture and because of her fear, the wife confesses to how she had betrayed her husband.

Bisclavret's human emotions are again underscored when no shape-shifting transformation occurs even when he is presented with his clothes. Again the sage readily understands that the creature would be ashamed to metamorphose in public. The beast's modesty becomes another endearing and really quite charming attribute. At the end of the lay, the wife's disfigurement and the treacherous couple's exile do not seem to constitute a sufficient sanction for their perfidy. Marie seems to join those readers of Genesis eager to condemn Eve more roundly than Adam, her spouse, for their sinful betrayal of their covenant with God. While the original sin of the first human parents is visited on all Adam and Eve's progeny—except, in orthodox Catholic belief, for Mary and Christ—numerous, not all, but numerous women, and only women, born from this couple suffer the horror of being born noseless.

This passage from the entry "Werewolf" in the two-volume *Dictionary of Literary Themes and Motifs* seems quite apt, especially if one replaces the word "greedy" with "fearful and treacherous": "Marie employs the werewolf theme to portray human qualities. The 'beast' is less feral than his greedy wife; and he regains his humanity through the sympathy and charity of the king . . . , who looks beneath physical ugliness to see moral beauty in the wolf."[1]

NOTE

[1]*Dictionary of Literary Themes and Motifs*, ed. Jean-Charles Seigneuret, Westport, CT: Greenwood Press, 1988, II, 1385.

On *Lanval*

Lanval is the first Arthurian lay in the collection. Like *Guigemar* and *Bisclavret*, it begins with a case of exceptionalism. At Pentecost, Arthur richly rewards all of his knights, yet he forgets one, Lanval, a foreigner who had given so liberally of his own wealth that he ends up penniless and sadly forgotten. Marie supplies a maxim to underscore the plight of this knight and others like him: ". . . a foreigner in distress in a foreign land is very sad, when he doesn't know where to turn for help."

As he sulks alone in a meadow, help does come to him in the form of an uncommonly beautiful woman to whom he is led by her handmaidens. Her exalted and otherworldly status is reflected in the luxuriously appointed tent she inhabits, a more costly dwelling than any "earthly" king could afford. Lanval enters and finds her lying provocatively in semi-undress on a bed that, like the tent, is of inestimable value. Told that she has left her own faraway country to come to him in order to love him, he is struck seemingly for the first time in his life by Love's spark that enflames his heart. Not only will he have her love but whatever goods he may wish to possess. And so in this one moment his life and status are utterly transformed; his depression, his isolation, and his penury are all at an end. His mysterious beloved will come to him wherever he calls for her, invisible to all but him.

But, of course, love is not simple, and the woman announces this proviso: he may not speak of her to anyone, and should he, he will not see her again and will thus lose possession of her body. The need for secrecy, especially in a nonadulterous relationship, seems to be a curious condition, but a clearly pervasive element in the amorous relationships in these lays.

Lanval breaks this stricture of absolute silence for no trivial reason, yet in so doing he incurs the promised consequence of an end to his relationship with his mistress and patron. There is a rival for his love and a rival who is a woman of no insignificance, but rather the queen, Arthur's wife, the unnamed Guinevere. When on the feast of Saint John, whose nativity is celebrated on the twenty-fourth of June, the queen offers herself to Lanval, he refuses outright, citing as his reason his loyalty to the king. He is on safe ground so far. Yet when the queen, in a retort surely aimed at bolstering her self-esteem in the face of this rejection, attributes his refusal as a proof of his homosexuality, Lanval speaks without thinking and repays the queen's insult with another: the least among his beloved's handmaidens is more worthy in all regards than the queen.

This first half of the lay ends with a variant of the biblical wife of Potiphar motif (see Genesis 39:1–20), wherein the spurned woman accuses the man she had attempted to seduce of having solicited her love. Lanval's prolonged trial for having slandered the queen occupies the second half of the lay. Arthur's barons will hear the case as Lanval's freedom of movement is assured when Gawain and others offer themselves as guarantors. In order to defend against the charge of calumny, Lanval will have to present proof that what he said about the beauty of the least of his mistress's handmaids was the truth.

A series of paired beauties arrive to announce the coming of their mistress. One finds a similar scene in the Tristan legend, where the coming of Isolde is preceded by the arrival of several more and more beautiful women. At each arrival in *Lanval*, Gawain assumes that one of these women of such extraordinary grace and beauty must surely be Lanval's beloved. Finally, a solitary woman arrives whose unsurpassed beauty Marie describes at length in a portrait filled with superlatives and concluding with the startling declaration that "Such great beauty had not been seen in Venus. . . ." Lanval, heretofore overcome by despair, declares himself cured at the very sight of his long-absent mistress. The lady by her very arrival, judged by all as the most beautiful woman in the world, and whose four serving maids were also seen as preternaturally beautiful, exonerates Lanval, whose boast was clearly fully justified.

This lay, like *Guigemar*, ends happily as Lanval now leaves the problematic world of mere mortals where secrets prove difficult to keep. His beloved leads him off to the isle of Avalon, and as Marie concludes, of these two no more is known.

On *Les Deus Amanz*

Marie cites her source for this story as a Breton lay of the same title, yet this lay alone is the only one among her twelve lays that does not take place in a Celtic locale, but rather in Normandy. In an unusual move, she also announces the dénouement, the death of the lovers, in the opening sentence of the lay. In *Les Deus Amanz*, Marie presents as the impediment to love not wifely sequestration, fear, or the fragility of secrecy, but rather a widowed father's almost unnatural attachment to his marriageable daughter. Even the king's court criticizes the sovereign's relationship with his only daughter. From Marie's description of this situation and of the king's efforts to thwart any possibility that his daughter will marry, it is easy to surmise that this tale concerns a case of only somewhat veiled father-daughter incest.

In order to secure his reputation, the worthy young man of the lay comes to court, wanting to take up the king's seemingly unmeetable challenge that his daughter may marry only the man able to carry her to the top of Mount Pistre. After the young man declares his love to the young woman, they become secret lovers, but his frustration at this situation prompts him to propose to her that they run off together because the bride-test is clearly undoable. Yet the daughter cannot abandon her father because, as she says, "I love him so much. . . ."

The solution to this dilemma requires a trip to Salerno, where the young man goes in search of a fortifying potion that the girl's aunt will supply. The potion when drunk will allow him to carry his beloved to the top of the mountain and thus win her hand. Thanks to medieval herbal medicine—dispensed, as potions often were, by women practitioners, like Isolde's mother in the celebrated Tristan legend, known by Marie—the young man presents himself to the king for the test. Despite the putative power of the potion and leaving nothing to chance, the king's daughter does what she can to help by dieting to lose weight in order to lighten her lover's load. How can they fail?

The girl carries the phial containing the potion as the young man sets off up the mountain. All goes well until they reach the second leg of the ascent when the girl urges him to drink the potion. Feeling strong, he declines, refusing to stop even ever so briefly in order to drink. Marie intervenes to identify for her readers the character flaw that subverts all the young man's efforts: ". . . in him there was no sense of moderation." Such a lack of a balanced and measured response to a dire situation is most often identified as the fatal flaw of the epic hero Roland, who refuses to call for reinforcements when confronted with an unexpected and overwhelming enemy force. In Marie's lay, the stakes are more private and more limited than the welfare of the entire Frankish rear guard as in *The Song of Roland,* yet the fatal consequence of *démesure,* lack of moderation, is the same: the death of the young man and the subsequent death of his intended. After the young man's heart bursts from his chest, as Roland's brains burst from his temples, the young woman dies of sorrow and loss like Aude, Roland's fiancée, when she is told of her intended's death in the Pyrenees. In the lay, the king's daughter lies down beside her dead lover and, like Isolde, who stretches out to die beside the corpse of Tristan, dies in his arms. Unlike King Mark, who has Tristan and Isolde buried in separate coffins, in this lay the king has his daughter and her lover placed in the same marble sarcophagus and buried on the mountain they were unable to conquer. That place henceforth bears their name: the Mountain of the Two Lovers. They lie there together, like the hero and heroine of *Yonec,* together at last in the same tomb.

On *Yonec*

Démesure, lack of moderation, proved fatal to the two lovers in the lay of that name (*Les Deus Amanz*), and this same flaw appears again as the cause of the bird-knight's mortal wounds and of his subsequent death in *Yonec*. Other motifs seen elsewhere recur as well in this lay: the secret nature of the liaison between the unhappily wedded wife and the mysterious bird-knight is a requisite condition for yet another adulterous affair; the knight tells the woman, just as the fairy mistress in *Lanval* and the king in *Equitan* say to the ones they love, that he loved her even before ever seeing her. Yet in *Yonec*, for some unexplained reason, he was able to come to see her, but only after she had expressed her wish to take a lover. The tunnel in the hillock through which the woman follows the wounded Muldumarec marks a boundary between the ordinary realm of mere mortals and the otherworldly region inhabited by exceptional beings, and so reminds the reader of the fairy mistress who crosses from her far-off home to love Lanval and who, at the end, takes him away to Avalon.

Yonec presents a variation on the situation of the wife in *Guigemar*, for in both lays a jealous husband has imprisoned his beautiful young wife—in *Yonec* for the past seven years—in order to prevent his being cuckolded. This woman yearns for a love affair like those recounted in stories of old in which the women incurred no blame whatsoever because of the secret nature of such relationships. This lay alone, among all those attributed to Marie, offers the most striking example of adulterous, courtly love considered as existing in a wholly separate realm and utterly distinct from society's predominant, Catholic, sexual moral code. By having the knight receive Communion in order to prove his good intentions and to ratify by this act of religion his sworn oath in which he declared his belief in God, the sequestered wife appears much less ready than Lanval did, for example, simply to accept a relationship with a mysterious stranger, without some proof of this stranger's religious orthodoxy. Marie's juxtaposition of the knight's reception of the "Body of the Lord our God" as a prelude to and a condition for adultery makes this lay the most remarkably audacious of any in the Marian canon.

The usual enemies of true love haunt the lovers' existence. Marie reserves one of the most virulent authorial condemnations found in any of her lays for these characters, asking rhetorically: "What ills will befall those on whom they wish to spy in order to betray and entrap them!"

Later on, she speaks of the "treachery that the felons had planned" to dispose of the wife's lover.

The lay's dénouement takes place only years after Muldumarec's death. His posthumous son, born to his bereft mistress, and believed by her husband to be his own son, learns the story of his stepfather's perfidy from his mother as the family visits an abbey containing Muldumarec's tomb. Having recounted the entire story to Yonec, the mother faints and dies, while to avenge the death of his parents, Yonec uses his dead father's sword to cut off his stepfather's head, the head that had hatched the cruel plan of how to dispose of his rival. One is reminded of what some now forgotten critic said of Equitan's lover: having hatched the plan for the seneschal's death, she is plunged head first into the boiling bathwater.

In Marie's one-sentence epilogue to *Yonec*, she underscores a key aspect of the nature of love in these lays; namely, the pain and sadness that this couple had to suffer because of their love. Once again, the love of Muldumarec and his beloved involves suffering, as did also, and most especially, the love of their homologues Guigemar and his unhappily married paramour.

On *Laüstic*

The lady's husband plays a major role in the cruel dénouement of this lay, and yet just a brief statement toward the beginning of the lay is enough to suggest to the reader his true personality. Whenever their next-door neighbor, a young knight, is in residence, the wife is kept under strict surveillance. And so, the knight and his beloved have to become satisfied with a quite rarified relationship, limited to seeing each other from their facing windows, speaking together from this distance, and exchanging love tokens by tossing them from window to window.

One of the lady's reasons for accepting her young neighbor as her lover, when he first begged her to love him, may seem curious at first, but it too suggests the kind of husband to whom she is wedded. She became persuaded to love her neighbor because of his good reputation and fine personality and also because "he lived so near to her." What might seem humorous at first reading—love based on the convenience of geography—upon reflection, suggests that she, like other women in *The Lays*, is closely watched and kept sequestered by a jealous husband.

The proximity of the lovers' houses assured the secret nature of their affair which seems to have consisted of nothing more than looking at each other and speaking together long into the night. More contact than that seems not to have been possible. When questioned by her spouse about her nocturnal behavior, the lady explains the irresistible appeal of the nightingale's song, an attraction that will not allow her to sleep. The nightingale with its sweet song that surpasses all earthly joy becomes a metaphor for the love between the lady and her neighbor. There is little surprise then when the husband decides to trap the bird, marshaling all in his household to take part in this maniacal undertaking. Yet instead of caging the trapped bird to limit its singing, the husband kills the nightingale in front of his wife most brutally by wringing its neck and then throws the bloody carcass at her, staining her dress. She now laments the loss of the bird's song and of her great joy, both the joy she felt from hearing the song, but especially the concomitant and greater joy derived from her nightly interludes with her lover. The nightingale trapped by the jealous husband and then killed by him replicates in another register the scene in which the jealous husband in *Yonec* fatally wounds Muldumarec, the bird-knight, as he passes through the window into the room of his sequestered beloved.

The nightingale, which had been a metaphor for the love of this lady for her neighbor, now becomes an actual love token for the young knight. The dead bird will now symbolize the impossibility of even a limited and rarified kind of liaison, like the one they had enjoyed at their respective windows. Love is fragile and cruelly interdicted, in this lay and in others, by the enemies of true love.

All the young knight will now have is the dead nightingale whose cadaver the lady had wrapped in a silk cloth embroidered with gold writing. Just as Tristan's exact message in *Chievrefueil* is unclear, the text of this writing remains unstated by Marie, but the messenger does recount to the knight the story of what had happened, lest he think his beloved's faintness of heart explains her absence from her window. To enshrine properly the symbol of their impossible love, the knight has a golden casket made, and in it he seals the dead nightingale, in an amorous imitation of the honor accorded to saints' relics, likewise reserved in reliquaries for veneration. Marie's final statement before the lay's epilogue that he keeps the casket with him always underscores the survival and, indeed, the endurance of this forbidden love which now exists as intensely as ever but in a way even more rarified and virtual than when they could only talk to each other long into the night from their respective windows.

On *Milun*

The lovers in *Milun*, like in *Yonec*, are united at the end of the lay by the actions of their adult son. Yet there are some important differences between the two lays. At the outset of *Milun*, the unmarried and, as is often the case, the unnamed woman, having never seen Milun but knowing of his fine reputation, offers him her love. They keep a secret of their relationship which consists of encounters in her garden where "she and Milun often arranged to talk together." In Marie's next sentence, she describes the outcome of these conversations in this quite under- stated and slyly humorous way: "Milun came there so often and loved her so much that the girl became pregnant." While Yonec, although the product of adultery, was raised unbeknownst to his mother's hus- band as his and his wife's legitimate offspring and heir, the unwed girl in *Milun* is faced with two serious problems. What will become of the child, and what, when she does marry, will be the consequence of her lost virginity?

There is no question in the lay of her ever thinking like Frêne's mother, whose first solution for ridding herself of one of her daughters is infanticide. Rather, after the child's birth, he is, like Frêne, given a ring and placed in a basket, not to be abandoned like Frêne, but to be deliv- ered to his aunt, his mother's sister, in Northumbria along with a letter containing the story of the child's parents and of his birth for the aunt to read and to use later to educate their son about his origins. Milun's men travel with the child from South Wales to Northumbria, stopping, as Marie points out in order to underscore the great care taken of the infant, seven times each day in villages on their route where the child is nursed and bathed and his linen changed.

When Milun's beloved does subsequently marry, her husband seems unaware that she is no longer *virgo intacta*, yet there are some familiar indications that as a married woman she is hardly able to act freely in her dealings with anyone beyond the household. When a fowler comes with word from Milun, the porter tells him that no one may speak with the lady of the house. Then later, when she wants to write a reply to Milun, "by art and guile she managed to get ink and parchment."

The picturesque nature of their twenty-year correspondence lends a charming detail to the lay, and the three-day period of imposed fasting that the swan is made to observe prior to each flight suggests the cleverness of these faithful and devoted lovers. Despite the dangers of meeting, the lovers do manage to meet but only several times in a score of years. Marie offers a maxim-like explanation of their persistence: "People cannot be so isolated nor so closely observed that they cannot find an opportunity to meet."

The second half of the lay focuses on the adult son of Milun and his beloved. After reading his mother's letter that his aunt gives him, the son's decision to set off in search of chivalric fame is also explained in a maxim: "Little does a man value himself, being the son of such an esteemed father, if he does not set for himself a higher goal beyond his own land and his own country." His exploits earn him both the name Peerless and, in a kind of reversal of the Oedipus complex, the intense resentment felt by Milun, who is angry at this young knight's great prowess and jealous of his widespread reputation.

Even as father and son do battle incognito, Milun admires the physical beauty of his young adversary. Unhorsed by Peerless, Milun is treated with great respect when his son sees Milun's grey hair. Milun recognizes the ring on the youth's finger and elicits from Peerless a résumé of the young man's story.

Peerless' plan to kill his mother's husband seems harsh, for despite some clues about her possible sequestration, all that Marie says of the husband directly is that he was very rich, "powerful and quite famous," and therefore nothing like the jealous and murderous husband beheaded by Yonec to avenge his dead parents. A fortuitous and not very plausible deus ex machina—"When he heard the news, it seemed to Milun to be too good to be true"—renders Peerless' plan moot since his mother's husband conveniently dies. Without delay, the son unites his parents "giving his mother to his father" in a kind of extra-ecclesial marriage ceremony. And so, like *Guigemar*, *Le Frêne*, *Lanval*, and *Eliduc*, this lay too ends in a union of the lovers who live henceforth in great good fortune after twenty years of separation, secrecy, and yearning.

On *Chaitivel*

Chaitivel, like *Eliduc* as we shall see, lays claim to an alternate title. In each case the choice of title reflects how one reads the lay. *Chaitivel, The Unfortunate One*, describes the sole survivor among four knights all in love with, and encouraged in their love by, the same woman. Marie uses this title and thereby suggests, at least until the very end of the lay, that she, like the surviving knight in her lay, reads the story primarily as the tale of his predicament and not as an account, as the alternate title *The Four Lamentations* would suggest, of the lady's suffering.

Chaitivel presents an extended study of the nature and the effects of coquetry. Already in *Guigemar*, Marie had allowed her eponymous hero to excoriate the woman he loves for her apparent inability to decide and to make a commitment to him: "A coquettish woman who makes a practice of this kind of thing insists on being pursued for a long while, to make herself more desirable, so that a man will not think that she frequently grants this kind of pleasure." *Chaitivel* constitutes an extended gloss on this general statement.

In a tournament each of the four knights is so valiant and expert that even on this extraordinary occasion, the lady as usual cannot decide which one of the four to prize the most. The coquette is obsessed even after their deaths by the three knights whom she had lost in a single day. The fourth knight, like Guigemar, is wounded in the thigh. Unlike Guigemar, for whom a woman's suffering is required for his wound to be cured, the surviving knight will have no cure, because the lady is intent on memorializing her own bereavement in a lay entitled *The Four Lamentations*. The heretofore docile surviving knight breaks his silence and angrily denounces the woman. Perhaps because his wounded thigh connotes sexual impotence or simply because her ego is so overweening that she cannot think of him and his needs but only of herself and her loss, she grants him no favors except that he may speak with her. He therefore insists that the lay be named for him and be called *The Unfortunate One*. And, amazingly, she agrees to this, thereby suggesting that Marie also condemns the lady's coquettish behavior. In the brief epilogue, however, Marie makes the comment that each title suits the lay well but adds that *The Unfortunate One* is the customary name. Point of view is everything.

Chaitivel stands alone among Marie's twelve lays as the only one in which the love situation remains utterly unresolved. And in this, *Chaitivel* is a precursor of a later French text in which the author presents the portrait par excellence of the coquette. In *The Misanthrope*, Molière's dark comedy, Célimène, the archetypal coquette, and Alceste, the misanthrope of the title, cannot end up together because each type incarnates the antithesis of the other. The surviving lover in *Chaitivel* is no misanthrope, yet surely the coquettish lady is incapable of focusing her love on one man even when he alone remains as the only survivor of the four worthies. The lady's very nature requires that she be the sole object of the unfulfilled desires of a number of suitors, even, it would seem, of dead suitors whose ardor and desires to please her led them to risk their lives for her. In life, their ardent and unflagging desire, sustained by her resistance, certified her worth; in death, their loss perpetuates, in a sense, her concept of her extraordinary appeal and her ability to keep lovers in her thrall. Her very authorship of the lay underscores and is a testament to her unbridled ego.

Marie fails to condemn the coquette in anything like very strong terms. Yet the title of the lay does certify the view that the fourth knight is, indeed, the unfortunate one in this tale of cruel indecision and frustrated desire.

On *Chievrefueil*

Chievrefueil is Marie's shortest lay. It recounts an episode of the Tristan legend not extant in any other Old French version of the story of Tristan and his love for Isolde, his uncle's wife. This episode describes the separation of the lovers, a strategy for communication, and a brief encounter, followed again by the inevitability of separation.

Unable to be with the queen, Tristan's thoughts turn to death and destruction, for as the maxim Marie uses states: ". . . he who loves faithfully is very sad and pensive, when his sexual desires are unsatisfied." To announce his return to Cornwall from South Wales, Tristan fashions a wand from the branch of a hazelnut tree on which he carves his name. This sign will remind Isolde of other such signals sent to her by Tristan, and she will know the meaning of this message; namely, that the two of them are one, bound together like the honeysuckle entwined on the hazelnut. If the two plants are separated, they die, just as the lovers, if separated, cannot survive.

After a brief interlude in the woodlands, Tristan and Isolde must again leave each other, and it is this motif of their prior separations and this new parting that predominate in this lay. Even they cannot deny the impossible nature of their forbidden love. As they are about to part once again, they both begin to weep. The lay that Tristan then composes about the words of his message to Isolde testifies to the pain of separation and the consequent inevitability of the death of the lovers. It also stands in antithesis to the egocentric lay *Chaitivel* composed by that lay's coquettish and self-centered heroine. *Chievrefueil* surely calls to mind *Laüstic*, where another impossible love is symbolized by the dead nightingale entombed in its casket. In *Chievrefueil*, the two possible states of the hazelnut and the honeysuckle—entwined or sundered—represent the possible conditions of the relationship of Tristan and Isolde. "[N]either you without me, nor I without you" is their ideal, yet this is an unsustainable ideal. The two plants can be pulled apart, just as the lovers often are. When this happens, the plants wither; the lovers will die.

This brief lay is charged throughout with sadness. The fragile ideal of union surely cannot endure, and separation will lead to the death of the lovers. This is the whole of the legend.

On *Eliduc*

Marie opens her final lay with an unequivocal declaration that the original title of this lay, *Eliduc*, was replaced by another. According to the author, the lay's real title is *Guildeluec and Guilliadun*, the names, respectively, of Eliduc's wife and of the young woman with whom he falls in love, for, as Marie says, "the story on which the lay was based happened to the women."

From the outset too, Marie states that the married couple, Eliduc and his wife, loved each other loyally. Unlike other apparently happily wedded spouses like Bisclavret's wife and the seneschal's wife in *Equitan*, Eliduc will, despite his intense feelings for another woman, remain faithful to his wife. The crux of the lay will be the working out of this dilemma of how to reconcile conjugal and courtly, adulterous love.

The daughter of the king of Exeter falls in love with Eliduc upon seeing him, and Eliduc too is terribly unsettled upon meeting this girl. Although he remembers his promise of fidelity to his wife, he nonetheless accepts the love tokens the girl sends him: a gold ring and a belt.

Both Eliduc and the girl feel the pangs of love, yet neither knows for certain whether the other has the same feelings. One recalls a similar lovers' standoff in *Guigemar*. During their conversation at court, the girl offers Eliduc her body, as she had offered him the love tokens she had earlier sent to him. Marie is careful to indicate that their relationship consists of nothing more than wooing and conversing and exchanging gifts. Eliduc knows that he cannot wed the young woman because Christianity will not tolerate such a bigamous marriage. He remains faithful to his wife because of his promise to her, and he sustains a chaste relationship with the girl because he serves her father, the king, to whom he wishes to remain loyal. The tension between conjugal and feudal fidelity, on the one hand, and the power of love, on the other, permeates this lay. When Eliduc reveals to the girl that he has been recalled to his own country, she faints and he relents but then insists on leaving, promising to return by a date of her choosing.

Once reunited with his wife, Eliduc appears despondent and behaves strangely, explaining that he must return to Exeter because of a promise made to the king he served there. Once back in England, Eliduc sends for the girl and takes her aboard his ship to return with him to Brittany. A storm at sea is the backdrop for the most cruel scene of this lay. A sailor explains their plight by the presence on board of Eliduc's beloved when, in fact, he already has a legitimate wife. Hearing this, the girl faints and Eliduc in an uncontrollable furor kills the sailor and throws his body into the sea.

What to do with his beloved, now in a state of suspended animation —looking as if dead, yet having lost but little of her natural color? He has her laid out on a bed in a hermitage deep in the woods near his residence where he visits her repeatedly. His wife discovers the girl and seems hardly surprised by her husband's devotion to this girl whose beauty is like a gemstone. Imitating the weasel who, in a most charming scene, resuscitates its companion by putting a red flower into the dead weasel's mouth, Eliduc's wife, having wrested the flower from the weasel, resuscitates her husband's beloved. The dilemma of the love triangle still awaits a resolution, as the girl explains all to the wife and concludes with the observation that "whoever believes a man is quite foolish."

The wife resolves the seemingly irresolvable situation by deciding, in a kind of psychological deus ex machina, to enter a convent, thereby freeing her husband to marry his beloved. One remarkable example of conjugal love is now followed by another as Eliduc marries and lives with his new wife for many years, sharing once again a most perfect love.

Marie ends her lay with a most unusual second dénouement. This married couple, like Eliduc's first wife, now turn toward God and decide that they too will enter religious life where they will strive to love God with deep fidelity. In the end all three of these characters have, Marie tells her readers, a happy death. For the first and only time in *The Lays*, divine love supersedes terrestrial love and earthly renunciation leads to celestial happiness. In her final lay, Marie, the putative author of *The Life of Saint Audrey*, seems to have made a foray—albeit a brief one— into hagiography. At the end of *Eliduc*, the three principals exhibit saintly traits of extraordinary abnegation and conversion of life within a most orthodox Catholic context. It is not at all clear whether Marie's reader is to see this final example of the resolution of a complicated love situation as the ideal or simply as yet another example of how to resolve a complex triangular relationship, one in which all three parties are worthy and honorable. Interestingly, a strikingly similar situation will constitute the core story of Madame de Lafayette's 1678 novel *The Princess of Clèves*, where yet another unexpected dénouement will perplex and challenge readers' attempts to interpret that story, just as Marie's *Eliduc* leaves her readers uncertain about, and perhaps unsatisfied with, the pious resolution of the love triangle she describes at such length in her longest lay.

Two Anonymous
Breton Lays

The Lay of Melion

An Anonymous Werewolf Lay

Introduction

Prudence Mary O'Hara Tobin begins her Old French edition of *Melion* by situating the composition of this lay sometime between 1170 and 1267. She then refines her dating of the text and narrows the most likely date of its composition to the years between 1190 and 1204.[1] Evaluating the literary skill of the *Melion* author, Tobin writes, "his talent does not reach the level of Marie de France's" (p. 292). Later in a concluding sentence, she offers only rather faint praise for this lay: "*Melion* attains neither the loftiness nor the elegance of the best lays of Marie de France; nonetheless, it does have a certain charm" (p. 296).

For my translation, I have used the Old French text contained in *Lai d'Ignaurès, suivi des lais de Melion et du Trot*, eds. J. L. N. Monmerqué and Francisque Michel, Paris: Silvestre, 1832, 43–67. Amanda Hopkins has edited and translated into English both *Melion* and the *Bisclarel* episode of the Renard the Fox tradition. These texts and her exhaustive and superb comparative study of *Bisclavret, Melion,* and *Bisclarel* are available online in the Liverpool Online Series, Critical Editions of French Texts, number 10, at http://www.liv.ac.uk/sml/los/.

NOTE

[1] Prudence Mary O'Hara Tobin, *Les lais anonymes des XIIe et XIIIe siècles: édition critique de quelques lais bretons*, Geneva: Droz, 1976, 292. Translations from Tobin's study in this introduction are mine.

Melion

At the time when King Arthur reigned, who conquered lands, and gave rich gifts to knights and to barons, he had with him a squire; I've heard him called Melion. He was most courteous and brave, which made him loved by all; he was very chivalrous and a courtly companion. The king had a very splendid household; prized by all for its courtliness and prowess, its worth and its largesse. On the day the squires made their vows— and know for certain that they kept them—Melion made one of those boastful vows¹ that turned back upon him with great harm. He said he'd never love a maiden, no matter how highborn or how beautiful, whom any other man had loved or about whom any man had spoken. Matters remained this way for quite some time. Those who had heard the vow repeated it in a number of places and recounted it to maidens, and when the maidens heard it, they hated Melion very much because of it. Those who lived in castle rooms and who served the queen—of whom there were over a hundred—had a discussion about this vow; they said they would never love him nor speak with him. Women did not wish to look at him, maidens did not wish to speak to him. When Melion heard this he became terribly discouraged; he no longer wished to seek out adventures, nor did he have any interest in bearing arms; he was much saddened, much discouraged and lost something of his prestige. The king learned of this, it troubled him greatly, he sent for Melion and spoke with him.

"Melion," said King Arthur, "Have you lost your senses, your self-esteem, and your knightly dignity? Say what's wrong with you; don't keep it hidden. If you wish to have land or a manor house, or anything else that someone can possess, if it is in my royal power to grant, you shall have it to your liking. I would gladly satisfy you," the king said, "were I able. I have a castle which opens onto the sea, in all the world there is none its equal; it is rich in woodlands and in water fowling and in forest land which you value greatly; I shall give this to you in order to cheer you; you will certainly be able to enjoy yourself there."

The king granted him this fief; Melion thanked him for it. He went straight to his castle, he led a hundred knights there. The region pleased him greatly, as did the forest that he loved very much. After he had been there for a year, he developed a great affection for the region, for truly he sought no pleasure that he could not find in the forest.

One day Melion and his foresters had gone hunting; with him were his huntsmen who loved Melion deeply, for he was their liege lord in whom they saw reflected all honor. Soon they spotted a large deer, they immediately took after it and unleashed the dogs. Melion stopped in a prairie to wait for the pack of hounds. There was a squire with him, with his hand the squire held on to two greyhounds. On the plain, which was verdant and beautiful, Melion saw a maiden coming toward him on a handsome palfrey. Her appearance was magnificent. She was dressed in a rich crimson garment, very nicely stitched with ribbons; at her neck she wore an ermine cloak: never had a queen donned a nicer one. She had a lovely body and beautiful shoulders, and blond hair; a small, quite shapely, rose-colored mouth; she had bright and twinkling green eyes: she was in all aspects most beautiful. She was most noble and quite slender and rode alone without companions.

Melion rode toward her, he greeted her most fittingly: "Fairest one," he said, "I greet you in the name of Jesus, the glorious king; tell me where you were born and what has led you here."

She answered: "I shall tell you, and I shall not say one untrue word. I am of quite high birth and born of noble lineage; I have come to you from Ireland. Know that I am indeed your beloved; I have never loved, nor will I ever love, any man save you. I have heard you greatly praised; I never wanted to love another, save you alone, never shall I feel love for any other man."

When Melion heard that his wishes had been granted, he put his arms around her waist and kissed her more than thirty times; then he called all his household and told them this adventure. They saw the maiden, there was none so beautiful in the kingdom; Melion led her to his castle; they all felt very great joy. He married her amid great pomp, and because of this he felt very great joy. The celebration lasted two weeks. He held her dear for three years during which he had two sons. One day he went into the forest, he took his dear wife with him; he spotted a deer, and they pursued it, and the deer fled with its head down. He had with him a squire who carried his bow and his arrows. They came onto a plain; he looked into a thicket, he saw standing there a very large deer; laughing, he looked to his wife.

"Lady," he said, "if I wished to, I could show you a very large deer; see he is in that thicket."

"Believe me, Melion," she said, "and know that, if I do not eat some of that deer, I shall never eat again."

She fell from her palfrey into a faint, and Melion picked her up, unable to console her; she began to cry most uncontrollably. "Lady," he said, "for God's sake, please! Do not cry anymore, I beg of you. I wear on my hand a ring, see it on the finger of my hand; it has two stones in its setting; no one ever saw anything made like it; one stone is white, the other red; you shall hear a great marvel about it. You shall press the white one against me, and you will put it on my head when I am stripped completely naked. I shall become a wolf, large and strong; for love of you I shall take the deer, and I shall bring you some flesh. For God's sake, I pray you, wait here for me, and watch over my clothes. I entrust you with my life and my death. There would be no solace, were I not touched with the other stone; I would never again be a man."

He called his squire, and ordered the squire to remove Melion's boots. The squire came forward, and took the boots off; and Melion went into the forest, he removed his clothes, he remained naked, he donned his cloak. When she saw him naked and undressed, his wife touched him with the ring; he then became a wolf, large and strong; he rushed off into great difficulty.

The wolf went running very speedily to where he saw the deer lying; he was soon on its trail. The strife will be great when he has taken and seized it, and before he has its meat.

The wife said to the squire: "Now let him hunt to his satisfaction."

She mounted, she tarried no longer, and she took the squire with her. The lady went straight toward Ireland, her country. She came to the harbor, she found a ship; at once she spoke to the sailors, who took her to Dublin, a city on the coast, which belonged to her father, the king of Ireland: thereupon she had what she asked for. As soon as she arrived at the port, she was received with great joy. We shall now leave her; we shall speak further of Melion.

Melion, who hunted the deer, chased after it prodigiously. He followed after it onto the plain, then he utterly felled it; he then took a large portion of its meat, he carried the meat in his mouth. He quickly returned to where he had left his wife, but he did not find her there: she had left for Ireland. He was most wretched, he didn't know what to do when he didn't find her where he had left her; though a wolf, he nonetheless had the intelligence and the memory of a man. So he waited till nightfall. He saw a ship that was being loaded, which was to put to sea that night, headed straight for Ireland. He went toward the port and waited for nightfall. Undaunted, he boarded the ship, for he had no concern for his life; he hide under some wicker baskets, crouching down and concealing himself. The sailors made haste, for they had a very good wind. Then they headed toward Ireland; each one had all that he required. They hoisted their sails; they navigated by the heavens and the stars, and on the following day, at dawn, they saw the land of Ireland; and when they came into port, Melion waited no longer;

he immediately left his hiding place, he jumped from the ship to the shore. The sailors shouted at him, and threw their oars at him; one sailor struck him with his staff; they almost caught him. Happy was he when he escaped from them; he went to the top of a mountain, he looked over all the country where he knew his enemies to be. He still had the chunk of meat which he had brought from his country; he was famished, and he ate it. The sea had tired him greatly.

He went into a forest, he found cows and oxen there; he tore out the throats of many of them and killed them. He began his campaign; here he killed more than a hundred of them at this first encounter. People who were in the woods saw the loss of animals; they came running into the city, they recounted the story to the king that there was a wolf in the forest who was devastating the entire region; he had killed many of their livestock, but the king considered all this of no importance. Often Melion went through the forest, over mountains and across deserts, accompanied by ten wolves; he befriended them and praised them so much that he took them along with him, and they did all he bade them to do. They wandered all over the country, terrorizing men and women. They acted like this for an entire year, they devastated the entire country. They killed men and women, they destroyed the entire country, they knew well how to keep on guard. The king was unable to outwit them. One night they had wandered broadly in a woodland near Dublin on a hill near the coast; they were tired and worn out. The woods were next to a plain; there were many people about. The wolves entered there to rest. They will be betrayed and outwitted. A peasant spotted them; he ran immediately to the king: "Sire," he said, "the eleven wolves are asleep in the nearby woods." When the king heard this, he was most delighted; he spoke to his men about it.

The king addressed his men: "Barons," he said, "hear this: know for certain that this man saw the wolves in my forest—all eleven of them." In the woods they hung nets that they used to trap boars. As soon as they had hung all the nets, they then mounted, they tarried there no more; the king's daughter said she would accompany them and observe the wolf hunt. Without delay they entered the woods quite silently and stealthily, they encircled the woods entirely; for indeed the king had plenty of men, who carried axes and clubs, and some wielded naked swords. Now there were a thousand hounds, urged on with shouts, who soon located the wolves. Melion saw that he had been betrayed, and knew well that he was in a sorry plight. The dogs pursued the wolves fiercely, and the wolves went fleeing into the nets. They were all slashed and slaughtered; not a single one escaped alive, save for Melion who did escape: he jumped over the nets; he went into a vast wooded area; by cunning he escaped from them. The huntsmen returned to the city; the king was quite joyful.

The king felt great joy that of the eleven wolves ten had been killed, for he had avenged himself most fittingly upon the wolves; there escaped from him but a single one. His daughter said: "That's the largest; he will again make us all grieve." When Melion escaped, he climbed to the top of a mountain; he was most sad, the loss of his wolves weighed upon him greatly. He had labored long and hard, but now he will soon have help. Arthur was heading to Ireland, for he wished to establish peace there. They were in conflict in that country, Arthur decided to reconcile the warring parties; he wished to enlist them in his war, he wished to conquer the Romans. Arthur came without ostentation, he brought along but a handful of great men, he brought twenty knights with him. The weather was very fine; there was a favorable wind; the ship was most splendid and grand, there were worthy seamen, it was very well equipped, well furnished with men and weapons. The knights' shields were on display. Melion knew them: first he recognized Gawain's shield, and then noticed Yvain's, and then the shield of King Yder; all this pleased him and was welcomed by him. He recognized Arthur's shield; know that he felt great joy at this sight: he was most joyful, he rejoiced, for henceforth he thought he would find pardon. They came sailing toward the shore; they now had a headwind; they couldn't bring the ship into port; for this reason there was great distress. They headed toward another port, located two leagues from the town. There had once been a large castle there, but now it was all in ruins; and when they arrived, it was night, and it was dark.

The king arrived at the port; he was extremely tired and worn out, for the ship had made him quite ill. He called his seneschal: "Go forth," he said, "and find where I may rest tonight." The seneschal went back to the ship, he spoke to the chamberlains: "Come on shore with me," he said, "and prepare the king's lodging." They left the ship, and came to the lodging; they had two candles brought, and had them lit immediately. They brought feather beds and rugs; quickly it was nicely furnished. Then the king left the ship, he went directly to his lodging, and as soon as he had entered, he was happy to find it so beautiful.

Melion did not tarry, he went right toward the ship, he stopped near the castle, he recognized them quite well; he was quite aware that if he received no help from the king, he would meet his death in Ireland. But he didn't know how to proceed, he was a wolf and he could not speak, and nonetheless he would still go, he would put himself at risk. He came to the king's door, he recognized all of the king's barons; he stopped for nothing, he went right up to the king; he risked death. He fell down at the king's feet. To the amazement of all, he did not wish to get up. The king said this: "I am witness to a marvelous thing; this wolf has come to me. Now know full well that he is tame, he is not to be struck or seized." When the food was ready, and the barons had washed, the king had washed, and had sat down, the napkins were set before them. The king called Yder, and had him sit at his side.

Melion lay at the king's feet; he knew all the barons well. The king looked at him often; he gave him bread, and Melion took it. Then he began to eat it. The king began to marvel, he said to King Yder: "Look, be assured that this wolf is tame." The king gave him a piece of meat, and he gladly ate it. Then Gawain said: "My lord, look, this wolf is not at all true to type." All the barons said among themselves that never had they seen such a well-behaved wolf.

The king had wine brought to the wolf in a basin. The wolf looked at it, he drank some. Know that he wanted it very much; he drank a great deal of the wine, and the king observed him closely.

When they had gotten up from table, and the barons had washed, they went outside onto the shore. The wolf was always with the king; the king could never go any place where anyone could keep the wolf from him. When the king wished to retire, he ordered his bed prepared. He went to retire, he was very tired, and the wolf went with him; no one could ever separate him from the king, he went to lie down at the king's feet.

The king of Ireland was astonished that Arthur had come to him; he was quite happy about it, and was joyful; he rose at the crack of dawn, he went from his castle to the port, he took his barons with him, he came riding straight to the port. They looked warmly at each other. Arthur showed great affection for him and paid him very great honor. When Arthur saw him coming toward him he did not want to appear at all proud, but got up, and kissed him. The horses were readied, they no longer tarried, they mounted, and now went toward the city.

Arthur got onto his palfrey; he took good care of his wolf, he did not in the least want to leave him; the wolf was always at the king's stirrup. The king of Ireland was very happy about Arthur; the company was magnificent and grand. They came to Dublin and dismounted at the imposing castle. When Arthur went up into the tower, the wolf held on to him by the flap of his clothing; when Arthur was seated, the wolf took his place at the king's feet.

The king looked at his wolf, he summoned him next to the head table. Together the two kings sat on the royal dais. They had very sumptuous provisions there. The barons provided excellent service; in all parts of the castle they were bountifully served; but Melion watched, he noticed in the middle of the hall the man whom his wife had led away. He well knew that he had crossed the sea, and had gone to Ireland. He went and seized him by the shoulder; this man could not hold his own against the wolf. In the great hall, Melion assailed him. He would already have overcome the man and killed him, were it not for the king's men-at-arms who arrived there in profusion from all parts of the palace; they carried clubs and yokes: they would indeed have killed the wolf when King Arthur shouted: "By God, never is he to be touched," he said, "know that the wolf is mine."

Yder, son of Yrien, said: "My lord, you do little good; if the wolf didn't hate him, he wouldn't attack him." And the king said: "Yder, you are right." Arthur turned away from the high table, from there he went to where the wolf was, he said to the young man: "You will confess why the wolf seized you, or you will die now."

Melion looked at the king, he grasped the servant, and the servant screamed. The youth asked pardon of the king, he said he would reveal the truth. Now he told the king how the lady had brought him, how she touched the ring to the wolf and brought the young man to Ireland. He told him everything and revealed all that had happened to him.

Arthur called to the king of Ireland: "Now I know well what the truth is. I am very pleased with my baron. Have the ring delivered to me; your daughter, who took it, tricked him wickedly. The king of Ireland left there, he entered her room; he took King Yder with him. He cajoled and flattered her so much that she gave him the ring. He took it to King Arthur. Melion clearly recognized the ring, as soon as he saw it. He came to the king, and knelt, and kissed both his feet. King Arthur wanted to touch him, Gawain did not want to permit that: "Dear uncle," he said, "you will not do that; you will lead him into a room, all alone and in private, so that he may have no shame before men."

The king summoned Gawain, and he took Yder with him. They led the wolf into a room; when he was inside, the king closed the door. He put the ring on the wolf's head; his face took the shape of a man's, his entire body changed; he then became a man, and he spoke. He fell down before the king's feet; they covered him with a cloak. When he saw he was formed like a man, they felt very great joy. The king cried out of pity, and while crying he asked Melion what had happened to him; they had lost him through misfortune. He had his chamberlain summoned, he had sumptuous garments given to Melion; he dressed him fittingly and groomed him and led him into the great hall. Throughout the castle they were amazed when they saw Melion approaching.

The king of Ireland brought his daughter in, she was presented to King Arthur for him to deal with her as he wished, be it to burn her or to mutilate her. Melion said: "I will touch her with the stone, I will never desist for anything." Arthur said to him: "No, you shall not; for your dear children's sake, you will abandon her." All the barons asked this of him; Melion agreed to do so. King Arthur stayed long enough that the war was soon settled; he went back to his country, he took Melion with him; he was quite happy about this, he felt great joy. Melion left his wife in Ireland; he consigned her to the devils because she had treated him so badly, as you have heard in this tale. She will never be loved by him for even one day. He never wished to take her back, but would leave her to be burned or hanged. Melion said: "Never will it fail: he who believes his wife in everything will be mistreated in the end; he ought not believe all she says." *The Lay of Melion* is true; all the barons attest to this.

Here *Melion* ends.

NOTE

[1] In his notes to his translation of *Melion*, Alexandre Micha suggests that "vow" is a variant of Old French "gab," that is, a "boast" made during a celebration when each knight speaks of accomplishing an extraordinary exploit. See *Lais féeriques des XIIe et XIIIe siècles*, Paris: Flammarion, 1992, p. 159, note 1.

Commentary on *Melion*

The anonymous author seems to have borrowed motifs for this lay directly from Marie de France or from some source common to them both or from an intermediary source between Marie and the *Melion* author.

Melion, like *Lanval*, is set at the court of King Arthur, and like Lanval, Melion is the beneficiary of the largesse of another, not of a lover like Lanval's fairy mistress, but of Arthur himself. Lanval's service to the king goes unrewarded and so his consequent dejection and penury are therefore all the more undeserved. Melion's neediness, on the other hand, is emotional rather than pecuniary, and it is also self-inflicted, for it is his boastful vow that alienates many, and it is this alienation that leads to his state of deep despair. By his bountiful gift to Melion of a castle, Arthur jolts the hero from his morose state. The hunting motif at the beginning of Melion certainly calls to mind the celebrated early hunt scene of Guigemar, but it too and more especially evokes comparisons with Lanval's solitary sortie, and this because of the unexpected arrival of a woman, come from afar—in Melion's case from Ireland, not from Avalon as in Lanval—who has fallen in love with the hero.

All sorts of magical rings, like the one that allows for Melion's metamorphosis from man to werewolf, constitute a commonplace in Old French narrative literature. In one of Marie's own lays, Muldumarec, for example, assures protection for the mother of his posthumous son, Yonec, by giving her on his deathbed a ring that prevents her jealous husband from suspecting her of infidelity.

Withholding from Melion the ring's restorative second stone prevents him from regaining his human form, just as depriving Bisclavret of his clothes keep him captive in his beastly form. While fear motivates Bisclavret's wife to betray her husband, no motivation at all is given for why Melion's Irish wife betrays him by absconding with his bi-gemmed ring with its restorative red stone.

Bisclavret admits without going into detail that, on those days of the week when he assumes his lupine form, he lives off prey and pillage. The author of Melion describes in quite gory detail how Melion rips out the throats of a hundred cattle and oxen during his first rampage in Ireland. Melion is also distinguished from the solitary Bisclavret by his subsequent leadership of a band of ten other wolves. The description of the hunting down and the destruction of Melion's band of bloodthirsty wolves occupies a significant part of this lay.[1] The dénouement of this hunt allows the author of Melion to attribute to his werewolf a human emotion more endearing than the anger and vengeance that prompt both him and Bisclavret to attack those responsible for their plights. Bereft following the slaughter of his fellow marauding wolves, whose loss "weighed upon him greatly," Melion, the reader learns, is "most sad."

Marie de France has other characters point out that her werewolf has the intelligence of a man. In Melion it is left to the narrator to tell the reader that Melion, "though a wolf, [had nonetheless] the intelligence and the memory of a man."

Both Bisclavret and Melion are depicted lying at the feet of their respective patrons (the unnamed king in Bisclavret, and in Melion Arthur). And at both royal courts, the astounded nobles comment on the surprising tameness of each beast. Bisclavret's actual diet at court is never mentioned, yet Melion's eating bread and his relishing the drink-ing of "a great deal" of wine reinforce the idea of the beast's hidden humanity.

Each werewolf regains his human form in private—Bisclavret by again donning his clothes, Melion by having the magical red stone of the ring touched to him—thus highlighting the modesty and sensibility of each. Yet the dénouement of *Melion* lacks the drama and brutality of Marie's lay. Melion attacks the squire who had accompanied his wife to Ireland, but the wife is spared the mutilation wrought by Bisclavret on his treacherous wife who not only loses her nose but passes along this terrible disfigurement to many women descended from her.

Marie does not supply a moral at the conclusion of *Bisclavret*. The enormity of Bisclavret's wife's crimes—her fear of his lycanthropy; her subsequent assurances that, in revealing to her the whereabouts of his clothes, Bisclavret will be doing the right thing; and her cynical deci-sion to marry a man she does not love but who will help her betray Bisclavret—justify the punishment meted out to her at the end of the lay. Marie leaves it to her readers, if they care to do so, to formulate the moral of this powerful tale of love betrayed. In *Melion*, the author has the eponymous hero offer at the very end of that lay the rather pedes-trian reminder that a man ought not believe his spouse in all she says. This rule of human behavior seems to echo the lapidary dictum offered from the distaff side by Eliduc's beloved: "Whoever believes a man is quite foolish."

NOTE

[1]Matthieu Boyd studies the significance of this lay's Irish setting in some detail in his article "*Melion* and the Wolves of Ireland," *Neophilologus*, 93, 2009, 555–70.

The Lay of Tyolet

Introduction and Translation by
Margo Vinney

Introduction

The *Lay of Tyolet* is composed of 704 lines and divided into two parts that are preceded by a prologue of forty lines in which the narrator recounts how and why the Bretons of former days used to compose lays. The first part of the lay relates the eponymous hero's upbringing, and the second part constitutes one of the numerous variants of a widespread Celtic tale. Although *Tyolet* shares a certain number of parallel episodes with Marie de France's *Lanval* and contains echoes of both Chrétien de Troyes' *Perceval* (where the youthful hero and his widowed mother live isolated in the forest) and the Tristan legend (where a false claimant uses a purloined proof), it seems reasonable to conclude that because of its predominant Arthurian nature, *Tyolet* offers only a pale reflection of Marie's lay.

The translation that follows was made from the Old French text edited by Gaston Paris and published in *Romania* in 1879 as "Lais inédits de *Tyolet*, de *Guingamor*, de *Doon*, du *Lecheor* et du *Tydorel*." After completing my translation, I came across Jessie Weston's which dates from 1900 and is part of an old collection entitled *Four Lais Rendered into English Prose from the French of Marie de France and Others*, published by David Nutt in London. Miss Weston's rendition is quite archaic in comparison to mine, and we often derive different interpretations of problematic syntactic structures. Since the publication of my translation in 1978, others have published translations of *Tyolet*.

As a narrative work, the *Lay of Tyolet* has merit. It furnishes the reader with some knowledge of elements of the Arthurian cycle, and it contains a certain number of key themes that are evidenced in diverse texts of the Middle Ages. Moreover, the lay is not devoid of humor.

The story, though, is sometimes abrupt and elliptical and lacks clear transitions between scenes. Considering the brevity of the genre, however, this abruptness of style is nothing abnormal.

In general, I have followed the text strictly but permitted myself to translate freely where necessary. As every reader of Old French knows, the syntax of the ancient language differs greatly from that of modern French, and very often one encounters a juxtaposition or a mélange of verb tenses in the narrative portions of these old texts. There is a mixing of the present with the past tense, and within scenes narrated in the past tense, one finds what appear to be arbitrary shifts among the compound past, the simple past, and the imperfect, as well as the past anterior and the pluperfect.

I have attempted to translate the text with precision while respecting the syntax and maintaining the mélange of verb tenses, and to remain faithful to its simplicity in order to retain as much of the tone and flavor of the Old French original as possible.

This is *The Lay of Tyolet*

Long ago, during the time when Arthur reigned and governed Britain, which is called England, it was not then, in my opinion, at all so populated as it is now. But Arthur, who was highly esteemed, had with him knights who were very courageous and undaunted. In our day there are a great many knights who are quite valiant and renowned, but not of the same mettle as those in the days of yore when the most powerful, best, and fiercest knights frequently used to venture forth at night to search for and discover adventures. They used to venture forth also during the day at a time when they did not have squires. And they would not journey all day long without finding a house or tower, or two or three of them perchance. And likewise, in the dark of the night they would find marvelous adventures which they used to tell and relate.

At court the adventures were recounted just as they were experienced; the learned clerks who were there wrote them all down. They were put into Latin and written on parchment, for there would again be a time when people would willingly listen to them. Now they are told and recounted, translated from Latin into Romance. The Bretons composed several lays from these adventures, so say our ancestors.

I will tell you one of them which they composed, according to the story that I know, about a fine and clever young man, hardy, bold, and courageous. Tyolet was his name. He knew a great deal about how to capture beasts, and it was by whistling that he would take all the beasts that he wanted. A fairy bestowed this gift upon him and taught him how to whistle. God never made any beast that Tyolet could not capture by whistling.

His mother was a lady who lived at that time in the woods. A knight she had for a husband, who lived there night and day. He stayed all alone in the forest; there was not a house within ten leagues. Fifteen years had passed since his death, and Tyolet had grown fair and tall. But never an armed knight had he seen during his whole life, nor had he seen other people very often. He stayed in the woods with his mother and never did he leave them. In the forest he had remained, for his mother loved him very much. Hence, he went about the forest when it pleased him, and he had no other activity. When the beasts heard him whistle they would all come to him immediately, and those that he wanted he would kill and take to his mother. In this way they lived, he and his mother; he had not sister or brother.

The lady was very noble and always conducted herself with courtesy. One day she graciously asked her son, because she loved him very much, that he go into the woods and capture a stag. He carried out her wish; straightway he went into the woods just as his mother directed. Until nine o'clock in the morning he wandered in the woods, and found neither beast nor stag. He was very angry with himself because he found no beast. Straight toward home he wanted to go, when, under a tree, he saw a stag standing that was big and meaty.

He whistled immediately. The stag heard him and looked, paid no attention to him, then went away. It left the woods slowly, and Tyolet followed the stag in such a way that it has led him right to a river. The stag has crossed the river. The river was big, swift flowing, wide, long, and dangerous. The stag crossed the river; Tyolet turned around and saw coming quickly a roebuck which was fleshy, long, and big. He stopped and whistled, and the roebuck came toward him. Tyolet put out his hand and then killed the beast. He thrust his knife and plunged it into the body. While he flayed the roebuck, the stag, who had crossed the river, transformed itself.

It appeared as a knight, having completely donned its mail near the water's edge; mounted upon a warhorse with a flowing mane, it was armed like a knight. The youth saw it; never before had he seen such a sight. He looked at it in wonderment and stared for a long time. He marveled at such a thing that he had never before seen and watched it intently.

The knight addressed him and spoke first in a good and kind way and asked Tyolet who he was, what he went about in search of, and what his name was. And Tyolet, who was very valiant and courageous, and the son of the widowed woman who lived in the great forest, answered him.

"Those that want to call me by name call me Tyolet. Now tell me, if you know, who you are and what name you have."

And the one who was standing on the shore answered him forthwith that he was called a knight. And Tyolet asked what kind of beast a knight was, where it lived, and whence it came.

"By my faith," he says, "I will tell you and will not lie to you about a word of it. It is a very dreaded beast which takes and eats other beasts, and it quite often inhabits the woods as well as the plain."

"By my faith," says Tyolet, "I hear marvels. For never, after I learned how to go and after I took to going through the woods, did I succeed in finding such a beast, even though I know bears and lions and all other game. There is not a beast in the woods that I do not know, and I capture them all effortlessly, except you that I scarcely know. You look very much like a courageous beast. Now tell me, Sir Beast, what is this on your head and what is this that hangs around your neck that is so red and so very shiny?"

"By my faith," says the knight, "I will tell you and will not lie to you about a word of it. This is a headpiece called a helmet, and it is made of steel all around. And this is the mantle that I put on; and this is a shield decorated with gold."

"And what is that you are wearing which is full of little holes?"

"It is a tunic of finely wrought iron which is called by the name hauberk."

"And what are you wearing on your feet? Kindly tell me."

"They are called greaves; well-made they are and well wrought."

"And what is that you have at your waist? Tell me if you will."

"It is called a sword and is very beautiful; sharp and sturdy is its blade."

"And this long piece of wood that you carry? Tell me and do not keep it from me."

"Do you want to know?"

"Yes, indeed."

"It is a lance that I carry with me. Now I have told you the truth about everything that you have asked me."

"Sir," says Tyolet, "I thank you. For would to God who does not lie that I might have a raiment such as you have, so beautiful, so fine; would that I might have a tunic and a mantle such as you have, and the same kind of hat! Now tell me, Sir Beast, for the sake of God and for His feast day, if there are other such beasts or ones as beautiful as you."

"Yes," says the knight, "verily. I will show you more than a hundred of them."

At that very instant, just as the story tells us, two hundred armed knights, who were coming from the court of the King, came forth into the middle of a meadow. The King's order they had carried out: a strongly defended house they had taken, put it to the torch and reduced it to ashes; and they are all returning from there armed, in three very tightly formed squadrons.

The Knight-Beast thus spoke to Tyolet and ordered that he go just a bit farther on and look across the river. Tyolet has obeyed the order, looks rapidly about, and sees the knights coming who are fully armed on their chargers.

"By my faith," he says, "I see the beasts who all have casques on their heads. Never before did I see such beasts nor such headpieces as I see here. Would to God that I were a Knight-Beast!"

The Knight-Beast, who was on the shore armed, has spoken to Tyolet again: "Would you be valorous and bold?"

"Yes, by my faith, I swear it to you."

And so the Knight-Beast has said: "Now you will leave. And when you see your mother again, and when she speaks to you, she will say: 'Fair son, tell me about what you are thinking and what is bothering you.' And you will say to her forthwith that you have much to think about, that you would like to resemble the Knight-Beast that you saw, and that for this reason you were pensive. And she will tell you immediately that it weighs on her very heavily that you have seen such a beast that preys upon others and kills them. And you will tell her, by your faith, that you will be the cause of her sadness if you cannot be such a beast and have such a casque on your head. And as soon as she hears this, at once, she will bring you a completely new garb—tunic and mantle, casque and belt, boots and a long, flat lance—such as you have seen here."

Then Tyolet departs and when he arrives home it is very late. Then he gave his mother the roebuck which he had brought and told her his adventure exactly as it had happened. His mother, for this weighs on her very heavily, immediately exclaims, "You have seen a beast like this which takes and eats others!"

"By my faith," says Tyolet, "now this is so. If I cannot be such a beast as the one I saw, know this and understand it well, you will be unhappy on my account."

But his mother, when she heard this, answered him forthwith. All of the arms that she had—those which had belonged to her lord husband—she immediately brought to him. She has armed her son very well with them, and when he had mounted the horse, he indeed resembled a Knight-Beast.

"Do you know now, fair son, what you will do? You will go straight to King Arthur, and I will tell you this: do not take any man as your companion, nor speak of love with any woman who is of the common sort."

Thereupon, Tyolet has turned away from her; she has kissed and embraced him. So far he has journeyed, for so many days, over hills, through flat lands and valleys, that he has come to the court of the King, who was a noble king and a valiant one. The King was sitting at dinner, having himself served magnificently. And Tyolet entered, fully armed, just as he had come. On horse he came before the Round Table, there, where Arthur the King was sitting. Never a word did he utter, nor did he address him.

"Friend," says the King, "dismount and come eat with us, and tell me what you are in search of, who you are, what name you have."

"By my faith," says Tyolet, "I will tell you, but will not eat before so doing. King, I am Knight-Beast by name, I have cut off many heads, and people call me Tyolet; I know very well how to capture game. I am the son, Noble Sir, if it please you, of the widow of the forest. To you she sends me with confidence to learn all I must know. I want to become wise and learn of chivalry and of knighthood, and how to tourney and to joust, to spend and to give [generously]. For I was never before at the court of a king, nor was there ever, I firmly believe, a place where there was so much wealth and culture, chivalry, and learning. Now I have told you what I am seeking. King, now tell me your opinion."

The King says to him, "Lord Knight, I take you into my service. Come and eat."

"Sire," says Tyolet, "I thank you."

So Tyolet dismounted, has disarmed himself, and has dressed in a tunic and a light mantle. He washes his hands and goes to eat.

Behold, there was a maiden there—a haughty damsel; of her beauty I do not wish to speak . . . never did Dido, this is my opinion, nor Helen have so radiant a face. The daughter of the King of Logres she was; on a white palfrey she was seated with a small white hound behind her. She had hung a small bell of gold around the neck of the white hound whose coat was very delicate and pure. On horseback she has come before the King, and she greets him.

"King Arthur, Sire, may God, the all-powerful who reigns on high, save you."

"Beautiful friend, may He care for you. He who protects the just."

"Sire, I am a maiden, the daughter of a king and queen; of Logres my father is King. He and my mother have no other children, and so out of love they ask you—a king, greatly esteemed—if there is among your knights, any one who would be bold and fierce enough to cut off the white foot of a stag and give it to me. Noble Sir, that one I would take as my lord, and for no other would I have any concern. Never will any man have my love if he does not give me the white foot of the stag, who is both beautiful and big, and who has such a shiny coat that it looks almost golden. By seven lions it is well guarded."

"By my faith," says the King, "I promise you that such will be the pledge. He who gives you the foot of the stag will have you as a wife."

"And I, Lord King, for my part, promise that such is the pledge."

Such a covenant they have sworn to and, between the two of them, established. In the hall there was not a knight, who considered himself of any value, who did not say that he would go look for the stag if he knew where it was to be found.

"This hunting dog," she said, "will lead you to where the stag lives and grazes."

Lodoer desired the adventure very much and he was the first to go looking for the stag. He has asked King Arthur, and the King did not forbid him to do it. He took the small hound, has mounted his horse, and has gone looking for the foot of the stag. The hound, who accompanied him, led him straight to a river that was both big and quite wide, black, menacing, and swollen; it was four hundred fathoms wide and at least a hundred fathoms deep. And the hound went into the water. According to its instincts it thought surely that Lodoer would plunge in as well, but he did nothing of the sort. He says that he will not go in, for he has no desire to die. He says to himself thoughtfully: "He who does not have his life has nothing; he who has a good castle, it seems to me, watches over it so that it not be harmed." So the hunting dog has left the water and has come back to Lodoer; and Lodoer has gone away and carried the hound behind him.

Straight to the court he came without delay, where there were assembled many barons. He returns the small hound to the maiden who was very courteous and beautiful. Then the King asked him if he had brought the foot, and Lodoer answered him that still another would be ridiculed because of it. Throughout the hall they made fun of him, and Lodoer, annoyed, shook his head at them, and told them that they should go look for the foot and bring it back.

Many went to look for the stag, and they asked for the maiden. There was no one else who would go there and sing a song different from that which Lodoer—who was a valiant knight—had sung, except one knight who was very brave and agile; Knight-Beast he was called and Tyolet was his name.

Tyolet has gone directly to the King and asked straightway that the maiden in the King's care be his, for he would go in quest of the white foot. He says that he will never return until he has cut off the white foot of the stag. The King has given him leave, and Tyolet has donned his mail, and with his armor was well protected. Then he went to the maiden and asked her for the small white hound. She has willingly given it to him and he has taken leave of her.

They have ridden and journeyed for so long that they have both come to the ford at the wide, swift-flowing river, which was very deep

and menacing. The hunting dog has jumped into the water and goes
along swimming for some time. Tyolet jumps in after it. On his charger,
where he sat, he has so followed the hound that he reached land. Then
the hound led him in such a way that it showed him the stag.

Seven big lions used to guard the stag, and they loved the beast
greatly. And Tyolet keeps watch and sees it in the middle of a meadow
where it was grazing. Not one of the seven lions was there.

Tyolet strikes his spurs and guides his horse to the stag. He then
begins to whistle, and the stag, very innocently, comes toward him at
once. Tyolet whistled seven times and the stag stopped in its tracks.
Quickly, Tyolet drew out his sword. He took the white right foot of
the stag, cut it through the joint, and pushed it into his hose. The stag
wailed loudly, and the lions, all at once, have swiftly come there and
have spotted Tyolet.

One of the lions has so wounded the horse on which Tyolet sat
armed that it goes off carrying the horse's right shoulder, both hide and
flesh. When Tyolet saw this, he struck one of the lions so fiercely with
the sword that he carried that he cut all the way through the nerves of
its chest. With this lion he no longer had any quarrel.

Tyolet's horse collapses beneath him to the ground, so he abandons
it. And the lions have attacked Tyolet; from all sides they assailed him.
They have torn off his sturdy hauberk as well as the skin of his arms and
ribs. In several places he is brutally wounded; they very nearly devoured
him. They ripped all his flesh, but Tyolet has killed every one of them.
It was with difficulty that he freed himself from them. He fell beside the
lions who had mistreated him so, and his body was so ravaged that he
will never be able to make it whole again.

Behold a knight riding, seated on a steel gray charger. He stopped
and looked about; he pities Tyolet and lamented. And Tyolet, who had
fallen asleep from fatigue, opened his eyes and has recounted to him
his adventure; he has told it from beginning to end. From his hose he
pulled out the foot and gave it to the knight. And the knight thanked
him very much for it because he greatly valued the foot. He takes leave
of Tyolet and goes off.

On the way, he thought to himself that if the knight, who had given
him the foot, should live, and if he himself did not want to flee, misfor-
tune could befall him for having the foot. He turns back immediately,
having considered the matter, and decides that he will kill the knight.
Never will Tyolet challenge him. He thrust his sword into the body. In
fact, Tyolet will be cured of this wound, but the knight thought for cer-
tain that he had killed him. Then, he has started on his way, and he has
so followed the direct road that to the court of the King he has come.

He asked the King for the maiden and showed him the white foot of the stag; but he did not have the small white hound that had led Tyolet to the stag. He watched for it morning and night, but about this he cannot be concerned. He who had brought the foot—whoever it might be who had cut it off—by the agreement, wanted the maiden, who is so very noble and beautiful. But the King, who was so wise, asked him for a week's delay on behalf of Tyolet who had not come. Then his court will assemble. At that time, there was no one there but his retinue, that was quite noble and learned. So the knight has granted the delay and has sojourned at the court.

But Gawain, who was so well bred and well versed in all aspects of chivalry, has gone in search of Tyolet, for the hunting dog had returned and he has taken it with him. Quickly, the small hound has led him so that he has found Tyolet in a swoon in the meadow beside the lions.

When Gawain sees the knight and the slaughter that he had accomplished, he greatly pities the valiant knight. At once, he dismounts from his charger and very gently spoke to Tyolet who responded feebly. Nevertheless, of his adventure he has told him the whole story.

Now, behold a maiden on a fine and handsome mule. She graciously greeted Gawain and he has returned her greeting in kind. Then he called her to his side and embraced her, holding her tightly. He beseeches her very gently and lovingly to take this knight—who was so esteemed—to the doctor in the black mountain. And she has done as he asked; she has carried the knight from this place and has put him in the care of the doctor. In Gawain's name she entrusted Tyolet to the doctor, who has received him willingly. He has stripped him of his armor, laid him on a table, and has cleansed his wounds which were very bloody. When he thoroughly examined his body and removed the caked blood which covered Tyolet, he saw that he would recover. At the end of a month's time he would be completely well.

In the meantime, Gawain had arrived at the court of the King and dismounted in the hall. There he has found the knight who had brought the white foot, and who has sojourned at court long enough for the week to have passed by. Then the knight came to the King, greeted him, and spoke about the agreement that the maiden had devised, and that the King, for his part, had accepted: that he who would give her the white foot, him she would take as her lord.

The King said, "This is so."

When Gawain had heard all this, he immediately stepped forward and said to the King, "This is not so. For this reason—even though I ought never, here, before you who are King, refute a knight, sergeant, knave, or squire—I would say that he is mistaken. He never took the foot of the stag in the manner which he maintains. He causes knights great shame who for others' deeds wants to be praised, and who dons another's mantle; he who wishes to draw another's crossbow, and have himself praised for another's action; and he who wants to joust by another's hand and drag from the bushes the serpent which is so dreaded. Now, this kind of behavior will never be seen here. What you say is worthless. You shall make your assault elsewhere; elsewhere you shall go to get what you desire, for you will not have the maiden."

"By my faith," says the knight, "Sir Gawain, now you take me for a villain, you who tell me that I do not dare carry my lance into combat to do battle, that I know well how to draw another's crossbow, and by another's hand, from the bushes, draw out the serpent of which you have spoken. But this is not at all true, so I believe and maintain. If against me one wanted to prove this charge, why, on the field of battle, could he not find me and settle it?"

While engaged in this dispute, they look through the hall and see Tyolet, who had arrived and dismounted outside before the steps. The King has risen to meet him, thrown his arms around his neck, and then kisses him as a sign of his great love for him. The King bows to Tyolet as one does before a lord. Gawain kisses him; Urien, Kay, Yvain, the son of Morgan, and Lodoer went up to kiss him, and so did all of the other knights.

When he sees this, the knight who wanted to have the maiden by virtue of the foot he had brought—which Tyolet had given him—spoke again to King Arthur and made his request. But Tyolet, when he learned this—that the knight had asked for the maiden—spoke to him very gently and asked him calmly: "Lord Knight, tell me this, now as you stand before the King. I want to know for what reason you wish to claim the maiden."

"By my faith," he responds, "I will tell you. It is because I have brought her the white foot from the stag and waited here at court. Both she and the King promised it."

"Did you cut the foot from the stag? If this is the truth, let it not be denied."

"Yes," he says, "I cut it off and I brought it here with me."

"And the seven lions, who killed them?"

The knight looked at him and said not a word, but he blushed and turned red with embarrassment.

Tyolet then spoke again: "Lord Knight, and who was it that was struck by the sword, and who was it that struck him with it? Tell me this if you please. It seems to me that it was you."

The knight hid his face and was much ashamed.

"But this was indeed a treacherous blow when you committed such an outrage. Willingly I had given you the foot that I had cut from the stag, and you deemed it so valuable that you very nearly killed me for it. In fact I did almost die. I gave the foot to you; now I regret it. Through my body you thrust the sword which you carried, and you certainly believed me dead. If you want to justify yourself, prove it before these assembled barons. I tender my pledge to King Arthur."

The knight knows that Tyolet is telling the truth and has suddenly begged for mercy. He fears death more than shame and in no way gainsays Tyolet's story. In the King's presence, he submits to Tyolet and promises to do his bidding. And Tyolet pardoned him on the advice which he accepted on this matter from the King and from all of his barons. And the knight falls to his knees and, then, would have kissed Tyolet's foot because of his magnanimity when Tyolet makes him stand up and kisses him with great affection. I never again heard this affair spoken of.

The knight returns the foot to Tyolet, and Tyolet takes it, and has given it to the maiden. She surpassed in beauty both the lily and the blossoming rose when they first bloom in the summertime. So Tyolet has asked for the damsel, and King Arthur has granted her to him. And the maiden acknowledged him and brought him into her country where he became king and she, queen.

Of Tyolet the lay ends here.

Glossary of Proper Names

Abbreviations used:

B	Bisclavret	Lau	Laüstic
Chai	Chaitivel	Ln	Lanval
Chev	Chievrefueil	Mel	Melion
DA	Les Deus Amanz	Mil	Milun
El	Eliduc	Prol	Prologue
Eq	Equitan	Tyol	Tyolet
F	Le Frêne	Y	Yonec
G	Guigemar		

Aaron, Saint (Y): Welsh martyr during the persecution of Diocletian; feast day, July 1.

Adam (Y): The first man.

Alexandria (G, Ln): City in Egypt founded by Alexander the Great.

Anjou (Chai, G): French province.

Arthur (Ln, Mel, Tyol): The legendary Celtic king of England.

Avalon (Ln): The magic island sometimes identified as Glastonbury in Somerset.

Barfleur (Mil): (Spelled Barbefluet in the manuscript) port city in Normandy.

Boulogne (Chai): Boulogne-sur-mer in Pas-de-Calais in northern France.

Brabant (Chai): Duchy whose main towns were Antwerp, Brussels, and Louvain.

Brangien (Chev): Isolde's nurse and confidant.

Breton (B, DA, Eq, G, Lau, Ln, Mil, Tyol): Inhabitant of Brittany.

Britain (Tyol, Y): England; includes Monmouthshire in *Yonec*.

Brittany (B, Chai, El, Eq, F, G, Mil): The Celtic-inhabited province in northwestern France whose capital was Rennes.

Burgundy (G): Duchy in west central France whose capital was Dijon.

Caerleon (Mil, Y): Caerleon-on-Usk in Monmouthshire in South Wales, a town where Arthur frequently holds court.

Caerwent (Y): Town in Monmouthshire.

Carlisle (Ln): Residence of Arthur in Cumberland.

Christ, Body of (Y): The Eucharist host. In her second reference to the host in this scene, Marie uses the Latin expression *Corpus Domini*.

Clement, Saint (El): Pope and martyr, tied to an anchor and thrown into the sea.

Coldre (F): The sister of Frêne. The word means hazelnut tree.

Constantinople (F): Istanbul in Turkey, evocative of the riches of the East.

Cornwall (Chev): Peninsula in southwest England, jutting into the Atlantic.

Cornwall, Duke of (Ln): Character in *Lanval*.

Dido (Ln, Tyol): According to Virgil, she fell in love with Aeneas, whose descendants founded Rome.

Dol (F): City in Brittany.

Dol, archbishop of (F): Character in *Le Frêne*.

Dublin (Mel): Major city of Ireland.

Duclas (Y): River on which Caerwent is located.

Eastertide (Chai, Mil): The period following the Christian feast celebrating the resurrection of Christ.

England (Mil, Tyol): Celtic land where Arthur ruled.

Exeter (El): The major city in Devon in southwest England.

Flanders (Chai, Mil): Principality in the southwest of the Low Countries, including what is now the French department of Nord, parts of Belgium, and the Dutch province of Zeeland.

Fortune (F, G): The goddess often pictured turning her wheel on which people rise and fall.

Gascony (G): Duchy in southwest France; the ducal title passed in the twelfth century to the Plantagenêt kings of England.

Gawain (Ln, Mel): The ideal of knighthood and the most famous member of the Round Table.

Gotelef (Chev): Marie's transliteration into English of the French *chèvrefeuille* (honeysuckle), literally "goat leaf."

Guildeluec (El): Eliduc's wife.

Guilliadun (El): Eliduc's beloved.

Gurun (F): Frêne's lover and later her husband.

Hainault (Chai): Region in southwest Belgium.

Helen (Tyol): Wife of Menelaus; her abduction by Paris precipitated the Trojan War.

Hoël (G): King of Brittany in *Guigemar*.

Ireland (Mel, Mil, Y): Celtic land west of England.

Ireland, king of (Mel): Father of Melion's wife.

Jesus (Mel): The Christ.

John, Saint (Ln): The Baptist, whose feast day is June 24.

Jutland (Mil): Danish peninsula.

Kay (Tyol): Arthur's seneschal.

Lavinia (Ln): Wife of Aeneas.

Lincoln (Y): Cathedral town in the East Midlands.

Liun (G): Saint-Pol-de-Léon in Finisterre, in northwest France.

Lodoer (Tyol): One of Arthur's knights.

Logres (El, Ln, Mil, Tyol): England.

Lorraine (G): Province in eastern France, called Lohringia by Marie.

Love (G, El, Eq, Ln): Personification of the power of this passion.

Mark, King (Chev): King of Cornwall, husband of Isolde, and uncle of Tristan.

Mary, Blessed Mother (El): The Blessed Virgin Mary, the Mother of God.

Meriaduc (G): Guigemar's rival.

Mont Saint Michel (Mil): The celebrated French monastery located on the border between Normandy and Brittany.

Muldumarec (Y): The bird-knight and father of Yonec.

Nantes (Chai): City in Brittany.

Nanz (Eq): People ruled over by Equitan.

Neustria (DA): Alternative name for Normandy.

Nicholas, Saint (El): Fourth-century bishop of Myra and patron saint of sailors; his feast day is December 6.

Noguent (G): Guigemar's sister.

Normandy (DA, Mil): Province in northern France.

Normans (B, Chai): Inhabitants of Normandy.

Northumbria (Mil): The English county of Northumberland.

Norway (Mil): The Scandinavian nation.

Octavian (Ln): The Roman emperor Caesar Augustus.

Oridial (G): Guigemar's father.

Ovid (G): The Roman poet and author of *Ars amatoria* and *Remedia amoris*.

Peerless (Mil): Milun's son.

Pentecost (Chev, Ln): The Christian feast celebrating the coming of the Holy Spirit to the Apostles fifty days after Easter.

Picts (Ln): Ancient inhabitants of eastern and northeastern Scotland.

Pistre, Vale of (DA): Region in Normandy around the town of Pistre.

Pistrians (DA): Inhabitants of the Norman region of Pistre.

Priscian (Prol): The sixth-century Latin grammarian, author of the *Institutiones grammaticae*.

Queen, the [Guinevere] (Ln): Arthur's wife, who offers her love to Lanval.

Queen, the [Isolde] (Chev): Mark's wife and Tristan's beloved.

Romance (Tyol): The French language, in contrast to Latin.

Romans (Mel): The people Arthur wishes to conquer.

Round Table (Ln, Tyol): According to Geoffrey of Monmouth, the gathering place of Arthur's knights.

Saint Malo (Lau): Channel port in Brittany.

Salerno (DA): Italian city famous for its medical school.

Scotland (Mil): The nation occupying the northern third of the isle of Great Britian. In *Milun*, Marie uses the Gaelic name "Albany."

Scots (Ln): The inhabitants of Scotland.

Seine (DA): The river in northern France that empties into the Channel.

Semiramis, Queen (Ln): Ninth-century B.C. Assyrian queen, legendary builder of Babylon.

Southampton (M): Town in Hampshire on the Channel.

Tintagel (Chev): King Mark's residence in Cornwall.

Totness (El): Town in Devonshire.

Tristan (Chev): Mark's nephew and Isolde's lover.

Urien (Tyol): One of Arthur's knights.

Venus (G, Ln): Roman goddess, identified with Aphrodite, the Greek goddess of love.

Wales, South (Chev, Mil): Birthplace of both Milun and Tristan.

Yder (Mel): One of Arthur's knights (spelled Ydel in the manuscript); son of Yrien (see Urien).

Yvain (Ln, Mel): One of the chief knights of the Round Table and cousin of Gawain. In *Tyolet*, he is called the son of Morgan (le Fey).

Glossary of Specialized Terms

birdlime: A glutinous substance spread upon twigs, by which birds may be caught and held fast.

burgher: An inhabitant of a burgh, borough, or town.

castellan: The lord of a castle.

chamberlain: An officer charged with the management of the private chambers of a sovereign or nobleman.

chapter house: A building attached to a monastery in which are held meetings of the chapter, the duly constituted assembly of the members of the monastic order for consultation and transaction of the affairs of that order.

constable: The chief officer of the military forces of a ruler.

fief: An estate, held on condition of homage and service to a superior lord, by whom it is granted and in whom the ownership remains.

fowler: One who hunts wild birds, for sport or food, especially with nets.

gauntlet: A glove thrown down in the act of challenging an opponent

goatleaf: A literal translation of the French *chèvrefeuille* (honeysuckle).

goshawk: A large short-winged hawk.

greave: Armor for the leg below the knee.

guarantor: A person answerable for the performance of an obligation by another person, who is in the first instance liable to such an obligation.

hauberk: A coat of mail.

hound-swain: A male servant charged with the care of hunting dogs.

league: A measure of distance, usually estimated roughly at about three miles.

The *Oxford English Dictionary* has been quite useful in supplying a number of these definitions.

liegeman: A vassal sworn to the service and support of his superior lord, who in return was obliged to afford him protection.

mail: Armor composed of interlaced rings or chainwork or of overlapping plates fastened upon a groundwork, as in a coat of mail.

marten (fur): The fur or dressed skin of any animal of the mustelid genus Martes, which comprises furry, bushy-tailed mammals found in forests of Eurasia.

office: The prayers of the breviary for each of the canonical hours of the day, comprising psalms, collects, and lessons which vary for each day of the liturgical year.

palfrey: A horse for ordinary riding, as distinct from a warhorse.

psalter: A volume containing the Psalms, especially as arranged for liturgical or devotional use.

question, the: The application of torture as part of a judicial examination.

rote: A musical instrument, probably of the violin class.

seneschal: An official in the household of a sovereign, to whom the administration of justice and the entire control of domestic arrangements were entrusted.

Solomonic: Characteristic of Solomon; suggestive of the splendor of that Israelite king.

squire: A young man of good birth attendant upon a knight.

troth: One's faith as pledged in a solemn agreement or undertaking; one's word.

vassal: One holding land from a superior on conditions of homage and allegiance.

werewolf: A person who is transformed or is capable of self-transformation into a wolf. The first element of the word has usually been identified as Old English *wer*, meaning man.

Appendix

Selected Old French Texts

Prologue

Qui Deus a duné esciënce
e de parler bone eloquence,
ne s'en deit taisir ne celer,
ainz se deit voluntiers mustrer.
5   Quant uns granz biens est mult oïz,
dunc a primes est il fluriz,
e quant loëz est de plusurs,
dunc a espandues ses flurs.
Custume fu as anciëns,
10   ceo testimoine Preciëns,
es livres que jadis faiseient
assez oscurement diseient
pur cels ki a venir esteient
e ki apendre les deveient,
15   que peüssent gloser la letre
e de lur sen le surplus metre.
Li philesophe le saveient,
par els meïsme l'entendeient,
cum plus trespassereit li tens,
20   plus serreient sutil de sens
e plus se savreient guarder
de ceo qu'i ert, a trespasser.
Ki de vice se vuelt defendre,
estudiër deit e entendre
25   e grevose oevre comencier;
par ceo s'en puet plus esloignier
e de grant dolur delivrer.
Pur ceo començai a penser
d'alkune bone estoire faire
30   e de Latin en Romanz traire;
mais ne me fust guaires de pris:
itant s'en sunt altre entremis.
Des lais pensai qu'oïz aveie.
Ne dutai pas, bien le saveie,
35   que pur remembrance les firent
des aventures qu'il oïrent
cil ki primes les comencierent

145

e ki avant les enveierent.
Plusurs en ai oïz conter,
40   nes vueil laissier ne obliër.
Rime en ai e fait ditié,
soventes feiz en ai veillié.

En l'onur de vus, nobles reis,
ki tant estes pruz e curteis,
45   a qui tute joie s'encline,
e en qui quer tuz biens racine,
m'entremis des lais assembler
par rime faire e reconter.
En mun quer pensoe e diseie,
50   sire, ques vos presentereie.
Se vos les plaist a receveir,
mult me ferez grant joie aveir;
a tuz jurs mais en serrai liee.
Ne me tenez a surquidiee,
55   se vos os faire icest present.
Ore oëz le comencement!

Guigemar

Ki de bone matire traite,
mult li peise, se bien n'est faite.
Oëz, seignur, que dit Marie
ki en sun tens pas ne s'oblie.
5   Celui deivent la genz loër,
ki en bien fait de sei parler.
Mais quant il a en un païs
hume ne femme de grant pris,
cil ki de sun bien unt envie
10   sovent en dïent vileinie.
Sun pris li vuelent abaissier:
pur ceo comencent le mestier
del malvais chien coart, felun,
ki mort la gent par traïsun.
15   Nel vueil mie pur ceo laissier,
si jangleür u losengier
le me vuelent a mal turner;
ceo est lur dreiz de mesparler.

Les contes que jo sai verais,
20   dunt li Bretun unt fait les lais,
vos conterai assez briefment.
El chief de cest comencement
sulunc la letre e l'escriture
vos mosterrai une aventure,
25   ki en Bretaigne la Menur
avint al tens anciënur.
En cel tens tint Hoëls la terre,
sovent en pais, sovent en guerre.
Li reis aveit un suen barun,
30   ki esteit sire de Liün.
Oridials esteit apelez.
De sun seignur ert mult amez;
chevaliers ert pruz e vaillanz.
De sa moillier out dous enfanz,
35   un fiz e une fille bele.

Noguent ot nun la dameisele;
Guigeimar noment le dancel:
el reialme nen out plus bel.
A merveille l'amot sa mere,
40   e mult esteit bien de sun pere.
Quant il le pout partir de sei,
si l'enveia servir le rei.
Li vadlez fu sages e pruz;
mult se faiseit amer de tuz.
45   Quant fu venuz termes e tens
que il aveit eage e sens,
li reis l'adube richement;
armes li dune a sun talent.
Guigemar se part de la curt;
50   mult i dona ainz qu'il s'en turt.
En Flandres vait pur sun pris querre:
la out tuz jurs estrif e guerre.
En Lohereigne n'en Burguigne
ne en Anjou ne en Gascuigne
55   a cel tens ne pout hom truver
si bon chevalier ne sun per.
De tant i out mespris nature
que unc de nule amur n'out cure.
Suz ciel n'out dame ne pucele,
60   ki tant par fust noble ne bele,
se il d'amer la requeïst,
que volentiers nel retenist.
Plusurs l'en requistrent suvent,
mais il n'aveit de ceo talent;
65   nuls ne se pout aparceveir
que il volsist amur aveir.
Pur ceo le tienent a peri
e li estrange e si ami.
En la flur de sun meillur pris
70   s'en vait li ber en sun païs
veeir sun pere e sun seignur,
sa bone mere e sa sorur,
ki mult l'aveient desiré.
Ensemble od els a sujurné,
75   ceo m'est a vis, un meis entier.
Talenz li prist d'aler chacier.

La nuit somunt ses chevaliers,
ses veneürs e ses berniers.
Al matin vait en la forest;
80   kar cil deduiz forment li plest.
A un grant cerf sunt aruté,
e li chien furent descuplé.
Li veneür current devant;
li dameisels se vait tarjant.
85   Sun arc li portë uns vaslez,
sun hansac e sun berserez.
Traire voleit, si mes eüst,
ainz que d'iluec se remeüst.
En l'espeisse d'un grant buissun
90   vit une bisse od sun foün.
Tute fu blanche cele beste;
perches de cerf out en la teste.
Pur l'abai del brachet sailli.
Il tent sun arc, si trait a li.
95   En l'esclot la feri devant;
ele chaï demeintenant.
La saiete resort ariere:
Guigemar fiert en tel maniere
en la quisse desqu'al cheval,
100 que tost l'estuet descendre a val.
A terre chiet sur l'erbe drue
delez la bisse qu'out ferue.
La bisse, ki nafree esteit,
anguissuse ert, si se plaigneit.
105 Aprés parla en itel guise:
«Oï, lasse! Jo sui ocise!
E tu, vassal, ki m'as nafree,
tels seit la tue destinee:
ja mais n'aies tu medecine!
110 Ne par herbe ne par racine,
ne par mire ne par poisun
n'avras tu ja mes guarisun
de la plaie qu'as en la quisse,
de si que cele te guarisse,
115 ki suferra pur tue amur
si grant peine e si grant dolur,
qu'unkes femme tant ne sufri;

e tu referas tant pur li,
dunt tuit cil s'esmerveillerunt,
120   ki aiment e amé avrunt
u ki puis amerunt aprés.
Va t'en de ci! Lai m'aveir pes!»

Guigemar fu forment blesciez.
De ceo qu'il ot est esmaiez.
125   Comença sei a purpenser
en quel terre purra aler
pur sa plaie faire guarir;
kar ne se volt laissier murir.
Il set assez e bien le dit
130   qu'unkes femme nule ne vit,
a qui il aturnast s'amur
ne kil guaresist de dolur.
Sun vaslet apela avant.
«Amis,» fait il, «va tost poignant!
135   Fai mes compaignuns returner;
kar jo voldrai a els parler.»
Cil point avant, e il remaint.
Mult anguissusement se pleint.
De sa chemise estreitement
140   bende sa plaie fermement.
Puis est muntez, d'iluec s'en part;
qu'esloigniez seit, mult li est tart;
ne vuelt que nuls des suens i vienge,
kil desturbast ne kil retienge.
145   Le travers del bois est alé
un vert chemin, ki l'a mené
fors de la landë. En la plaigne
vit la faleise e la muntaigne
d'une ewe ki desuz cureit.
150   Braz fu de mer; hafne i aveit.
El hafne out une sule nef,
dunt Guigemar choisi le tref.
Mult esteit bien aparilliee;
defors e dedenz fu peiee,
155   nuls huem n'i pout trover jointure.
N'i out cheville ne closture

ki ne fust tute d'ebenus;
suz ciel n'a or ki vaille plus.
La veile fu tute de seie:
160 mult est bele, ki la despleie.
Li chevaliers fu mult pensis;
En la cuntree n'el païs
n'out unkes mes oï parler
que nes i peüst ariver.
165 Il vait avant, si descent jus;
a grant anguisse munta sus.
Dedenz quida humes truver,
ki la nef deüssent guarder:
n'i aveit nul, ne nul ne vit.
170 En mi la nef trova un lit,
dunt li pecol e li limun
furent a l'uevre Salemun
taillié a or, tut a trifoire,
de ciprés e de blanc ivoire.
175 D'un drap de seie a or teissu
ert la coilte ki desus fu.
Les altres dras ne sai preisier;
mes tant vos di de l'oreillier:
ki sus eüst sun chief tenu
180 ja mais le peil n'avreit chanu.
Le cuverturs de sabelin
volz fu du purpre Alexandrin.
Dui chandelabre de fin or
(le pire valeit un tresor)
185 el chief de la nef furent mis;
desus out dous cirges espris.
De ceo s'esteit il merveilliez.
Il s'est sur le lit apuiez;
repose sei, sa plaie duelt.
190 Puis est levez, aler s'en vuelt.
Il ne pout mie returner;
la nes est ja en halte mer,
od lui s'en vat delivrement.
Bon oré ot e suëf vent,
195 n'i a niënt de sun repaire;
mult est dolenz, ne set que faire.
N'est merveille se il s'esmaie,

kar grant dolur a en sa plaie.
Sufrir li estuet l'aventure.
200   A Deu prie qu'en prenge cure,
qu'a sun poeir l'ameint a port
e sil defende de la mort.
El lit se colche, si s'endort
Hui a trespassé le plus fort;
205   ainz la vespree arivera
la u sa guarisun avra,
desuz une antive cité,
ki esteit chiés de cel regné.

Li sire, ki la mainteneit,
210   mult fu vielz huem e femme aveit,
une dame de halt parage,
franche, curteise, bele e sage.
Gelus esteit a desmesure;
car ceo purporte la nature
215   que tuit li vieil seient gelus;
mult het chascuns que il seit cus:
tels est d'eage li trespas.
Il ne la guardout mie a gas.
En un vergier suz le donjun
220   la out un clos tut envirun.
De vert marbre fu li muralz,
mult par esteit espés e halz.
N'i out fors une sule entree;
cele fu nuit e jur guardee.
225   De l'altre part fu clos de mer;
nuls n'y pout eissir ne entrer,
se ceo ne fust od un batel,
se busuin eüst al chastel.
Li sire out fait dedenz le mur,
230   pur mettre i sa femme a seür,
chambre; suz ciel n'aveit plus bele.
A l'entree fu la chapele.
La chambre ert peinte tut en tur.
Venus, la deuesse d'amur,
235   fu tresbien mise en la peinture;
les traiz mustrot e la nature

cument hom deit amur tenir
e leialment e bien servir.
Le livre Ovide, u il enseigne
240   coment chascuns s'amur estreigne,
en un fu ardant le getout,
e tuz icels escumenjout
ki ja mais cel livre lirreient
ne sun enseignement fereient.
245   La fu la dame enclose e mise.
Une pucele a sun servise
li aveit sis sire bailliee,
ki mult ert franche e enseigniee,
sa niece, fille sa sorur.
250   Entre les dous out grant amur;
od li esteit quant il errout.
De ci la que il repairout,
hume ne femme n'i venist
ne fors de cel murail n'issist.
255   Uns vielz prestre blancs e floriz
guardout la clef de cel postiz:
les plus bas membres out perduz:
altrement ne fust pas creüz.
Le servise Deu li diseit
260   e a sun mangier la serveit.

Cel jur meïsme ainz relevee
fu la dame el vergier alee.
Dormi aveit aprés mangier,
si s'ert alee esbaneier,
265   ensemble od li la meschine.
Guardent a val vers la marine;
la nef virent al flot muntant,
ki el hafne veneit siglant
ne veient rien ki la cunduie.
270   La dame vuelt turner en fuie:
se ele a poür, n'est merveille;
tute en fu sa face vermeille.
Mes la meschine, ki fu sage
e plus hardie de curage,
275   la recunforte e aseüre.

Cele part vunt grant aleüre.
Sun mantel oste la pucele,
entre en la nef ki mult fu bele.
N'i trova nule rien vivant
280   fors sul le chevalier dormant.
Arestut sei, si l'esguarda;
pale le vit, mort le quida.
Ariere vait la dameisele,
hastivement sa dame apele.
285   Tute l'aventure li dit,
mult pleint le mort que ele vit.
Respunt la dame: «Or i alums!
Se il est morz, nus l'enforruns;
nostre prestre nus aidera.
290   Se vif le truis, il parlera.»
Ensemble vunt, ne targent mes,
la dame avant e cele aprés.
Quant ele est en la nef entree,
devant le lit est arestee.
295   Le chevalier a esguardé;
mutl pleint sun cors e sa belté.
Pur lui esteit triste e dolente
e dit que mar fu sa juvente.
Desur le piz li met sa main;
300   chalt le senti e le quer sein,
ki suz les costes li bateit.
Li chevalier, ki se dormeit,
s'est esveilliez, si l'a veüe.
Mult en fu liez, si la salue;
305   bien set qu'il est venuz a rive.
La dame, pluranz e pensive,
li respundi mult bonement;
demande li cumfaitement
il est venuz e de quel terre
310   e s'il est eissilliez pur guerre.
«Dame,» fet il, «ceo n'i a mie.
Mes se vus plest que jeo vus die
m'aventure, vus cunterai;
nïent ne vus en celerai.
315   De Bretaigne la Menur sui.
En bois alai chacier jehui.

Une blanche bisse feri,
e la saiete resorti;
en la quisse m'a si nafré,
320 ja mes ne quid aveir santé.
La bisse se pleinst e parla,
mult me maldist e si ura,
que ja n'eüsse guarisun
se par une meschine nun.
325 Ne sai u ele seit trovee!
Quant jeo oï la destinee,
hastivement del bois eissi.
En un hafne ceste nef vi;
dedenz entrai, si fis folie;
330 od mei s'en est la nes ravie.
Ne sai u jeo sui arivez,
coment a nun ceste citez.
Bele dame, pur Deu vus pri,
cunseilliez mei, vostre merci!
335 Kar jeo ne sai quel part aler,
ne la nef ne puis governer.»
El li respunt: «Bels sire chiers,
cunseil vus durrai volentiers.
Ceste citez est mun seignur
340 e la cuntree tut en tur.
Riches huem est de halt parage,
mes mult par est de grant eage.
Anguissusement est gelus,
par cele fei que jeo dei vus.
345 Dedenz cest clos m'a enseree.
N'i a fors une sule entree;
uns vielz prestre la porte guarde:
ceo doinse Deus que mals feus l'arde!
Ici sui nuit e jur enclose;
350 ja nule feiz nen ierc si ose
que j'en isse, s'il nel comande,
se mis sire ne me demande.
Ci ai ma chambre e ma chapele,
ensemble od mei ceste pucele.
355 Se vus i plest a demurer
tant que vus mielz puissiez errer,
volentiers vus sojurnerum

e de bon quer vus servirum.»
Quant il a la parole oïe,
360   dulcement la dame en mercie;
od li sujurnera, ceo dit.
En estant s'est dreciez del lit;
celes li aïent a peine.
La dame en sa chambre l'en meine.
365   Desur le lit a la meschine,
triers un dossal ki pur cortine
fu en la chambre apareilliez,
la est li dameisels culchiez.
En bacins d'or ewe aporterent:
370   sa plaie e sa quisse laverent.
A un bel drap de cheinsil blanc
li osterent en tur le sanc;
puis l'unt estreitement bendé.
Mult le tienent en grant chierté.
375   Quant lur mangiers al vespre vint,
la pucele tant en retint,
dunt li chevaliers out asez:
bien est peüz e abevrez.
Mes amurs l'ot feru al vif;
380   ja ert sis quers en grant estrif,
kar la dame l'a si nafré,
tut a sun païs ublié.
De sa plaie nul mal ne sent;
mult suspire anguissusement.
385   La meschine, kil deit servir
prie qu'ele le laist dormir.
Cele s'en part, si l'a laissié.
Puis qu'il li a duné cungé,
devant sa dame en est alee,
390   ki alkes esteit reschalfee
del feu dunt Guigemar se sent
que sun quer alume e esprent.

Li chevaliers fu remés sous.
Pensis esteit e anguissous;
395   ne set uncore que ceo deit;
mes nepurquant bien s'aparceit;

se par la dame n'est guariz,
de la mort est seürs e fiz.
«A las!» fet il, «quel le ferai?
400 Irai a li, si li dirai
que ele ait merci e pitié
de cest chaitif descunseillié.
S'ele refuse ma preiere
e tant seit orgoilluse e fiere,
405 dunc m'estuet il a doel murir
u de cest mal tuz jurs languir.»
Lors suspira; en poi de tens
li est venuz novels purpens,
e dit que sufrir li estoet;
410 kar issi fait ki mielz ne poet.
Tute la nuit a si veillié
e suspiré e travaillié;
en sun quer alot recordant
les paroles e le semblant,
415 les uiz vairs e la bele buche,
dunt la dolçurs al quer li tuche.
Entre ses denz merci li crie;
pur poi ne l'apele s'amie.
Se il seüst qu'ele senteit
420 e cum amurs la destreigneit,
mult en fust liez, mun esciënt;
un poi de rasuagement
li tolist alques la dolur
dunt il ot pale la colur.
425 Se il a mal pur li amer,
el ne s'en puet niënt loër.
Par matinet einz l'ajurnee
esteit la dame sus levee.
Veillié aveit, de ceo se pleint;
430 ceo fet amurs ki la destreint.
La meschine, ki od li fu,
al semblant a aparceü
de sa dame, que ele amout
le chevalier ki sojurnout
435 en la chambre pur guarisun;
mes el ne set s'il l'eime u nun.
La dame est entree el mustier,

e cele vait al chevalier.
Asise s'est devant le lit;
440   e il l'apele, si li dit:
«Amie, u est ma dame alee?
Pur quei est el si tost levee?»
A tant se tut, si suspira.
La meschine l'araisuna.
445   «Sire,» fet ele, «vus amez!
Guardez que trop ne vus celez!
Amer poëz en itel guise,
que bien iert vostre amurs assise.
Ki ma dame vodreit amer,
450   mult devreit bien de li penser.
Ceste amurs sereit covenable,
se vus amdui fussiez estable.
Vus estes bels, e ele est bele.»
Il respundi a la pucele:
455   «Jeo sui de tel amur espris,
bien me purra venir a pis,
se jeo n'ai sucurs e aïe.
Cunseilliez mei, ma dulce amie!
Que ferai jeo de ceste amur?»
460   La meschine par grant dulçur
le chevalier a conforté
e de s'aïe aseüré,
de tuz les biens qu'ele puet faire;
mult ert curteise e de bon'aire.

465   Quant la dame a la messe oïe,
ariere vait, pas ne s'ublie.
Saveir voleit que cil faiseit,
se il veillout u il dormeit,
pur qui amur sis quers ne fine.
470   Avant l'apele la meschine;
al chevalier la fait venir:
bien li purra tut a leisir
mustrer e dire sun curage,
turt li a pru u a damage.
475   Il la salue e ele lui.
En grant esfrei erent amdui.

Il ne l'osot nïent requerre;
pur ceo qu'il ert d'estrange terre,
aveit poür, s'il li mustrast,
480   qu'el l'enhaïst e esloignast.
Mes ki ne mustre s'enferté,
a peine puet aveir santé.
Amurs est plaie dedenz cors
e si ne piert nïent defors;
485   ceo est uns mals ki lunges tient,
pur ceo que de nature vient.
Plusur le tienent a gabeis,
si cume cil vilain curteis,
ki jolivent par tut le mund,
490   puis s'avantent de ceo que funt;
n'est pas amurs, einz est folie
e malvaistiez e lecherie.
Ki un en puet leial trover,
mult le deit servir e amer
495   e estre a sun comandement.
Guigemar eime durement:
u il avra hastif sucurs,
u li estuet vivre a reburs.
Amurs li dune hardement:
500   il li descuevre sun talent.
«Dame,» fet il, «jeo muerc pur vus;
mis quers en est mult anguissus.
Se vus ne me volez guarir,
dunc m'estuet il en fin murir.
505   Jo vus requier de druërie:
bele, ne m'escundites mie!»
Quant ele l'a bien entendu,
avenantment a respundu.
Tut en riant li dit: «Amis,
510   cist cunseilz sereit trop hastis,
d'otreier vus ceste peiere:
jeo n'en sui mie custumiere.»
«Dame,» fet il, «pur Deu, merci!
Ne vus ennuit, se jol vus di!
515   Femme jolive de mestier
se deit lunc tens faire preier,
pur sei cherir, que cil ne quit

que ele ait usé cel deduit.
Mes la dame de bon purpens,
520 ki en sei ait valur ne sens,
s'ele trueve hume a sa maniere,
ne se fera vers lui trop fiere,
ainz l'amera, si'n avra joie.
Ainz que nuls le sace ne l'oie,
525 avrunt il mult de lur pru fait.
Bele dame, finum cest plait!»
La dame entent que veir li dit,
e li otreie senz respit
l'amur de li, e il la baise.
530 Des ore est Guigemar a aise.
Ensemble gisent e parolent
e sovent baisent e acolent;
bien lur covienge del surplus,
de ceo que li altre unt en us!

535 Ceo m'est a vis, an e demi
fu Guigemar ensemble od li.
Mult fu delituse la vie.
Mes fortune, ki ne s'oblie,
sa roe turnë en poi d'ure,
540 l'un met desuz, l'altre desure.
Issi est de cels avenu;
kar tost furent aparceü.

Al tens d'esté par un matin
jut la dame lez le meschin.
545 La buche li baise e le vis,
puis si li dit: «Bels, dulz amis,
mis quers me dit que jeo vus pert;
veü serum e descovert.
Se vus murez, jeo vueil murir;
550 e se vis en poëz partir,
vus recoverrez altre amur,
e jeo remeindrai en dolur.»
«Dame,» fet il, «nel dites mes!
Ja n'aie jeo joie ne pes,
555 quant vers nule altre avrai retur!

N'aiez de ceo nule poür!»
«Amis, de ceo m'aseürez!
Vostre chemise me livrez!
El pan desuz ferai un pleit;
560   cungié vus doins, u que ceo seit,
D'amer cele kil desfera
e ki despleier le savra.»
Il li baille, si l'aseüre;
le pleit i fet en tel mesure,
565   nule femme nel desfereit,
se force u cultel n'i meteit.
La chemise li dune e rent,
il la receit par tel covent
qu'el le face seür de li
570   par une ceinture altresi,
dunt a sa char nue la ceint:
parmi les flans alkes l'estreint
Ki la bucle purra ovrir
senz depescier e senz partir,
575   il li prie que celui aint.
Il l'a baisiee; a tant remaint.

Cel jur furent aparceü,
descovert, trové e veü
d'un chamberlenc mal vezïé
580   que sis sire i out enveié.
A la dame voleit parler,
ne pout dedenz la chambre entrer.
Par une fenestre les vit;
vait a sun seignur, si li dit.
585   Quant li sire l'a entendu,
unques mes tant dolenz ne fu.
De ses privez demande treis.
A la chambre vait demaneis;
il en a fet l'us depescier:
590   dedenz trova le chevalier.
Pur la grant ire que il a
a ocire le cumanda.
Guigemar est en piez levez;
ne s'est de nïent esfreez.

595   Une grosse perche de sap,
        u suleient pendre li drap,
        prist en ses mains, e sis atent.
        Il en fera alkun dolent:
        ainz que il d'els seit aprismiez,
600   les avra il tuz mahaigniez.
        Li sire l'a mult esguardé;
        enquis li a e demandé
        ki il esteit e dunt fu nez
        e coment est laienz entrez.
605   Cil li cunte cum il i vint
        e cum la dame le retint;
        tute li dist la destinee
        de la bisse ki fu nafree
        e de la nef e de sa plaie.
610   Ore est del tut en sa manaie.
        Il li respunt que pas nel creit
        e s'issi fust cum il diseit,
        se il peüst la nef trover,
        il le metreit giers en la mer:
615   s'il guaresist, ceo li pesast,
        e bel li fust, se il neiast.
        Quant il l'a bien aseüré,
        al hafne sunt ensemble alé.
        La barge truevent, enz l'unt mis:
620   od lui s'en vet en sun païs.
        La nes eire, pas ne demure
        Li chevaliers suspire e plure;
        la dame regrete sovent,
        e prie Deu omnipotent
625   que il li doinst hastive mort
        e que ja mes ne vienge a port,
        s'il ne repuet aveir s'amie,
        qu'il desire plus que sa vie.
        Tant a cele dolur tenue,
630   que la nes est a port venue
        u ele fu primes trovee.
        Asez ert pres de sa cuntree.
        Al plus tost qu'il pout s'en issi.
        Un damisels qu'il ot nurri,
635   errot aprés un chevalier;

en sa mein menot un destrier.
Il le conut, si l'apela,
e li vaslez se reguarda.
Sun seignur veit, a pié descent;
640 le cheval li met en present.
Od lui s'en vait; joius en sunt
tuit si ami ki trové l'unt.
Mult fu preisiez en sun païs;
mes tuz jurs ert maz e pensis.
645 Femme voleient qu'il presist;
mes il del tut les escundist:
ja ne prendra femme nul jur,
ne pur aveir ne pur amur,
se ele ne puet despleier
650 sa chemise senz depescier.
Par Bretaigne vait la novele;
il n'i a dame ne pucele
ki n'i alast pur asaier:
unc ne la porent despleier.

655 De la dame vus vueil mustrer,
que Guigemar puet tant amer.
Par le cunseil d'un suen barun
sis sire l'a mise en prisun
en une tur de marbre bis.
660 Le jur a mal e la nuit pis.
Nuls huem el mund ne purreit dire
la grant peine ne le martire
ne l'anguisse ne la dolur
que la dame suefre en la tur.
665 Dous anz i fu e plus, ceo quit;
unc n'i ot joie ne deduit.
Sovent regrete sun ami:
«Guigemar, sire, mar vus vi!
Mielz vueil hastivement murir
670 que lungement cest mal sufrir!
Amis, se jeo puis eschaper,
la u vus fustes mis en mer
me neierai!» Dunc lieve sus;
tute esbaïe vient a l'us;

675 n'i trueve clef ne serreüre:
fors s'en eissi par aventure.
Unques nuls ne la desturba.
Al hafne vint, la nef trova;
atachiee fu al rochier
680 u ele se voleit neier.
Quant el la vit, enz est entree;
mes d'une rien s'est purpensee
qu'ilec fu sis amis neiez;
Dunc ne puet ester sur ses piez:
685 se desqu'al bort peüst venir,
el se laissast defors chaïr.
Asez suefre travail e peine.
La nes s'en vet, ki tost l'en meine.
En Bretaigne est venue al port
690 suz un chastel vaillant e fort.
Li sire a qui li chastels fu
aveit a nun Meriadu.
Il guerreiot un suen veisin;
pur ceo fu levez par matin,
695 sa gent voleit fors enveier
pur sun enemi damagier.
A une fenestre s'estot
e vit la nef ki arivot.
Il descendi par un degré;
700 sun chamberlein a apelé.
Hastivement a la nef vunt;
par l'eschiele muntent a munt.
Dedenz unt la dame trovee,
ki de belté resemble fee.
705 Il la saisist par le mantel;
od lui l'en meine en sun chastel.
Mult fu liez de la troveüre,
kar bele esteit a desmesure;
ki que l'eüst mise en la barge,
710 bien set qu'ele est de grant parage.
A li aturna tel amur,
unques a femme n'ot greignur.
Il out une serur pucele;
en sa chambre, que mult fu bele,
715 la dame li a comandee.

Bien fu servie e honuree,
richement la vest e aturne;
mes tuz jurs ert pensive e murne.
Il vait sovent a li parler
720 kar de bon quer la puet amer.
Il la requiert; el n'en a cure,
ainz li mustre de la ceinture:
ja mes hume nen amera,
se celui nun ki l'uverra
725 senz depescer. Quant il l'entent,
si li respunt par maltalent:
«Altresi a en cest païs
un chevalier de mult grant pris:
de femme prendre en itel guise
730 se defent par une chemise,
dunt li destre pan est pleiez;
il ne puet estre deslïez,
ki force u cultel n'i metreit.
Vus feïstes, ceo quit, cel pleit!»
735 Quant el l'oï, si suspira,
pur un petit ne se pasma.
Il la reçut entre ses braz.
De sun blialt trencha les laz;
la ceinture voleit ovrir,
740 mes n'en poeit a chief venir.
Puis n'ot el païs chevalier,
que il n'i feïst essaier.

Issi remist bien lungement
de ci qu'a un turneiement,
745 que Meriadus afia
cuntre celui qu'il guerreia.
Mult i ot semuns chevaliers;
Guigemar fu tuz li primiers.
Il l'i manda par gueredun
750 si cum ami e cumpaignun,
qu'a cel busuin ne li faillist
e en s'aïe a lui venist.
Alez i est mult richement;
chevaliers meine plus de cent.

755   Meriadus dedenz sa tur
le herberja a grant honur.
Encuntre lui sa serur mande;
par dous chevaliers li comande
qu'ele s'aturt e vienge avant,
760   la dame meint qu'il eime tant.
Cele a fet sun comandement.
Vestues furent richement,
main a main vienent en la sale;
la dame fu pensive e pale.
765   Ele oï Guigemar nomer:
ne pout desur ses piez ester;
se cele ne l'eüst tenue,
ele fust a terre chaüe.
Li chevaliers cuntre els leva;
770   la dame vit e esguarda
e sun semblant e sa maniere.
Un petitet se traist ariere.
«Est ceo,» fet il, «ma dulce amie,
m'esperance, mis quer, ma vie,
775   ma bele dame ki m'ama?
Dunt vient ele? Ki l'amena?
Ore ai pensé mult grant folie;
bien sai que ceo n'est ele mie:
femmes se resemblent asez;
780   pur nïent change mis pensez.
Mes pur cele qu'ele resemble,
pur qui mis quers suspire e tremble,
a li parlerai volentiers.»
Dunc vet avant li chevaliers.
785   Il la baisa, lez lui l'asist;
unques nul altre mot ne dist
fors tant que seeir la rova.
Meriadus les esguarda;
mult li pesa de cel semblant.
790   Guigemar apele en riant.
«Sire,» fet il, «se vus plaiseit,
ceste pucele essaiereit
vostre chemise a despleier,
s'ele i purreit rien espleitier.»
795   Il li respunt: «E jeo l'otrei!»

Un chamberlenc apele a sei,
ki la chemise ot a guarder;
il li comande a aporter.
A la pucele fu bailliee;
800   mes ne l'a mie despleiee.
La dame conut bien le pleit.
Mult est sis quers en grant destreit;
kar volentiers s'i essaiast,
s'ele peüst u ele osast.
805   Bien se aparceit Meriadus;
dolenz en fu, ainz ne fu plus.
«Dame,» fait il, «kar assaiez,
se desfaire le purriëz!»
Quant ele ot le comandement,
810   le pan de la chemise prent;
legierement le despleia.
Li chevaliers s'esmerveilla.
Bien la conut; mes nequedent
nel poeit creire fermement.
815   A li parla en tel mesure:
«Amie, dulce creature,
estes vus ceo? dites mei veir!
Laissiez mei vostre cors veeir,
la ceinture dunt jeo vus ciens!»
820   A ses costez li met ses meins,
si a trovee la ceinture.
«Bele,» fet il, «quels aventure
que jo vus ai ici trovee!
Ki vus a ici amenee?»
825   Ele li cunte la dolur,
les granz peines e la tristur
de la prisun u ele fu,
e coment li est avenu,
coment ele s'en eschapa,
830   neier se volt, la nef trova,
dedenz entra, a cel port vint,
e li chevaliers la retint;
guardee l'a a grant honur,
mes tuz jurs la requist d'amur.
835   Ore est sa joie revenue.
«Amis, menez en vostre drue!»

Guigemar s'est en piez levez.
«Seignurs,» fet il, «or m'escultez!
Ci ai m'amie cuneüe
840   que jeo quidoue aveir perdue.
Meriadu requier e pri,
rende la mei, sue merci!
Sis huem liges en devendrai;
dous anz u treis li servirai
845   od cent chevaliers u od plus.»
Dunc respundi Meriadus.
«Guigemar,» fet il, «bels amis,
jeo ne sui mie si suzpris
ne si destreiz pur nule guerre
850   que de ceo me deiez requerre.
Jeo la trovai, si la tendrai
e cuntre vus la defendrai.»

Quant il l'oï, hastivement
comanda a munter sa gent.
855   D'iluec se part; celui desfie.
Mult li peise qu'il lait s'amie.
En la vile n'out chevalier,
ki fust venuz pur turneier,
que Guigemar n'en meint od sei.
860   Chescuns li afie sa fei:
od lui irunt quel part qu'il alt;
mult est huniz ki or li falt.
La nuit sunt al chastel venu
ki guerreiout Meriadu.
865   Li sire les a herbergiez,
ki mult en fu joius e liez
de Guigemar e de s'aïe;
bien set que sa guerre est finie.
El demain par matin leverent,
870   par les ostels se cunreerent.
De la vile issent a grant bruit;
Guigemar primes les cunduit.
Al chastel vienent, si l'asaillent;
mes forz esteit, al prendre faillent.
875   Guigemar a la vile assise;

n'en turnera, si sera prise.
Tant li crurent ami e genz
que tuz les afama dedenz.
Le chastel a destruit e pris
880   e le seignur dedenz ocis.
A grant joie s'amie en meine.
Ore a trespasse sa peine.
De cest cunte qu'oï avez
fu Guigemar li lais trovez,
885   que hum fait en harpe e en rote;
bone en est a oïr la note.

Bisclavret

Quant des lais faire m'entremet,
ne vueil ubliër Bisclavret.
Bisclavret a nun en Bretan,
Garulf l'apelent li Norman.
5   Jadis le poeit hume oïr
e sovent suleit avenir,
hume plusur garulf devindrent
e es boscages maisun tindrent.
Garulf, ceo est beste salvage;
10 tant cum il est en cele rage,
humes devure, grant mal fait,
es granz forez converse e vait.
Cest afaire les ore ester;
del Bisclavret vus vueil cunter.

15 En Bretaigne maneit uns ber,
merveille l'ai oï loër.
Beals chevaliers e bons esteit
e noblement se cunteneit.
De sun seignur esteit privez
20 e de tuz ses veisins amez.
Femme ot espuse mult vaillant
e ki mult faiseit bel semblant.
Il amot li e ele lui;
mes d'une chose ot grant ennui,
25 qu'en la semeine le perdeit
treis jurs entiers qu'el ne saveit
que deveneit ne u alout,
ne nuls des soens niënt n'en sout.
Une feiz esteit repairiez
30 a sa maisun joius e liez;
demandé li a e enquis.
«Sire,» fait el, «bealz, dulz amis,
une chose vus demandasse
mult volentiers, se jeo osasse;
35 mes jeo criem tant vostre curut

que nule rien tant ne redut.»
Quant il l'oï, si l'acola,
vers lui la traist, si la baisa.
«Dame,» fait il, «or demandez!
40   Ja cele chose ne querrez,
se jo la sai, ne la vus die.»
«Par fei,» fet ele, «or sui guarie!
Sire, jeo sui en tel esfrei
les jurs quant vus partez de mei.
45   El cuer en ai mult grant dolur
e de vus perdre tel poür,
se jeo nen ai hastif cunfort,
bien tost en puis aveir la mort.
Kar me dites u vus alez,
50   u vus estes e conversez!
Mun esciënt que vus amez,
e se si est, vus meserrez.»
«Dame,» fet il, «pur Deu, merci!
Mals m'en vendra, si jol vus di;
55   kar de m'amur vus partirai
e mei meïsmes en perdrai.»
Quant la dame l'a entendu,
ne l'a niënt en gab tenu.
Suventes feiz li demanda.
60   Tant le blandi e losenja
que s'aventure li cunta;
nule chose ne li cela.
«Dame, jeo devienc bisclavret.
En cele grant forest me met
65   al plus espés de la gualdine,
s'i vif de preie e de ravine.»
Quant il li aveit tut cunté,
enquis li a e demandé
s'il se despueille u vet vestuz.
70   «Dame,» fet il, «jeo vois tuz nuz.»
«Dites pur Deu, u sunt voz dras?»
«Dame, ceo ne dirai jeo pas;
kar si jes eüsse perduz
e de ceo fusse aparceüz,
75   bisclavret sereie a tuz jurs.
Ja nen avreie mes sucurs,

de si qu'il me fussent rendu.
Pur ceo ne vueil qu'il seit seü.»
«Sire,» la dame li respunt,
80   «jeo vus eim plus que tut le mund.
Nel me devez niënt celer,
ne mei de nule rien duter;
ne semblereit pas amistié.
Qu'ai jeo forfait, pur quel pechié
85   me dutez vus de nule rien?
Dites le mei! Si ferez bien!»
Tant l'anguissa, tant le suzprist,
ne pout el faire, si li dist.
«Dame,» fet il, «delez cel bois,
90   lez le chemin par unt jeo vois,
une viez chapele i estait,
ki meinte feiz grant bien me fait.
La est la piere cruese e lee
suz un buissun, dedenz cavee.
95   Mes dras i met suz le buissun,
tant que jeo revienc a maisun.»
La dame oï cele merveille,
de poür fu tute vermeille.
De l'aventure s'esfrea.
100   En maint endreit se purpensa
cum ele s'en peüst partir;
ne voleit mes lez lui gisir.
Un chevalier de la cuntree,
ki lungement l'aveit amee
105   e mult preiee e mult requise
e mult duné en sun servise,
(ele ne l'aveit unc amé
ne de s'amur aseüré),
celui manda par sun message,
110   si li descovri sun curage.
«Amis,» fet ele, «seiez liez!
Ceo dunt vus estes travailliez
vus otrei jeo senz nul respit;
ja n'i avrez nul cuntredit.
115   M'amur e mun cors vus otrei:
vostre drue faites de mei!»
Cil l'en mercie bonement

      e la fiance de li prent,
      e el le met a sairement.
120 Puis li cunta cumfaitement
      sis sire ala e qu'il devint.
      Tute la veie que il tint
      vers la forest li enseigna;
      pur sa despueille l'enveia.
125 Issi fu Bisclavret traïz
      e par sa femme malbailliz.
      Pur ceo qu'um le perdeit sovent,
      quidouent tuit comunalment
      que dunc s'en fust del tut alez.
130 Asez fu quis e demandez:
      mes n'en porent mie trover,
      si lur estut laissier ester.
      La dame a cil dunc espusee,
      que lungement aveit amee.

135 Issi remest un an entier,
      tant que li reis ala chacier.
      A la forest ala tut dreit
      la u li Bisclavret esteit.
      Quant li chien furent descuplé,
140 le Bisclavret unt encuntré.
      A lui cururent tutejur
      e li chien e li veneür,
      tant que pur poi ne l'ourent pris
      e tut deciré e malmis.
145 Des que il a le rei choisi,
      vers lui curut querre merci.
      Il l'aveit pris par sun estrié,
      la jambe li baise e le pié.
      Li reis le vit, grant poür a;
150 ses cumpaignuns tuz apela.
      «Seignur,» fet il, «avant venez
      et ceste merveille esguardez,
      cum ceste beste s'umilie!
      Ele a sen d'ume, merci crie.
155 Chaciez mei tuz cez chiens ariere,
      si guardez que hum ne la fiere!

Ceste beste a entente e sen.
Espleitiez vus! Alum nus en!
A la beste durrai ma pes:
160   kar jeo ne chacerai hui mes.»

Li reis s'en est turnez a tant.
Li Bisclavret le vet siwant;
mult se tint pres, n'en volt partir,
il n'a cure de lui guerpir.
165   Li reis l'en meine en sun chastel.
Mult en fu liez, mult li est bel,
kar unkes mes tel n'ot veü;
a grant merveille l'ot tenu
e mult le tint a grant chierté.
170   A tuz les suens a comandé
que sur s'amur le guardent bien
e ne li mesfacent de rien
ne par nul d'els ne seit feruz;
bien seit abevrez e peüz.
175   Cil le guarderent volentiers;
tuz jurs entre les chevaliers
e pres del rei s'alout culchier.
N'i a celui ki ne l'ait chier;
tant esteit frans e de bon'aire,
180   unkes ne volt a rien mesfaire.
U que li reis deüst errer,
il n'out cure de desevrer;
ensemble od lui tuz jurs alout:
bien s'aparceit que il l'amout.

185   Oëz aprés cument avint.
A une curt que li reis tint
tuz les baruns aveit mandez,
cels ki furent de lui chasez,
pur aidier sa feste a tenir
190   e lui plus bel faire servir.
Li chevaliers i est alez,
richement e bien aturnez,
ki la femme Bisclavret ot.
Il ne saveit ne ne quidot

195 qu'il le deüst trover si pres.
Si tost cum il vint al palais
e li Bisclavret l'aparceut,
de plein eslais vers lui curut:
as denz le prist, vers lui le trait.
200 Ja li eüst mult grant laid fait,
ne fust li reis ki l'apela,
d'une verge le manaça.
Dous feiz le volt mordre le jur.
Mult s'esmerveillent li plusur;
205 kar unkes tel semblant ne fist
vers nul hume que il veïst.
Ceo diënt tuit par la maisun
qu'il nel fet mie senz raisun,
mesfait li a, coment que seit,
210 kar volentiers se vengereit.
A cele feiz remest issi,
tant que la feste departi
e li barun unt pris cungié;
a lur maisun sunt repairié.
215 Alez s'en est li chevaliers,
mien esciënt tut as premiers,
que li Bisclavret asailli;
n'est merveille s'il le haï.

Ne fu puis guaires lungement,
220 (ceo m'est a vis, si cum j'entent),
qu'a la forest ala li reis,
ki tant fu sages e curteis,
u li Bisclavret fu trovez,
e il i est od lui alez.
225 La nuit quant il s'en repaira,
en la cuntree herberja.
La femme Bisclavret le sot.
Avenantment s'apareillot.
El demain vait al rei parler,
230 riche present li fait porter.
Quant Bisclavret la veit venir,
nul huem nel poeit retenir:
vers li curut cum enragiez.

Oëz cum il s'est bien vengiez!
235 Le nes li esracha del vis.
Que li peüst il faire pis?
De tutes parz l'unt manacié;
ja l'eüssent tut depescié,
quant uns sages huem dist al rei:
240 «Sire,» fet il, «entent a mei!
Ceste beste a esté od vus;
n'i a ore celui de nus
ki ne l'ait veü lungement
e pres de lui alé sovent.
245 Unkes mes hume ne tucha
ne felunie ne mustra,
fors a la dame qu'ici vei.
Par cele fei que jeo vus dei,
alkun curuz a il vers li
250 e vers sun seignur altresi.
Ceo est la femme al chevalier
que tant suliëz aveir chier,
ki lung tens a esté perduz,
ne seümes qu'est devenuz.
255 Kar metez la dame en destreit,
s'alcune chose vus direit,
pur quei ceste beste la het.
Faites li dire s'el le set!
Meinte merveille avum veüe
260 ki en Bretaigne est avenue.»
Li reis a sun cunseil creü.
Le chevalier a retenu;
de l'autre part la dame a prise
e en mult grant destresce mise.
265 Tant par destresce e par poür
tut li cunta de sun seignur,
coment ele l'aveit traï
e la despueille li toli,
l'avenutre qu'il li cunta,
270 e que devint e u ala;
puis que ses dras li ot toluz,
ne fu en sun païs veüz;
tresbien quidot e bien creeit
que la beste Bisclavret seit.

275 Le reis demande la despueille.
      U bel li seit u pas nel vueille,
      ariere la fet aporter,
      al Bisclavret la fist doner.
      Quant il l'orent devant lui mise,
280 ne se prist guarde en nule guise.
      Li prozdum le rei apela,
      cil ki primes le cunseilla.
      «Sire, ne faites mie bien.
      Cist nel fereit pur nule rien,
285 que devant vus ses dras reveste
      ne mut la semblance de beste.
      Ne savez mie que ceo munte.
      Mult durement en a grant hunte.
      En tes chambres le fai mener
290 e la despueille od lui porter;
      une grant piece l'i laissuns.
      S'il devient huem, bien le verruns.»
      Li reis meïsmes l'en mena
      e tuz les hus sur lui ferma.
295 Al chief de piece i est alez;
      dous baruns a od lui menez.
      En la chambre entrerent tuit trei.
      Sur le demeine lit al rei
      truevent dormant le chevalier.
300 Li reis le curut enbracier;
      plus de cent feiz l'acole e baise.
      Si tost cum il pot aveir aise,
      tute sa terre li rendi;
      plus li duna que jeo ne di.
305 La femme a del païs ostee
      e chaciee de la cuntree.
      Cil s'en ala ensemble od li,
      pur qui sun seignur ot traï.
      Enfanz en a asez eüz,
310 puis unt esté bien cuneüz
      e del semblant e del visage:
      plusurs des femmes del lignage,
      c'est veritez, senz nes sunt nees
      e si viveient esnasees.

315 L'avenutre qu'avez oïe
    veraie fu, n'en dutez mie.
    De Bisclavret fu fez li lais
    pur remembrance a tuz dis mais.

Yonec

Puis que des lais ai comencié,
ja n'iert par nul travail laissié;
les aventures que j'en sai,
tut par rime les cunterai.
5   En pensé ai e en talant
que d'Yonec vus die avant
dunt il fu nez, e de sun pere
cum il vint primes a sa mere.
Cil ki engendra Yonec
10   aveit a nun Muldumarec.

En Bretaigne maneit jadis
uns riches huem, vielz e antis.
De Caruënt fu avuëz
e del païs sire clamez.
15   La citez siet sur Duëlas;
jadis i ot de nes trespas.
Mult fu trespassez en eage.
Pur ceo qu'il ot bon heritage,
femme prist pur enfanz aveir,
20   ki aprés lui fussent si heir.
De halte gent fu la pucele,
sage e curteise e forment bele,
ki al riche hume fu donee;
pur sa bealté l'a mult amee.
25   Pur qu'en fereie altre parole?
Nen ot sa per desqu'a Nicole
ne tresqu'en Yrlande de la.
Grant pechié fist ki li dona.
Pur ceo que ele ert bele e gente,
30   en li guarder mist mult s'entente.
Dedenz sa tur l'a enserree
en une grant chambre pavee.
Il ot une sue serur,
vieille ert e vedve, senz seignur;
35   ensemble od la dame l'a mise

pur li tenir plus en justise.
Altres femmes i ot, ceo crei,
en une altre chambre par sei;
mes ja la dame n'i parlast,
40   se la vieille nel comandast.

Issi la tint plus de set anz
(unques entre els n'ourent enfanz),
ne fors de cele tur n'eissi
ne pur parent ne pur ami.
45   Quant li sire s'alot culchier,
n'i ot chamberlenc ne huissier,
ki en la chambre osast entrer
ne devant lui cirge alumer.
Mult ert la dame en grant tristur,
50   od lermes, od suspir e plur
sa belté pert en tel mesure
cume cele ki n'en a cure.
De sei meïsme mielz volsist
que morz hastive la presist.

55   Ceo fu al meis d'avril entrant,
quant cil oisel meinent lur chant.
Li sire fu matin levez;
d'aler en bois s'est aturnez.
La vieille a faite lever sus
60   e aprés lui fermer les hus.
Cele a sun comandement fet.
En une altre chambre s'en vet;
en sa main portot sun psaltier,
u ele voleit verseillier.
65   La dame en plur e en esveil
choisi la clarté del soleil.
De la vieille est aparceüe
que de la chambre esteit eissue.
Mult se pleigneit e suspirot
70   e en plurant se dementot.
«Lasse,» fait ele, «mar fui nee!
Mult est dure ma destinee.
En ceste tur sui en prisun,

ja n'en istrai se par mort nun.
75 Cist vielz gelus de quei se crient,
ki en si grant prisun me tient?
Mult par est fols e esbaïz,
il crient estre tuz jurs traïz.
Jeo ne puis al mustier venir
80 ne le servise Deu oïr.
Se jo peüsse a gent parler
e en deduit od lui aler,
jo li mustrasse bel semblant,
ja n'en eüsse jeo talant.
85 Maleeit seient mi parent
e li altre comunalment,
ki a cest gelus me donerent
e a sun cors me mariërent!
A forte corde trai e tir!
90 Il ne purra ja mes murir;
quant il dut estre baptiziez,
si fu el flum d'enfern plungiez;
dur sunt li nerf, dures les veines,
ki de vif sanc sunt tutes pleines.
95 Mult ai oï sovent cunter
que l'em suleit jadis trover
aventures en cest païs,
ki rehaitouent les pensis.
Chevalier trovoënt puceles
100 a lur talent, gentes e beles,
e dames truvoënt amanz
beals e curteis, pruz e vaillanz,
si que blamees n'en esteient,
ne nul fors eles nes veeient.
105 Se ceo puet estre ne ceo fu,
se unc a nul est avenu,
Deus, ki de tut a poësté,
il en face ma volenté!»

Quant ele ot fait pleinte issi,
110 l'umbre d'un grant oisel choisi
parmi une estreite fenestre.
Ele ne set que ceo puet estre.

En la chambre volant entra.
Giez ot es piez, ostur sembla;
115   de cinc mues fu u de sis.
Il s'est devant la dame asis.
Quant il i ot un poi esté
e ele l'ot bien esguardé,
chevaliers bels e genz devint.
120   La dame a merveille le tint;
li sans li remut e fremi,
grant poür ot, sun chief covri.
Mult fu curteis li chevaliers:
il l'en araisuna primiers.
125   «Dame,» fet il, «n'aiez poür,
gentil oisel a en ostur,
se li segrei vus sunt oscur.
Guardez que seiez a seür,
si faites de mei vostre ami!
130   Pur ceo,» fet il, «vinc jeo ici.
Jeo vus ai lungement amee
e en mun quer mult desiree;
unkes femme fors vus n'amai
ne ja mes altre n'amerai.
135   Mes ne poeie a vus venir
ne fors de mun païs eissir,
se vus ne me eüssiez requis.
Or puis bien estre vostre amis!»
La dame se raseüra;
140   sun chief descovri, si parla.
Le chevalier a respundu
e dit qu'ele en fera sun dru,
s'en Deu creïst e issi fust
que lur amurs estre peüst.
145   Kar mult esteit de grant bealté;
unkes nul jur de sun eé
si bel chevalier n'esguarda
ne ja mes si bel ne verra.
«Dame,» fet il, «vus dites bien.
150   Ne voldreie pur nule rien
que de mei i ait achaisun,
mescreance ne suspesçun.
Jeo crie mult bien al creatur,

ki nus geta de la tristur
155 u Adam nus mist, nostre pere,
par le mors de la pume amere;
il est e iert e fu tuz jurs
vie e lumiere as pecheürs.
Se vus de ceo ne me creez,
160 vostre chapelain demandez!
Dites que mals vus a suzprise,
si volez aveir le servise
que Deus a el mund establi,
dunt li pecheür sunt guari.
165 La semblance de vus prendrai:
le cors Damedeu recevrai,
ma creance vus dirai tute.
Ja de ceo ne serez en dute!»
El li respunt que bien a dit.
170 Delez li s'est culchié el lit;
mes il ne volt a li tuchier
ne d'acoler ne de baisier.
A tant la vieille est repairiee.
La dame trova esveilliee,
175 dist li que tens est de lever,
ses dras li voleit aporter.
La dame dist qu'ele est malade;
del chapelain se prenge guarde,
sil face tost a li venir,
180 kar grant poür a de murir.
La vieille dist: «Or suferrez!
Mis sire en est el bois alez;
nuls n'enterra ça enz fors mei.»
Mult fu la dame en grant esfrei;
185 semblant fist qu'ele se pasma.
Cele le vit, mult s'esmaia.
L'us de la chambre a desfermé,
si a le prestre demandé;
e cil i vint cum plus tost pot,
190 Corpus Domini aportot.
Li chevaliers l'a receü,
le vin del chalice a beü.
Li chapeleins s'en est alez,
e la vieille a les us fermez.

195 La dame gist lez sun ami:
      unkes si bel cuple ne vi.
      Quant unt asez ris e jué
      e de lur priveté parlé,
      li chevaliers a cungié pris;
200 raler s'en vuelt en sun païs.
      Ele le prie dulcement
      que il la reveie sovent.
      «Dame,» fet il, «quant vus plaira,
      ja l'ure ne trespassera.
205 Mes tel mesure en esguardez,
      que nus ne seium encumbrez.
      Ceste vieille nus traïra
      e nuit e jur nus guaitera.
      Ele parcevra nostre amur,
210 sil cuntera a sun seignur.
      S'issi avient cum jeo vus di
      e nus sumes issi traï,
      ne m'en puis mie departir
      que mei n'en estuece murir.»

215 Li chevaliers a tant s'en vait;
      a grant joie s'amie lait.
      El demain lieve tute seine;
      mult fu haitiee la semeine.
      Sun cors teneit a grant chierté:
220 tute recuevre sa bealté.
      Or li plest plus a surjurner
      qu'en nul altre deduit aler.
      Sun ami vuelt suvent veeir
      e sa joie de lui aveir;
225 des que sis sire s'en depart,
      e nuit e jur e tost e tart
      ele l'a tut a sun plaisir.
      Or l'en duinst Deus lunges joïr!
      Pur la grant joie u ele fu,
230 que suvent puet veeir sun dru,
      esteit tuz sis semblanz changiez.
      Sis sire esteit mult veziëz;
      en sun curage s'aparceit

       qu'altrement ert qu'il ne suleit.
235 Mescreance a vers sa serur.
       Il la met a raisun un jur
       e dit que mult a grant merveille
       que la dame si s'apareille;
       demanda li que ceo deveit.
240 La vieille dist qu'el ne saveit
       (kar nuls ne pot parler od li
       ne ele n'ot dru ne ami)
       fors tant que sule remaneit
       plus volentiers qu'el ne suleit;
245 de ceo s'esteit aparceüe.
       Dunc l'a li sire respundue:
       «Par fei,» fet il, «ceo quit jeo bien.
       Or vus estuet faire une rien!
       Al matin quant jeo ierc levez
250 e vus avrez les hus fermez,
       faites semblant de fors eissir,
       si la laissiez sule gisir.
       En un segrei liu vus estez
       e si veez e esguardez,
255 que ceo puet estre e dunt ceo vient
       ki en si grant joie la tient.»
       De cel cunseil sunt departi.
       A las! Cum ierent malbailli
       cil que l'um vuelt si aguaitier
260 pur els traïr e engignier!

       Tierz jur aprés, ceo oi cunter,
       fet li sire semblant d'errer.
       A sa femme a dit e cunté
       que li reis l'a par brief mandé,
265 mes hastivement revendra.
       De la chambre ist e l'us ferma.
       Dunc s'esteit la vieille levee,
       triers une cortine est alee;
       bien purra oïr e veeir
270 ceo qu'ele cuveite a saveir.
       La dame jut, pas ne dormi,
       kar mult desire sun ami.

Venuz i est, pas ne demure,
ne trespasse terme ne hure.
275 Ensemble funt joie mult grant
e par parole e par semblant,
de si que tens fu de lever,
kar dunc l'en estuveit aler.
Cele le vit, si l'esguarda,
280 coment il vint e il ala.
De ceo ot ele grant poür
qu'ume le vit e puis ostur.
Quant li sire fu repairiez,
ki n'esteit guaires esluigniez,
285 cele li a dit e mustré
del chevalier la verité,
e il en est forment pensis.
Des engins faire fu hastis
a ocire le chevalier.
290 Broches de fer fist granz furgier
e acerer les chiés devant:
suz ciel n'a rasur plus trenchant.
Quant il les ot apareilliees
e de tutes parz enfurchiees,
295 sur la fenestre les a mises,
bien serrees e bien asises,
par unt li chevaliers passot,
quant a la dame repairot.
Deus, qu'il ne set la traïsun
300 que apareillent li felun!

El demain a la matinee
li sire lieve a l'ajurnee
e dit qu'il vuelt aler chacier.
La vieille le vait cunveier;
305 puis se reculche pur dormir,
kar ne poeit le jur choisir.
La dame veille, si atent
celui qu'ele eime leialment,
e dit qu'or purreit bien venir
310 e estre od li tut a leisir.
Si tost cum el l'ot demandé,

n'i a puis guaires demuré.
En la fenestre vint volant;
mes les broches furent devant.
315 L'une le fiert parmi le cors,
li sans vermeilz en sailli fors.
Quant il se sent a mort nafrez,
desferre sei, enz est entrez.
Devant la dame el lit descent,
320 que tuit li drap furent sanglent.
Ele veit le sanc e la plaie,
mult anguissusement s'esmaie.
Il li a dit: «Ma dulce amie,
pur vostre amur pert jeo la vie!
325 Bien le vus dis qu'en avendreit,
vostre semblanz nus ocireit.»
Quant el l'oï, dunc chiet pasmee;
tute fu morte une loëe.
Il la cunforte dulcement
330 e dit que duels n'i valt niënt.
De lui est enceinte d'enfant,
un fiz avra pruz e vaillant:
icil la recunfortera.
Yonec numer le fera.
335 Il vengera e lui e li,
il oscira sun enemi.
Il n'i puet dunc demurer mes,
kar sa plaie seignot adés.
A grant dolur s'en est partiz.
340 Ele le siut a mult halz criz.
Par une fenestre s'en ist;
c'est merveille qu'el ne s'ocist,
kar bien aveit vint piez de halt
iloec u ele prist le salt.
345 Ele esteit nue en sa chemise.
A la trace del sanc s'est mise,
ki del chevalier decureit
sur le chemin u ele esteit.
Icel sentier erra e tint,
350 de si qu'a une hoge vint.
En cele hoge ot une entree,
de cel sanc fu tute arusee;

ne pot niënt avant veeir.
Dunc quidot ele bien saveir
355   que sis amis entrez i seit.
Dedenz se met en grant espleit.
El n'i trova nule clarté.
Tant a le dreit chemin erré,
que fors de la hoge est eissue
360   e en un mult bel pre venue.
Del sanc trova l'erbe moilliee,
dunc s'est ele mult esmaiee.
La trace en siut parmi le pré.
Asez pres vit une cité.
365   De mur fu close tut en tur.
N'i ot maisun, sale ne tur
ki ne parust tute d'argent;
mult sunt riche li mandement.
Devers le burc sunt li mareis
370   e les forez e les defeis.
De l'altre part vers le dunjun
curt une ewe tut envirun;
ileoc arivoënt les nes,
plus i aveit de treis cenz tres.
375   La porte a val fu desfermee,
la dame est en la vile entree
tuz jurs aprés le sanc novel
parmi le burc desqu'al chastel.
Unkes nuls a li ne parla,
380   n'ume ne femme n'i trova.
El palais vient al paviment,
del sanc le trueve tut sanglent.
En une bele chambre entra;
un chevalier dormant trova.
385   Nel cunut pas, si vet avant
en une altre chambre plus grant.
Un lit i trueve e niënt plus,
un chevalier dormant desus;
ele s'en est ultre passee.
390   En la tierce chambre est entree;
le lit sun ami a trové.
Li pecol sunt d'or esmeré;
ne sai mie les dras preisier;

li cirgë e li chandelier,
395   ki nuit e jur sunt alumé,
valent tut l'or d'une cité.
Si tost cum ele l'a veü,
le chevalier a cuneü.
Avant ala tute esfreee;
400   par desus lui cheï pasmee.
Cil la receit ki forment l'aime,
maleürus sovent se claime.
Quant de pasmer fu respassee,
il l'a dulcement cunfortee.
405   «Bele amie, pur Deu, vus pri,
alez vus en! Fuiez de ci!
Sempres murrai enmi le jur;
ça enz avra si grant dolur,
si vus i esteiez trovee,
410   mult en seriëz turmentee;
bien iert entre ma gent seü
qu'il m'unt par vostre amur perdu.
Pur vus sui dolenz e pensis!»
La dame li a dit: «Amis,
415   mielz vueil ensemble od vus murir
qu'od mun seignur peine sufrir!
S'a lui revois, il m'ocira.»
Li chevaliers l'aseüra.
Un anelet li a baillié,
420   si li a dit e enseignié,
ja, tant cum el le guardera,
a sun seignur n'en memberra
de nule rien ki faite seit,
ne ne l'en tendra en destreit.
425   S'espee li cumande e rent;
puis la cunjurë e defent
que ja nul huem n'en seit saisiz,
mes bien la guart a oés sun fiz.
Quant il sera creüz e granz
430   e chevalier pruz e vaillanz,
a une feste u ele irra
sun seignur e lui amerra.
En une abbeïe vendrunt;
par une tumbe qu'il verrunt

435 orrunt renoveler sa mort
e cum il fu ocis a tort.
Iluec li baillera l'espee.
L'aventure li seit cuntee
cum il fu nez, ki l'engendra;
440 asez verrunt qu'il en fera.
Quant tut li a dit e mustré,
un chier blialt li a doné;
si li cumandë a vestir.
Puis l'a faite de lui partir.
445 Ele s'en vet; l'anel en porte
e l'espee ki la cunforte.
A l'eissue de la cité
n'ot pas demie liwe alé,
quant ele oï les seins suner
450 e le doel el chastel lever
pur lur seignur ki se moreit.
Ele set bien que morz esteit;
de la dolur que ele en a
quatre fiëes se pasma.
455 E quant de pasmeisuns revint,
vers la hoge sa veie tint.
Dedenz entra, ultre est passee,
si s'en revait en sa cuntree.
Ensemblement od sun seignur
460 demura meint di e meint jur,
ki de cel fet ne la reta
ne ne mesdist ne ne gaba.

Sis fiz fu nez e bien nurriz
e bien guardez e bien cheriz.
465 Yonec le firent numer.
El regne ne pot um trover
si bel, si pruz ne si vaillant,
si large ne si despendant.
Quant il fu venuz en eé,
470 a chevalier l'unt adubé.
En l'an meïsmes que ceo fu,
oëz cument est avenu!

A la feste seint Aaron,
qu'on celebrot a Karlion
475 e en plusurs altres citez,
li sire aveit esté mandez,
qu'il i alast od ses amis
a la custume del païs;
sa femme e sun fiz i menast
480 e richement s'apareillast.
Issi avint, alé i sunt.
Mes il ne sevent u il vunt;
ensemble od els ot un meschin,
kis a menez le dreit chemin,
485 tant qu'il vindrent a un chastel;
en tut le siecle n'ot plus bel.
Une abbeïe aveit dedenz
de mult religiüses genz.
Li vaslez les i herberja,
490 ki a la feste les mena.
En la chambre ki fu l'abé
bien sunt servi e honuré.
El demain vunt la messe oïr;
puis s'en voleient departir.
495 Li abes vait a els parler;
mult les prie de surjurner,
si lur musterra sun dortur,
sun chapitre, sun refeitur.
Si cum il sunt bien herbergié.
500 li sire lur a otrié.

Le jur quant il orent digné,
as officines sunt alé.
El chapitre vindrent avant.
Une tumbe troverent grant,
505 coverte d'un paile roé,
d'un chier orfreis par mi bendé.
Al chief, as piez e as costez
aveit vint cirges alumez.
D'or fin erent li chandelier,
510 d'ametiste li encensier,
dunt il encensouent le jur

cele tumbe pur grant honur.
Il unt demandé e enquis
a cels ki erent del païs
515   de la tumbe ki ele esteit,
e quel huem fu ki la giseit.
Cil comencierent a plurer
e en plurant a recunter,
que c'ert le mieldre chevaliers
520   e li plus forz e li plus fiers,
li plus beals e li plus amez
ki ja mes seit el siecle nez.
«De ceste terre ot esté reis;
unques ne fu nuls si curteis.
525   A Caruënt fu entrepris,
pur l'amur d'une dame ocis.
Unques puis n'eümes seignur,
ainz avum atendu meint jur
un fiz qu'en la dame engendra,
530   si cum il dist e cumanda.»
Quant la dame oï la novele,
a halte voiz sun fiz apele.
«Beals fiz,» fet ele, «avez oï
cum Deus nus a amené ci!
535   C'est vostre pere ki ci gist,
que cist villarz a tort ocist.
Or vus comant e rent s'espee;
jeo l'ai asez lung tens guardee.»
Oianz tuz, li ad coneü
540   qu'il l'engendra e sis fiz fu,
cum il suleit venir a li,
e cum sis sire le traï;
l'aventure li a cuntee.
Sur la tumbe cheï pasmee;
545   en la pasmeisun devia:
unc puis a hume ne parla.
Quant sis fiz veit que morte fu,
sun parastre a le chief tolu.
De l'espee ki fu sun pere
550   a dunc vengié lui e sa mere.
Puis que si fu dunc avenu
e par la cité fu seü,

a grant honur la dame unt prise
e el sarcu posee e mise
555 delez le cors de sun ami;
Deus lur face bone merci!
Lur seignur firent d'Yonec,
ainz que il partissent d'ilec.

Cil ki ceste aventure oïrent
560 lunc tens aprés un lai en firent,
de la peine e de la dolur
que cil sufrirent pur amur.